The Complete Guide to
BIBLE
TRANSLATIONS

Ron Rhodes

HARVEST HOUSE PUBLISHERS

EUGENE, OREGON

Cover by Dugan Design Group, Bloomington, Minnesota

THE COMPLETE GUIDE TO BIBLE TRANSLATIONS

Copyright © 2009 by Ron Rhodes
Published by Harvest House Publishers
Eugene, Oregon 97402
www.harvesthousepublishers.com

Library of Congress Cataloging-in-Publication Data

Rhodes, Ron.
The complete guide to Bible translations / Ron Rhodes.
    p. cm.
Includes bibliographical references.
ISBN 978-0-7369-2546-4 (pbk.)
1. Bible. English—Versions. I. Title.
BS455.R56 2009
220.5'2—dc22   2008045616

Printed in the United States of America
09 10 11 12 13 14 15 16 17 / BP-NI / 10 9 8 7 6 5 4 3 2 1

To Bible lovers everywhere!

Acknowledgments

During the writing of this book I sustained a rather painful injury to my right arm. I had just checked the mailbox out by the street, and I was *multitasking*—reading my mail while walking back up the front steps. I missed a single step and ended up taking a dive into solid concrete, mail flying in every direction, our cats scrambling for safety in the bushes, birds taking immediate flight, and shockwaves of pain pulsating— rather, *blasting*—through my right arm. During my rather prolonged time of recovery, my wife, Kerri, not only gave her usual encouragement and prayer support, but threw into the mix an abundance of extra kindnesses with which she blessed me greatly. *I am so, so appreciative!* I am also thankful for our two children, David and Kylie, who are an unceasing source of joy for me. Finally, I want to thank my many friends—from California to New York—who prayed for me daily during my time of recovery. I don't think I could have written this book without those prayers!

Contents

APPENDIXES

Why Choosing the Right Bible Translation Is Important

A CHRISTIAN WHO WALKS INTO a typical Christian bookstore these days will generally find no less than ten different English translations of the Bible on the bookshelves—sometimes 15 or more. Choosing between them is not an easy task. The moment one encounters all these translations, numerous questions flood the mind: Which translation is the best? Which one is the easiest to understand? Which is the most accurate? Why are they all different? Are newer translations better than older ones? How do I know I can trust the translators? Are some of these translations for specific denominations, or are they for all Christians? Are Bibles with the words of Christ in red better than Bibles that do not have this feature?[1]

Let's be honest: A person who walks into a Christian bookstore today can be virtually overwhelmed at the number of available choices for buying a Bible. And most Bible buyers haven't the foggiest idea about how to answer the questions above. For this reason, the book you

are holding in your hands has been custom designed to provide you—
the reader—with all the information necessary to make an *informed*
decision about which Bible translation might be best *for you*.

First, though, let us consider a brief survey of major Bible translations throughout church history. This will set the context for all that
follows.

Historical Insights on Translations

Bible translations are not a new thing. They have been around for
many centuries. For example, way back in the third century B.C., the
Jews produced a Greek translation of the Hebrew Old Testament for
the Jews living in Alexandria, a Greek-speaking city. This translation
was called the Septuagint—a term that means "seventy," referring
to the roughly seventy translators who produced the translation.[2]
The Septuagint was used for reading aloud in synagogues in Greek-
speaking cities, including Corinth and many cities in Rome. This
translation solved a big problem, for many of the Jews who grew up
in these cities could no longer speak Hebrew, but only Greek.

Later, Christians began producing translations of the Old and New
Testaments in different languages so they could fulfill their assign-
ment by Jesus to make disciples of all nations (Matthew 28:18-20).
Early in biblical history, Syriac or Aramaic translations of the Bible
became increasingly important as Christianity spread throughout Cen-
tral Asia, India, and China. As Christianity continued to spread even
further, the need developed for Egyptian (Coptic), Ethiopic, Gothic
(Germanic), Armenian, and Arabic translations.

Because Latin emerged as the common language in many parts of
the Roman Empire, a man by the name of Jerome was commissioned
by the Bishop of Rome to translate the Scriptures into Latin in A.D.
382. This translation continued to be an unofficial standard text of
the Bible throughout the Middle Ages.

A problem soon emerged, however. Prior to the 1500s, during
which the Roman Catholic Church dominated, translations were

generally unavailable in the languages *of most of the people.* (The exception would be the translations mentioned above that are limited to certain parts of the world.) Predominantly, church services and the Bible itself were in Latin, and this remained the case for many centuries. Church authorities feared that if everyone had a translation in their own language, they would come up with all kinds of strange and different interpretations. Such would be intolerable, many reasoned, for the Roman Catholic Church would then lose control of what the people believed.

Other brave souls, however, believed that the common people needed to have the life-changing truths of God's Word in their own language, and hence produced translations, even in the face of great threat from Roman Catholic authorities. Because of the invention of printing in the fifteenth century, it was just a matter of time before Bible translations were being produced *en masse* for the common people, and Catholic authorities could do nothing to prevent it.

John Wycliffe (born mid-1320s), a lecturer at Oxford University, is an example of one who sought to provide a translation of the Bible for English-speaking Christians. He desired the average English-speaking layman to have access to the Word of God rather than the Roman Catholic Church having sole access. He completed his English translation in A.D. 1382.[3] Wycliffe wrote:

> Those heretics who pretend that the laity need not know God's law but that the knowledge which priests have had imparted to them by word of mouth is sufficient, do not deserve to be listened to. For Holy Scriptures is the faith of the Church, and the more widely its true meaning becomes known the better it will be. Therefore since the laity should know the faith, it should be taught in whatever language is most easily comprehended...[After all,] Christ and His apostles taught the people in the language best known to them.[4]

Unfortunately, Wycliffe's translation was based not on the original Hebrew, Aramaic, and Greek manuscripts of the Bible,* but rather on Jerome's Latin translation of the original manuscripts, called the Vulgate. This means that as helpful as Wycliffe's translation was, it had some shortcomings. Scholar Daniel Wallace tells us that "Latin does not have the definite article. That is a gift that the Greeks gave to Europe. But the article occurs in the Greek NT almost 20,000 times—understanding its use is vital for hundreds of passages. And yet, Wycliffe knew none of this, since he only used the Latin text as his base."[5]

Wycliffe's work—general writings, sermons, and translation of the Bible—did not go unchallenged. Indeed, some twenty-four theses from his writings and sermons were condemned as heretical or erroneous by a synod held at Blackfriars, London in A.D. 1382. He was fired from his teaching position at Oxford that same year. Throughout the rest of his life, five edicts were issued for his arrest by the pope in Rome. Lucky for him, England had distanced itself from Rome somewhat, and he found a level of protection in powerful English nobles. Two years later, in 1384, he died of natural causes and was buried in the Lutterworth church cemetery, where he had been pastor. Tragically and unfairly, Wycliffe was ultimately denounced as a heretic, and in 1415 his Bible was condemned and burned. As if that were not enough, his body was exhumed from the grave over a decade later and burned, with his ashes being thrown into a river. However, as scholar Bruce Metzger notes, "just as his ashes were carried by that river to multiple points, so his message went far and wide during the following centuries."[6] Judging by the number of manuscripts that have survived, Wycliffe's translation was clearly widely circulated *and* widely read.

Sometime later, William Tyndale (1492–1536), who taught at Cambridge University, translated the New Testament based on the

---

* The Old Testament was originally written in Hebrew, along with some Aramaic, and the New Testament was originally written in Greek.

original Greek manuscripts. Tyndale had been trained in both Greek and Hebrew, earning a bachelor's degree from Oxford in 1512 and his master's degree in 1515. He later completed his studies at Cambridge. It was not long before he became fluent in some seven languages. Scholars are practically unanimous that Tyndale's contribution to the English Bible is unparalleled. As one scholar put it, "No one has made more impact on the translation of the Bible into English than William Tyndale."[7]

Tyndale found a model to imitate in the person of German Reformer Martin Luther (1483–1546). Luther had translated the New Testament into German—not the High German used in courtly circles but the vernacular German used by the common folk. Luther explained his philosophy this way: "I must let the literal words go and try to learn how the German says that which the Hebrew expresses...Whoever would speak German must not use Hebrew style. Rather he must see to it—once he understands the Hebrew author—that he concentrates on the sense of the text, asking himself, 'Pray tell, what do the Germans say in such a situation?'...Let him drop the Hebrew words and express the meaning freely in the best German he knows."[8] Tyndale wanted to do the same for English readers.

History reveals that Tyndale was highly motivated: "I had perceived by experience how that it was impossible to establish the lay people in any truth, except that the Scriptures were plainly laid before their eyes in their mother tongue, that they might see the process, order, and meaning of the text." Tyndale once told a Catholic antagonist: "I defy the Pope and all his laws. If God spare my life, before many years I will make sure that a boy who drives the plough knows more of the Scriptures than you do."[9]

In 1523 Tyndale sought to begin his work of translation in England. But after receiving a cold shoulder—indeed, a vigorous rebuff—from the bishop of London, he decided to permanently relocate to Hamburg. His translation of the New Testament was finally published in English in 1526 and was revised in 1534, 1535, and 1536. He made progress in translating portions of the Old Testament from the original Hebrew, but he died before he was able to complete it.

Once Tyndale's New Testament was published, it was publicly burned in England. Tyndale was arrested in 1535, imprisoned in a fortress just north of Brussels, and the following year was tried and found guilty of heresy. Some of his critics falsely claimed that he changed the Bible as he translated it. He was strangled and burned at the stake. His crime? Translating a "corrupt" version of the Scriptures.[10] The final words he uttered were, "Lord, open the King of England's eyes." Tyndale's martyrdom reminds us that many have paid the ultimate price to make God's Word available to everyone. Tyndale's work was not in vain, however. Modern biblical scholars tell us that about 90 percent of the New Testament of the King James Version was ultimately based on Tyndale's work. (For more on this, see chapter 4.)

Myles Coverdale (1488–1569), who had been Tyndale's assistant as well as an English clergyman, produced the first complete printed English Bible. This was a milestone in Bible translation history. Coverdale's New Testament was essentially a slight revision of Tyndale's translation, with minor changes introduced after comparing it to Luther's New Testament. Portions of Tyndale's translation of the Old Testament were also influential in Coverdale's Bible. The Bible was published in 1535, and as it contained a dedication to the king and queen in flattering phraseology, it met with no serious opposition. The second edition of Coverdale's Bible was published "with the king's most gracious license."[11]

Another Bible worthy of note is the Matthew's Bible, published in 1537. This translation is apparently the work of one John Rogers, a Cambridge graduate and friend of William Tyndale who (probably wisely) published the Bible using a pseudonym, Thomas Matthew. This Bible closely follows the Tyndale version. In fact, the Matthew's Bible incorporates more of Tyndale's work than does the Coverdale Bible.

Just a few years later, the Great Bible was published in 1539. It was deemed "great" because the Bible was so big, with pages measuring fifteen by ten inches, making it the biggest Bible yet to be published. The task of editing the Great Bible was entrusted to Coverdale at the behest of Thomas Cromwell. This was the first "authorized" English Bible to be published for the Church of England, and in the 1540 and subsequent editions, the title page boasted: "This is the Byble apoynted to the use of the churches." The Bible was produced mainly by revising the text of the earlier Matthew's Bible. Six further editions were published between 1540 and 1541. This Bible was exceedingly popular.

Not many years passed before the Geneva Bible was published, translated wholly from the original Hebrew, Aramaic, and Greek. This Bible would ultimately become "the Bible of the people." It became the official Bible of the Church of Scotland (Presbyterian), and it was used by such luminaries as Shakespeare (its language and cadences can be found throughout his plays and sonnets), John Bunyan, the Mayflower Compact, and Oliver Cromwell. Even though the names of the translators do not appear in the Geneva New Testament (1557), the work is primarily credited to William Whittingham, brother-in-law of French Reformer John Calvin. Whittingham was an able scholar and succeeded John Knox as minister to the English congregation at Geneva. The Old Testament was translated by a group of linguists, including Anthony Gilby, Thomas Sampson, and others of uncertain identity.

The Geneva Bible went through an astounding 140 editions and remained in demand for almost 100 years. It is noteworthy that instead of using heavy, black-letter (Gothic) type, as had been used in previous Bibles, Roman type was used for the first time in the Geneva Bible. Moreover, this was the first English Bible with verse divisions (with verse numbers), and because of this was able to offer cross-references. It was also the first Bible to use italics extensively for words that were not in the original text. The Bible was published with notes in the margins that explained difficult points in the text, such as historical and geographical references. Other notes were doctrinal in nature. Not unexpectedly, the notes were Calvinistic in tone, and some had an anti-papal bias. The Bible also contained maps, tables, chapter summaries, and running titles. Because of such features, as well as a relatively low cost, this became a very popular Bible in a short time. Amusingly, this Bible is also called the Breeches Bible because of its translation of Genesis 3:7, speaking of Adam and Eve: "They sewed fig tree leaves together and made themselves breeches."[12]

A very short time after the Geneva Bible was published, the Bishops' Bible was published in 1568. The popularity of the Geneva Bible irked some English church officials, and hence, in 1564, the archbishop of Canterbury initiated efforts to produce a translation of the Bible that would replace the Geneva and other Bibles. The Bishops' Bible was, in fact, the official Anglican response to the Geneva Bible. It was called the Bishops' Bible because it was a group of Anglican bishops along with some soon-to-become Anglican bishops that revised it. They used the Great Bible as the basis of their work, making changes only as required by the original Hebrew, Aramaic, or Greek. Production took four years, from 1564 to 1568.

Modern scholars have noted that the Bishops' Bible has an uneven quality, perhaps because of the exercise of individual freedom by the translators without adequate hands-on editorial supervision of the project. Some translators apparently followed the Great Bible quite closely, while others apparently departed from it quite freely. The translation of the New Testament is clearly superior in quality to the Old Testament. Nevertheless, despite such defects, this became the second "authorized" English version of the Bible, eventually displacing the Great Bible as the one "appoynted to be read in the Churches." However, as scholars Gordon Fee and Mark Strauss have noted, "it was seldom used outside the Anglican communion because of the superior quality of the Geneva Bible."[13]

A few decades later brought publication of a Roman Catholic translation, the Douay-Rheims Bible. This Bible represents an effort on the part of the Roman Catholic Church to replace the Geneva and other Bibles that were unacceptable to their Roman point of view. It was produced by Gregory Martin, a Roman Catholic scholar. It essentially became the "KJV" of the English-speaking Roman Catholic Church up through the mid-twentieth century. It was completed in 1582 at Rheims in France. The translation was made not from the original Hebrew, Aramaic, and Greek manuscripts but rather from the Latin Vulgate. Modern scholars observe that this translation is often too literal to be suitable for use in public worship, and also tends to use too many technical words.

Not long after this, the previously mentioned Geneva Bible was dethroned by the King James Version (1611). However, the Geneva Bible had a substantial influence on the King James Version. As one scholar put it:

> The influence of [the Geneva Bible] on the KJV was enormous. The KJV translators employed this as much as Tyndale's (of course, much of Tyndale was incorporated into the Geneva). And although King James despised the Geneva Bible, in the original preface to the KJV the Bible is quoted several times—and every time it is the Geneva version that is quoted, not the King James! This was an implicit and perhaps unwitting admission of the Geneva Bible's superiority.[14]

Of course, there is a lot more to say about the KJV. I will withhold further comment until chapter 4, the whole of which deals with this monumental translation.

If there is one thing we learn from this brief survey, it is that minor and sometimes major dissatisfactions with previous translations bring about the need for new translations. However, as we will see below, sometimes it is updated research that can cause the need for new and modern translations.

Updated Research and Updated Translations

There are three areas of research that have brought about the need for new and modern translations. First, more ancient manuscripts have been discovered that are more reliable than those used for the King James Version. The more accurate the manuscripts, the more accurate the translations!

Second, since the late 1800s there have been many archaeological discoveries that have cast doubt on some of the renderings found in the King James Version. Historical evidence is now conclusive that the Greek of the New Testament was the common language of that day. It was most certainly not a dialect that only the intellectual elite of the time could understand. This has led some scholars today to suggest that we should translate the Bible in the common language of *our* day. As one scholar put it, "If the apostles wrote in easy-to-understand terms, then translations of the Bible should reflect this. We ought not to translate with big 50-cent religious-sounding words if the original was not written that way."[15]

And third, in recent decades there have been changes regarding the philosophy of translation, with some holding to the *formal equivalence* theory and others holding to the *dynamic equivalence* theory. I will address these theories at length in chapters 1 and 2.

First, however, allow me to share a brief procedural note. You may notice that some chapters provide more background details on the translation they address than other chapters. This is only because some publishers provide more details than others. For every chapter, however, I provide all the important and relevant information that is available. In each case, I think you will have plenty of information to make an informed decision about a translation.

The Difficulty of Bible Translation

THE WORD *TRANSLATION* REFERS TO "the rendering of something into another language or into one's own from another language."[1] A Bible translation is "a rendering of the Bible in a language different than the one in which it was written."[2] More specifically, a Bible translation for native English-speakers takes the original Old Testament Hebrew and New Testament Greek texts and puts them into the English language. An *accurate* translation is one that communicates to today's readers the same meaning that the original author's text conveyed to his original readers. Most Bible scholars say Bible translations should aim to remain faithful to the original meaning of the text while at the same time use language that sounds as clear and natural to the modern reader as the Hebrew or Greek did to the original readers. They ought to sound *natural,* as though they had originally been written in English, but at the same time preserve a feel for the original cultural setting.

Translation: Not an Easy Task

One might initially think Bible translation is an easy task—as easy as lining up all the Hebrew or Greek words on one side of the page and then quickly placing similar-meaning English words on the other side of the page, and *voila,* an English translation emerges. The reality is that Bible translation *is not* an easy task. Professor Daniel Wallace explains that "most laymen today think that a faithful translation of the Bible means a word-for-word translation. If the original has a noun, they expect a noun in the translation. If the original has sixteen words, they don't want to see seventeen words in the translation."[3] Such a view involves incredible ignorance, Wallace says. Translation involves substantially more than merely substituting words from one language to another. Bible translation ultimately involves *interpretation* of the Bible's meaning into another language, and, frankly, translators differ with each other as to the best way to render the ancient biblical texts into English.[4]

Translations by Individuals versus Committees

Some translations have been produced by a single individual. An example is *The New Testament in Modern English,* by J.B. Phillips. Such translations often have more vibrancy of style than translations done by a committee. The problem is that there is always the possibility that—whether consciously or unconsciously—the translator might allow too many of his interpretive views to bias or at least influence his translation.*

Most believe there is great benefit in a translation being done as a team effort. Not only is there a greater breadth of knowledge in a team of translators, a team can also serve to guard against personal biases, theological or otherwise, that might exist in an individual translator. The benefit of a large number of scholars working on a translation is

---

* An excellent discussion regarding the possibility of theological bias in Bible translations may be found in Robert Thomas, *How to Choose a Bible Version* (Great Britain: Christian Focus Publications, 2000), chapter 4.

that each can cross-check the work of the others. Not only does this *increase* accountability, but it can *decrease* the likelihood of idiosyncratic renderings. However, as David Dewey observes, problems *can* emerge with translations done by committees:

> Committee translations can suffer from any of three problems. First, they are made by biblical exegetes rather than English-language specialists. Consultation with English stylists generally comes late in the process. Second, a committee structure has a leveling-out effect: the need for compromise between committee members tends toward a conservative approach and sometimes to a blandness of style. And third, in the case of revised versions, changes may be only cautiously accepted. Typically, revisions are accepted only if agreed on by a two-thirds majority of the translation committee.[5]

Be that as it may, most Bible translations on the market today were accomplished by a committee of top-notch Hebrew and Greek scholars who worked for years—even over a decade—to complete their task. In some cases these committees were composed of people from a single Christian denomination, or at least predominantly from one denomination. For example, the Jerusalem Bible, the New Jerusalem Bible, and the New American Bible were translated by committees that were predominantly Roman Catholic. In other cases, the committee involved scholars from a variety of denominations, as was the case with the New International Version, the New American Standard Bible, the Holman Christian Standard Bible, and the NET Bible, among others. Some committees—such as those who translated the New American Standard Bible, the New International Version, and the English Standard Version—were required to subscribe to the doctrine of biblical inspiration.

Even with a committee of top biblical experts, however, Bible translation is still a very difficult task. The reasons for this will become clear in what follows.

No One-to-One Parallel in Words

One reason Bible translation is a difficult task is that, in many cases, there is no direct one-to-one parallel between words in the original Hebrew or Greek languages and the English language. For example, while the English language has a singular word, *love*, the Greek language has a number of words for "love," each of which communicates a different aspect of love (such as *friend* love or *passionate* love). For this reason, Bible translators must use their interpretive skills, remaining constantly sensitive to which nuance of meaning is being communicated by the original Hebrew or Greek word in a particular context so that the proper English word can be chosen to render that meaning.

The Historical Barrier

Another reason Bible translation can be difficult is that there is a historical barrier between the original documents and the modern translator. We are separated from the original documents by thousands of years. In order for translators to best accomplish their task, therefore, it is necessary for them to be thoroughly conversant in both the grammar and culture of the language they are translating. The more they know about the history of the culture that produced the document, the easier it is to translate. As Alan Duthie put it, "We expect Bible translators to have an up-to-date knowledge of the original languages and cultures so as to understand the full meaning of the Bible message before translating."[6] Archeological discoveries alone have uncovered all kinds of useful information about people who lived in Bible times—including their money, marriage customs, burial rites, business practices, trade, agriculture, fishing, hunting, shepherding, religious practices, and more. Such information is of immense value to the Bible translator.

Idioms and Figures of Speech

Another translational problem is that many languages make use of idioms, or figures of speech, that mean something in the original language but not necessarily in the translated language. As one scholar put it, "The trouble with figures of speech such as metaphors and similes is that they are culturally dependent."[7] For example, in the English language we have quite a number of idioms. To communicate that something is easy, we say, "It's a piece of cake." To exhort someone to do a good job at something, we might say, "Break a leg." When we want someone to calm down, we might say, "Chill." When something goes wrong, we might say, "How did the wheels come off this thing?" If we are going on a trip, we might say, "Let's hit the road." Such idioms can be extremely confusing to non-English readers.

Scholars Gordon Fee and Mark Strauss show a sense of humor in providing us with a paragraph full of English idioms:

> My career had seen better days. I was skating on thin ice, scraping the bottom of the barrel, and ready to say uncle. The boss and I did not see eye to eye, and he told me to shape up or ship out. There was no silver bullet. It was a safe bet I was going to sink or swim. Nobody could save my bacon. My smart-aleck colleague was a stick-in-the-mud and a snake in the grass who would sell me down the river as soon as shake a stick at me. I could smell a rat, so I steered clear of him. I had one slim chance. It was a shot in the dark, but if I could keep a stiff upper lip, stick to my guns, and sail close to the wind, I would get a second chance. The saving grace was that at the last minute I got a second wind and was saved by the bell.[8]

A foreigner trying to translate an English document into his language might find it exceedingly difficult to translate such idioms into his language. The reason is that such phrases are likely *not* idioms in *his* language, and hence a strictly literal translation of the words would be confusing to his readers. Likewise, an English-speaking person seeking to translate a document from the French might come across French idioms that are meaningful to French people but meaning*less* to English-speaking people.

I bring all this up because there are also hundreds of idioms that were used among the ancients in Bible times, and these are not easy to render into modern English. For example, the Greek idiom "take up souls" carries the idea "keep in suspense" (John 10:24). To "have lifespan" is a Greek idiom that means a person is of age (John 9:21). "Those having badly" is a Greek idiom that means "those who were sick" (Mark 1:32).[9] "Having in belly" is a Greek idiom meaning "pregnant" (Matthew 1:18). Speaking "with a heart and a heart" is a Jewish idiom meaning to speak "with a double heart" or "with deception" (Psalm 12:2).

Daniel Wallace is thus correct in his assessment that "anyone who has ever learned a second language knows that a word-for-word translation is impossible much or most of the time. Idioms in one language need to be paraphrased. Even the King James translators realized this. In a couple of places in the OT, the Hebrew text literally reads, 'God's nostrils enlarged.' But the King James has something like, 'God became angry'—which is what the expression means."[10] Once a translator recognizes an idiom or a figure of speech in the original language, he must consider whether his readers would grasp the meaning correctly if he were to translate it word-for-word. In most cases involving idioms in the Bible, English readers *would not* grasp the original meaning, and so the *meaning* of the idiom must be communicated rather than the original *words*. Another option is to use a modern English idiom that communicates the same message as the ancient Jewish idiom. Eugene Peterson does this in his paraphrase, The Message.

Euphemisms

A euphemism is a culturally appropriate way of saying something that might otherwise be considered offensive, unpleasant, or perhaps too direct. For example, a person might say that "nature is calling" when he needs to urinate. A person might say "I need to visit the restroom" for the same purpose.

There are euphemisms in all cultures, including the Hebrew and Greek. For example, among the ancient Jews, to "cover your feet" refers to going to the bathroom. To "know" a woman is a euphemism for sexual intercourse. The "way of women" is a reference to a woman's monthly period.

Bible translators handle such euphemisms in one of several ways. Some Bible translations, such as formal equivalence (word-for-word) translations, render euphemisms quite literally and leave it up to the reader to figure out what is meant. Other Bible translations, such as dynamic equivalence (meaning-driven) translations, leave out the euphemism but rather describe the action. Still other translations, including some dynamic equivalence translations, might use an alternate modern euphemism that is known in the receptor language (like English). For example, a translation might render the Jewish euphemism "to cover his feet" by using the English euphemism "to relieve himself."[11]

Technical Words

Different Bible translation committees have different policies on how to handle technical language in the Bible. Those who subscribe to the formal equivalence philosophy believe technical words such as *justification, sanctification,* and *propitiation* should be retained in the biblical text since they are rich in theological meaning. By contrast, those who subscribe to the dynamic equivalence philosophy typically believe such terms are incomprehensible to the average reader and hence believe easier substitutes should be used.

Weights, Measures, and Money

Weights, measures, and money are unique to the Jewish cultural context and hence are not easy to translate into English. Formal equivalence translations may transliterate Jewish weights, measures, and money—that is, they spell out the Hebrew or Greek term in English letters (for example, monetary units would include *shekels, talents, denarii,* and *minas*). A footnote is typically included that provides the modern English equivalent of each respective term. Dynamic equivalence translations typically insert a modern equivalent, sometimes including a footnote that references the original Hebrew or Greek term. As well, many Bible versions provide tables that make all this more understandable to the English reader.

Acrostics

A common feature of Hebrew poetry involves the use of the alphabetic acrostic. This entails beginning each line with a successive letter of the Hebrew alphabet (see, for example, Psalm 119). Obviously, while this makes great sense and is easy to grasp by the ancient Hebrew mind, it is almost impossible to translate such acrostic forms into modern English. Most Bibles today simply insert some kind of footnote that clarifies the presence of an acrostic.

Wordplays

Another difficulty involved in translating from the biblical languages into English relates to wordplays. There are cases in the Bible in which there is an obvious wordplay, but it is nearly completely masked in English translations. To illustrate, one scholar notes that "the account of Jacob and Esau's birth and their fight for the rights of the firstborn (Gen. 25:24-34) has several [wordplays]. *Jacob* means 'grasping'; *Esau* means 'hairy'; and Esau's alternative name, *Edom,* means 'red'—hence the red stew exchanged for his birthright."[12]

Considering the Readership

An important consideration in Bible translation involves the target readership of the translation. Will the readers be old or young, new Christians or mature Christians, people who speak English as their first language or people for whom English is a second language? Will the reading be for devotions or for detailed study? Will the reading be done privately or in a public setting? The target readership will largely determine whether or not theological wording—words like *justification, sanctification,* and *redemption*—can be used in the translation. If not, then alternative words or expressions must be found. The benefit of including theological words is that they often communicate a wealth of doctrinal truth. The downside of using a substitution is that an entire descriptive phrase must often be inserted into the text (for example, *justification* becomes "be made right with God").

Generally, formal equivalence (literal) translations retain traditional Bible vocabulary, while dynamic equivalence (meaning-driven) translations seek alternatives in order to make the Bible more accessible to readers who are less familiar with the Scriptures or who have a lower reading ability.

All Translation Necessitates *Some* Interpretation

All translation involves *some* interpretation. After all, there is seldom a one-to-one correspondence between the ancient Hebrew and Greek languages and modern English. Before we can translate a single word from the Hebrew or Greek, we must interpret the meaning of that word in its proper context. One must realize that words get their nuanced meaning in dynamic relationship with other words. That is why context is so very important. Every phrase, clause, and idiom must be interpreted in its proper context before it can be translated accurately into the English language.[13]

It is not too much to say that translation without interpretation is an absolute impossibility. As one scholar put it, "At every turn the translator is faced with interpretative decisions in different manuscript readings, grammar, syntax, the specific semantic possibilities of a Hebrew or Greek word for a given context, English idiom, and the like."[14] Indeed, "a faithful translator is obliged to convey in clear and readable form, not only the meanings of individual words and phrases, but something also of the structure, rhythm, and emotive elements of the original text."[15]

To illustrate, if a Japanese man wanted to say something that carries the meaning, "That person is smart," he might use words *ano hito wa atama ga ii desu,* which, if translated literally into English, mean, "As for that person, his head is good." However, in the United States, no one ever says, "As for that person, his head is good." That is not the way we talk! An English person translating from the Japanese must therefore engage in a certain level of interpretation regarding this phrase, properly rendering it, "That person is smart."

We must do the same thing when translating biblical manuscripts from the original Hebrew or Greek languages. To convert Greek or Hebrew words and phrases into readable English, the translator must decide to some degree what each term means in its original context.[16] He must understand what something meant *in one culture* and then translate it in a way meaningful to *today's culture.* "Between biblical culture and modern western culture there is little overlap of concepts or of words. So in many cases it is difficult to find the right word in English."[17]

We might say, then, that all translation involves at least a two-step process. First, the translators must interpret the meaning of the text in its original context, taking into consideration not just the words themselves, but the literary genre, the culture of the author, the life-situation of the author, and the assumptions (theological and otherwise) that the author brings to the text. Second, then and *only then* is the translator in a position to determine how this meaning can best be conveyed in the receptor language (like English).

Because a certain amount of interpretation comes into play in any translation of the Bible, because there is no one-to-one parallel of words between languages, and because no two languages ever express themselves in exactly the same way, *no translation will ever be absolutely perfect.* It is simply impossible to carry every nuance of the original Hebrew or Greek into clear English. So, as one scholar laments, "Translation always involves a degree of compromise.

Inevitably, something is lost, added or altered in the task of translating from one language to another."[18]

A good policy—one that I will suggest several times throughout this book—is to regularly use several Bible translations, ranging from formal equivalence (word-for-word) translations to dynamic equivalence (meaning-driven) translations. This policy can help shed a great deal of light on what the original biblical author was seeking to communicate.

Why the Need for New Bible Translations?

It seems that new translations of the Bible are coming out with regularity. Is there really a need for such new translations? Christians no doubt have various opinions on the matter.

Some Christians say we need new translations because English is an *evolving* language. Indeed, all languages are in a continual state of flux. No language stays virtually the same throughout history. This necessarily means that every Bible translation will eventually become out of date because its use of language will become out of date. This is nowhere more evident than in the King James Version (KJV) of the Bible, which has language that is not only archaic but has many words whose meanings have completely changed over time. For example, in James 5:11 we are told that "the Lord is very pitiful." In current usage, the word *pitiful* means "lamentable," "deplorable," "woeful," or "pathetic." But back in King James' days the word meant "one who has pity on others." Moreover, in James 2:3 in the KJV we find reference to a man entering a church in "gay" clothing. Today this would be interpreted as having some kind of homosexual meaning, whereas in King James' days the phrase referred to fine clothes.

With each new edition of the major English dictionaries, thousands of new words are introduced. Some people contend that because people in our country have varying levels of reading ability, various translations—ranging from very easy (short words, short sentences, and short paragraphs) to more advanced—are necessary.

Yet another reason for the need for new translations is that there is an ever-increasing percentage of people in our society—generally in the 18- to mid-30s age group—who are on the verge of bailing out of the church altogether. It is suggested that new translations, couched in more relevant and contemporary language, might contribute toward communicating God's timeless truths to our present generation.

Toward this end, once a translation is complete, it in itself may eventually be updated and improved. For example, the New American Standard Bible was updated in 1995. The Revised Standard Version was eventually updated to a more conservative English Standard Version. The Living Bible was eventually updated to the New Living Translation, which itself went through a revision a few years after its initial publication. It is all about communicating God's Word in an *accurate* yet *readable* way!

Tempering Initial Resistance

New translations are sometimes met with initial resistance. When the Septuagint (the Greek translation of the Old Testament that predates the time of Christ) was published, one individual claimed it was "as calamitous for Israel as the day on which their fathers made the golden calf." When Jerome's Latin Vulgate was published, it was widely attacked as "heretical and subversive of the Christian faith." When Tyndale's translation of the New Testament was published, some claimed it was "so faulty a piece of work that revision was out of the question." All of this provides some helpful perspective regarding the loud criticisms often voiced against modern Bible translations.[19]

Theories of Bible Translation

A NEW TESTAMENT SCHOLAR ONCE SAID: "When we speak of faithfulness in translation, we need to clarify the question: *faithfulness to form* [translating word-for-word]? or *faithfulness to meaning?* Sometimes faithfulness to one involves lack of fidelity to the other."[1] Of course, ideally, a translation should be as literal as possible and highly readable. That, however, is easier said than done. Two translation philosophies have emerged among scholars seeking to accomplish the task: *formal equivalence* and *dynamic equivalence*. In what follows, I will briefly survey the cases for and against these philosophies.

The Case *For* the Formal Equivalence Philosophy

The formal equivalence philosophy advocates as literal a rendering of the original text as possible. The translator attempts to render the exact words from Hebrew, Aramaic, and Greek into English. This is why the word *formal* is used: the rendering is *form-for-form* or *word-for-word*. If there is a long sentence in the original Greek, there will be a long sentence in the translated English. As much as possible, the

English rendering will reflect the word order and grammatical structures of the original.

The goal of accurately reproducing the grammar and syntax of the original Hebrew or Greek text is a prime consideration for this philosophy. As one scholar put it, "If the Greek or Hebrew text uses an infinitive, the English translation will use an infinitive. When the Greek or Hebrew has a prepositional phrase, so will the English…. The goal of this translational theory is formal correspondence as much as possible."[2]

The King James Version (1611), the New American Standard Bible (1971, updated 1995), the Revised Standard Version (1952), and the English Standard Version (2001) all reflect the formal equivalence approach to Bible translation. Among the benefits of such translations are that they retain the writing style of the original writers. They also better preserve the original beauty of Scripture and retain theological terminology—terms that are necessary for a full-orbed understanding of what God intended to communicate. For example, such translations will utilize the theological word *justification* instead of inserting a simple substitute, like "being made right with God."

Formal equivalence translations can also be trusted not to mix too much commentary in with the text derived from the original Hebrew and Greek manuscripts. To clarify, while *all* translation entails *some* interpretation, formal equivalence translations keep to a minimum in intermingling interpretive additives into the text. As one scholar put it, "An essentially literal translation operates on the premise that a translator is a steward of what someone else has written, not an editor and exegete who needs to explain or correct what someone else has written."[3]

The Case *Against* the Formal Equivalence Philosophy

Eugene Nida (born 1914), the founder of the dynamic equivalence philosophy, has strong words for those who advocate a word-for-word translation from the original Hebrew and Greek. He alleges that such people "don't understand the text" and "worship words instead of worshiping God as revealed in Jesus Christ."[4]

Critics of the formal equivalence theory often say that a translation can be so literal that it does not truly communicate God's Word to people. If a translation is literal but cannot be understood, then it cannot be said to be accurate. After all, it has not done its job—it has not communicated the original meaning to today's audience. An example might be Robert Young's 1862 overly literal translation, which renders John 3:16 this way: "For God did so love the world, that His Son—the only begotten—He gave, that every one who is believing in him may not perish, but may have life age-during." This rendering is so literal that it is almost unintelligible.[5]

I have noticed that sometimes the debate between advocates of different translation philosophies can become a bit heated. For example, in the following statement against strictly literal translations, the author is not unkind, but there does seem to be a subtle undercurrent of sarcasm:

> Theological hyper-conservatives may prefer literal "translations" because they insist on "verbal inspiration" rather than scriptural inspiration (2 Tim. 3:16), as if the very words and grammatical patterns of language A were sacrosanct, irrespective of the meanings they express in that language; or because the traditional theological terms are maintained, almost as badges of orthodoxy (whether or not they are generally understood); or perhaps because they do not trust the average translation committee to translate meaning properly.[6]

Others counter:

> If a translation gives a *present* tense when the original gives a *past,* or a *past* when it has a *present*…an *a* for a *the,* or a *the* for an *a,* an *imperative* for a *subjunctive,* or a *subjunctive*

for an *imperative;* a *verb* for a *noun,* or a *noun* for a *verb,*
it is clear that verbal inspiration is as much overlooked as
if it had not existed. THE WORD OF GOD IS MADE
VOID BY THE TRADITIONS OF MEN.[7]

The debate continues...

The Case *For* the Dynamic Equivalence Philosophy

If you have purchased a Bible in recent years, there is a very good
chance that you have purchased a dynamic equivalence Bible. This
philosophy advocates a more readable translation that does not provide
an *exact rendering* of the text, but rather focuses on communicating the
meaning of the text. It is a thought-for-thought, meaning-driven translation that seeks to produce the same dynamic impact upon modern
readers as the original had upon its audience. Translators who subscribe to this philosophy hold that a word-for-word translation does
not always adequately capture the meaning of the original text, and
hence a dynamic equivalent rendering is necessary.

Eugene Nida describes dynamic equivalence translation as the
"closest natural equivalent to the source-language message" and insists
it is "directed primarily toward equivalence of response rather than
equivalence of form." He then affirms, "Dynamic equivalence is therefore to be defined in terms of the degree to which the receptors of the
message in the receptor language respond to it in substantially the
same manner as the receptors in the source language. This response
can never be identical, for the cultural and historical settings are too
different, but there should be a high degree of equivalence of response,
or the translation will have failed to accomplish its purpose."[8]

Dynamic equivalence translations generally use shorter words,
shorter sentences, and shorter paragraphs. They use easy vocabulary
and use simple substitutes for theological and cultural terminology.
They often convert culturally dependent figures of speech into easy,
direct statements. They seek to avoid ambiguity as well as biblical

jargon in favor of a natural English style. Translators concentrate on transferring *meaning* rather than mere *words* from one language to another.

One scholar thus suggests that the dynamic equivalence philosophy is superior to the formal equivalence philosophy:

> If we translate word for word and grammatical pattern for grammatical pattern, we often fail to translate the meaning of the original. Indeed, when a translator does not understand the full and precise meaning of a passage, he may take refuge in a word-for-word "translation," thereby passing the buck of understanding the original meaning to his reader, who is much less capable of working it out. A literal translator is like an engineer whose bridge across a river goes only halfway![9]

So, a dynamic equivalence translation seeks to provide easier-to-understand equivalents to phrases that one does not hear in common usage today. For example, in our day, we do not use phrases such as these: "And it came to pass"; "Truly, truly, I say unto you"; "Thus saith the Lord"; and so forth. Such phrases are unnatural to most people nowadays. Hence, in the interest of communication, the dynamic equivalence philosophy changes these into easier equivalents.

Dynamic equivalence translations also seek to clarify cultural customs within the text. For example, when Reuben "tore his clothes" upon discovering that his brothers had sold Joseph as a slave (Genesis 37:29), most readers do not realize that this was a cultural sign of grief. Some dynamic equivalence translations therefore qualify the statement in Scripture so readers know Reuben tore his clothes "in grief."

Dynamic equivalence translations also diverge from the word order of the original Hebrew and Greek to a far greater degree than formal equivalence translations. They do so in order to produce a natural English that is more readily understood. Keeping the English reader in mind, they choose a word order that is more logical not only to produce a clearer English style but also to make reading (and listening) easier. "Word order is especially important when a passage is being read aloud, say in church. While readers can go back to the beginning of a sentence and remind themselves of what is written, listeners have only one shot at understanding what is said."[10] Dynamic equivalence translations are thus widely read in church services today.

The Case *Against* the Dynamic Equivalence Philosophy

A primary criticism of the dynamic equivalence philosophy is that it often makes interpretive decisions for the reader and adds commentary into the text. Such translations might incorporate too much of the translator's personal interpretations, and hence it is less suitable for serious Bible study. As one New Testament scholar put it, "A dynamic equivalence translation is usually clear and quite understandable. But if the translators missed the point of the original—either intentionally or unintentionally—they will be communicating an idea foreign to the biblical text."[11] Another New Testament scholar adds, "Most readers of dynamic equivalent translations do not have any understanding as to the liberties that have been taken with the words of the original text. What dynamic translators give us is a translation plus a commentary, but we have no way of knowing where translation ends and the translation committee's commentary begins."[12]

Scholar Leland Ryken, an advocate of the formal equivalence philosophy, alleges that the dynamic equivalence philosophy takes liberties in translating the Bible that we would certainly not permit in other areas of our lives. He suggests that there are certain documents where the exact words are very important—such as "love letters, marriage vows, legal documents, contracts, accident reports, a memorable statement from a sermon, memoirs of a grandmother, recipes, a compliment or criticism, a quote from an interview, instructions for assembling an appliance."[13] If getting the words right on such documents is important, then how much more is it important that we get the words exactly right (as literal as possible) when translating the Bible? To do anything less is to engage in "linguistic license."

Among other criticisms I have come across on dynamic equivalence translations are the following:

- They convert long sentences into short (often choppy) ones, which can result in a flat, monotonous style, as well as mask the relationship between one sentence and another.

- They convert difficult or technical words into easy substitutes that often do not convey the full breadth of meaning of the original word, and often reduce the literary beauty of the Bible.

- They often convert figures of speech or metaphors into direct statements with the unwarranted assumption that readers will miss what is meant by the figure of speech.

- They convert specific gender references to more generic terminology.

A rather significant problem involves the possibility of interpretive mistakes entering into the picture. One only need observe that Bible commentators often disagree in regard to the proper interpretation of a biblical text. This being the case, it is entirely feasible that two different dynamic equivalence translations of the Bible could translate the same verse in a way that reflects two different interpretations.

A case in point is John 6:27, a verse which speaks of the Father and Jesus. The New American Standard Bible, a literal translation based on the formal equivalence philosophy, reads, "For on Him the Father, God, has set His seal." Dynamic equivalence translations, however, render this verse in a variety of ways. The Revised English Bible says, "For on him God the Father has set the seal of his authority." The Contemporary English Version says, "Because God the Father has given him the right to do so." The New Living Translation says, "For God the Father has given me the seal of his approval." The Message, taking the most liberty, renders it, "He and what he does are guaranteed by God the Father to last." With such widely divergent translations of the same verse, it quickly becomes clear that there is a notable level of subjectivity to dynamic equivalence translations.

It is often suggested that, contrary to the dynamic equivalence philosophy, the doctrine of the inspiration of Scripture best fits the formal equivalence (word-for-word) philosophy. This philosophy recognizes that God's revelation resides in the words and not merely thoughts or ideas.

As noted elsewhere in the book, the biblical Greek word for inspiration literally means "God-breathed." Because Scripture is breathed out by God—because it originates from Him—it is true and inerrant. Biblical inspiration may be defined as God's superintending of the human authors so that, using their own individual personalities and even their writing styles they composed and recorded without error His revelation to humankind in the words of the original autographs. In other words, the original documents of the Bible were written by men, who, though permitted to exercise their own personalities and literary talents, wrote under the control and guidance of the Holy Spirit, the result being a perfect and errorless recording of the exact message God desired to give to man.

The words themselves are important. In 1 Corinthians 2:13 the apostle Paul said he spoke "not in *words taught us by human wisdom* but in *words taught by the Spirit, expressing spiritual truths in spiritual words*" (emphasis added). In this passage Paul (who wrote over half of the New Testament) affirmed that his words were authoritative because they were rooted not in fallible men but infallible God (the Holy Spirit). Later, in 1 Corinthians 14:37, Paul said, "If anybody thinks he is a prophet or spiritually gifted, let him acknowledge that *what I am writing to you is the Lord's command*" (emphasis added). In 1 Thessalonians 2:13, Paul likewise said, "And we also thank God continually because, when you received the word of God, which you heard from us, you accepted it *not as the word of men,* but as it actually is, *the word of God,* which is at work in you who believe" (emphasis added).

Ryken is representative of those who argue against the dynamic equivalence philosophy by appealing to the inspiration of Scripture:

> This doctrine asserts not only that God inspired the thoughts of biblical writers, but that inspiration extends to their words. The impetus for restating this doctrine with vigor a century ago was the claims of liberal theology that only the general thought or ideas of the Bible are inspired, not the details. Numerous passages in the Bible, however, show the importance of the very words of the Bible. A good example is Jesus' response to Satan that "Man shall not live by bread alone, but by every word that comes from the mouth of God" (Matt. 4:4), or Jesus' statement that "the words that I have spoken to you are spirit and life" (John 6:63). (See also Exod. 19:6; Deut. 32:46-47; Prov. 30:5; John 17:8,17; Luke 21:33; Rev. 21:5; 22:15-19.)[14]

Dynamic equivalence enthusiasts counter, however, that such a view is way too strict. Gordon Fee and Mark Strauss comment,

> Much of this rhetoric represents a poor understanding of the doctrine of verbal inspiration, which historically does not refer to the words as "words in themselves," but "words as they convey meaning." It is precisely at this point that we would argue that a translation that places the priority of *meaning* over *form* is much more in keeping with the doctrine of inspiration, since at issue always is the "meaning" of the inspired words. The translation that best conveys that meaning is the most faithful to this historic doctrine.[15]

Critics of the dynamic equivalence philosophy rebut that such translations make it impossible to know with conviction what the Bible *means* because they have not truly been given what the Bible *says*. They claim that even though those who purchase such Bibles may assume when they read it that they are reading the words of the Bible, the reality is that when they read it they are digesting a combination of words from the Bible and insights inserted by the translation committee. Since the inserted insights are not distinguished from that which derives from the original Hebrew and Greek manuscripts, there is no way to know where the Bible words end and the interpretive words begin.

Some Translations Take a "Middle Road"

There is yet another approach that some Bible publishers advocate—an approach that basically has a foot in both camps (*word-for-word* and *thought-for-thought*). In this line of thinking, a word-for-word approach is used for those portions of Scripture where such an approach yields a clear rendering for the English reader. For those portions that get more difficult—that is, for those portions in which a word-for-word translation might seem harder to understand—a thought-for-thought approach is adapted. Such translations seek to be word-for-word when possible, and thought-for-thought when necessary. Some believe this policy achieves the best balance between accuracy and readability. Zondervan's New International Version claims to utilize this method, as does the Holman Christian Standard Version and the NET Bible.

Paraphrases

A few modern Bibles are not translations at all but rather are "paraphrases." To paraphrase a statement is to say it in different (and simpler) words than the author used. It involves more literary license than the dynamic equivalence philosophy.

Scholar Sid Litke is correct in his observation that paraphrases involve a heavy use of interpretation:

Paraphrases have more "interpretation" than translations. That makes paraphrases easier reading because it seems everything is explained. But for that reason, they also will be less reliable, because you only know what the person doing the paraphrase thought a particular verse or phrase means. So it is best to stick with translations for most study and reading...Paraphrases are valuable for younger readers and perhaps for reading through large portions at a time for getting the "big picture."[16]

Most paraphrases are characterized by a great freedom of expression, a use of contemporary idioms and colloquialisms, a highly communicative language style, and more interpretive additives than dynamic equivalence translations. A very popular paraphrase today is Eugene Peterson's *The Message*.

A Sampling of Translations

Having summarized some of the basic theories of translating the Bible, let us now turn our attention to how some of the more popular translations today render specific verses. The differences between the translations reflect their commitment to different philosophies of translation. I will zero in on the specific translation philosophies of individual translations throughout the rest of the book.

Isaiah 26:3

The King James Version: "Thou wilt keep him in perfect peace, whose mind is stayed on thee: because he trusteth in thee."

The New King James Version: "You will keep him in perfect peace, whose mind is stayed on You, because he trusts in You."

The Revised Standard Version: "Thou dost keep him in perfect peace, whose mind is stayed on thee, because he trusts in thee."

The New Revised Standard Version: "Those of steadfast mind you keep in peace—in peace because they trust in you."

The English Standard Version: "You keep him in perfect peace whose mind is stayed on you, because he trusts in you."

The Revised English Bible: "Lord, you keep those of firm purpose untroubled because of their trust in you."

The New International Version: "You will keep in perfect peace him whose mind is steadfast, because he trusts in you."

Today's New International Version: "You will keep in perfect peace those whose minds are steadfast, because they trust in you."

New International Reader's Version: "Lord, you will give perfect peace to anyone who commits himself to be faithful to you. That's because he trusts in you."

The New American Standard Bible: "The steadfast of mind You will keep in perfect peace, because he trusts in You."

The Amplified Bible: "You will guard him and keep him in perfect and constant peace whose mind [both its inclination and its character] is stayed on You, because he commits himself to You, leans on You, and hopes confidently in You."

The New Living Translation: "You will keep in perfect peace all who trust in you, all whose thoughts are fixed on you!"

The New Century Version: "You, Lord, give true peace to those who depend on you, because they trust you."

The NET Bible: "You keep completely safe the people who maintain their faith, for they trust in you."

The Holman Christian Standard Bible: "You will keep in perfect peace the mind [that is] dependent [on You], for it is trusting in You."

GOD'S WORD: "With perfect peace you will protect those whose minds cannot be changed, because they trust you."

The Message: "People with their minds set on you, you keep completely whole, steady on their feet, because they keep at it and don't quit."

The Good News Bible (Today's English Version): "You, LORD, give perfect peace to those who keep their purpose firm and put their trust in you."

The New Jerusalem Bible (Catholic translation): "This is the plan decreed: you will guarantee peace, the peace entrusted to you."

The New American Bible (Catholic translation): "A nation of firm purpose you keep in peace; in peace, for its trust in you."

2 Corinthians 5:8

The King James Version: "We are confident, I say, and willing rather to be absent from the body, and to be present with the Lord."

The New King James Version: "We are confident, yes, well pleased rather to be absent from the body and to be present with the Lord."

The Revised Standard Version: "We are of good courage, and we would rather be away from the body and at home with the Lord."

The New Revised Standard Version: "Yes, we do have confidence, and we would rather be away from the body and at home with the Lord."

The English Standard Version: "Yes, we are of good courage, and we would rather be away from the body and at home with the Lord."

The Revised English Bible: "We are confident, I say, and would rather be exiled from the body and make our home with the Lord."

The New International Version: "We are confident, I say, and would prefer to be away from the body and at home with the Lord."

Today's New International Version: "We are confident, I say, and would prefer to be away from the body and at home with the Lord."

New International Reader's Version: "We are certain about that. We would rather be away from our bodies and at home with the Lord."

The New American Standard Bible: "We are of good courage, I say, and prefer rather to be absent from the body and to be at home with the Lord."

The Amplified Bible: "[Yes] we have confident and hopeful courage and are pleased rather to be away from home out of the body and be at home with the Lord."

The New Living Translation: "Yes, we are fully confident, and we would rather be away from these earthly bodies, for then we will be at home with the Lord."

The New Century Version: "So I say that we have courage. We really want to be away from this body and be at home with the Lord."

The NET Bible: "Thus we are full of courage and would prefer to be away from the body and at home with the Lord."

The Holman Christian Standard Bible: "Yet we are confident and satisfied to be out of the body and at home with the Lord."

GOD'S WORD: "We are confident and prefer to live away from this body and to live with the Lord."

The Message: "Do you suppose a few ruts in the road or rocks in the path are going to stop us? When the time comes, we'll be plenty ready to exchange exile for homecoming."

The Good News Bible (Today's English Version): "We are full of courage and would much prefer to leave our home in the body and be at home with the Lord."

The New Jerusalem Bible (Catholic translation): "We are full of confidence, then, and long instead to be exiled from the body and to be at home with the Lord."

The New American Bible (Catholic translation): "Yet we are courageous, and we would rather leave the body and go home to the Lord."

Philippians 4:6

The King James Version: "Be careful for nothing; but in every thing by prayer and supplication with thanksgiving let your requests be made known unto God."

The New King James Version: "Be anxious for nothing, but in everything by prayer and supplication, with thanksgiving, let your requests be made known to God."

The Revised Standard Version: "Have no anxiety about anything, but in everything by prayer and supplication with thanksgiving let your requests be made known to God."

The New Revised Standard Version: "Do not worry about anything, but in everything by prayer and supplication with thanksgiving let your requests be made known to God."

The English Standard Version: "Do not be anxious about anything, but in everything by prayer and supplication with thanksgiving let your requests be made known to God."

The Revised English Bible: "Do not be anxious, but in everything make your requests known to God in prayer and petition with thanksgiving."

The New International Version: "Do not be anxious about anything, but in everything, by prayer and petition, with thanksgiving, present your requests to God."

Today's New International Version: "Do not be anxious about anything, but in every situation, by prayer and petition, with thanksgiving, present your requests to God."

New International Reader's Version: "Don't worry about anything. Instead, tell God about everything. Ask and pray. Give thanks to him."

The New American Standard Bible: "Be anxious for nothing, but in everything by prayer and supplication with thanksgiving let your requests be made known to God."

The Amplified Bible: "Do not fret or have any anxiety about anything, but in every circumstance and in everything, by prayer and petition (definite requests), with thanksgiving, continue to make your wants known to God."

The New Living Translation: "Don't worry about anything; instead, pray about everything. Tell God what you need, and thank him for all he has done."

The New Century Version: "Do not worry about anything, but pray and ask God for everything you need, always giving thanks."

The NET Bible: "Do not be anxious about anything. Instead, in every situation, through prayer and petition with thanksgiving, tell your requests to God."

The Holman Christian Standard Bible: "Don't worry about anything, but in everything, through prayer and petition with thanksgiving, let your requests be made known to God."

GOD'S WORD: "Never worry about anything. But in every situation let God know what you need in prayers and requests while giving thanks."

The Message: "Don't fret or worry. Instead of worrying, pray. Let petitions and praises shape your worries into prayers, letting God know your concerns."

The Good News Bible (Today's English Version): "Don't worry about anything, but in all your prayers ask God for what you need, always asking him with a thankful heart."

The New Jerusalem Bible (Catholic translation): "Never worry about anything; but tell God all your desires of every kind in prayer and petition shot through with gratitude."

The New American Bible (Catholic translation): "Have no anxiety at all, but in everything, by prayer and petition, with thanksgiving, make your requests known to God."

The Benefit of Multiple Translations

A number of biblical scholars have suggested that perhaps it is best to use *both* a formal equivalence translation and a dynamic equivalence translation, as well as a middle-of-the-road translation, comparing them constantly, so that we best understand the Word of God. As one scholar puts it, "There is great benefit in using more than one version. This is because no version can capture all of the meaning, and different versions capture different facets of meaning. It is especially helpful to use versions from across the translation spectrum: formal, functional, and mediating."[17] Another scholar adds, "By understanding the different translation philosophies which undergird various translations and the strengths and weaknesses of each philosophy, the believer can profitably use different translations to gain greater trust in God's Word, to understand God's Word better, and in turn to live a life which pleases Him."[18]

It is also good to remember that there are specific situations in which one translation might serve better than another. For example, one who is engaging in detailed Bible study would be best suited to use a more literal translation of the Bible, or a formal equivalence translation. On the other hand, for a person who knows very little about the Bible, and is unfamiliar with biblical history, a dynamic equivalence translation might be best. Middle-of-the-road translations might also be useful in both situations above.

In the next chapter, we will turn our attention to a matter of great controversy: *gender-inclusive language.*

The Debate over Gender-Inclusive Language

THE GREEK AND HEBREW original documents of the biblical text often use words like *man* and *brothers* to refer to human beings, male and female. A tremendous debate has erupted in recent years as to whether or not translators should use gender-inclusive language—that is, language that is "inclusive" of males *and* females—in translating those terms. Critics of gender-inclusiveness sometimes claim that their opponents are not only wrong in their linguistic judgments, but that they are actually compromising the truthfulness of God's Word. The debate has become so heated that even whole denominations have split over it.

Back in 2002, when the debate was at its hottest, well-known religion writer Richard Ostling commented, "Conservative Protestants often find themselves in theological arguments with liberals about the Bible's historical reliability. But an unholy squabble over Scripture has erupted in recent days that pits evangelicals against each other."[1] This squabble has been more complex, more confusing, and more divisive than any other I can remember. It seemed to explode upon Western culture in the spring of 1997 when it became public knowledge that Zondervan was publishing an inclusive-language edition of the popular New International Version (NIV). I am referring to Today's New International Version (TNIV). This was by no means the first Bible to adopt inclusive language (earlier the New Revised Standard Version had taken this approach), but the furor escalated to a fever pitch because, apparently, Zondervan was messing with a Bible that was a huge favorite among evangelicals. It quickly became a lightning rod of controversy.

I will address the TNIV more comprehensively later in the book (see chapter 21). At this juncture, it is enough to note that many evangelical scholars publicly denounced this version of the Bible. A *U.S. Newswire* report stated: "One hundred Christian leaders have issued a joint statement that claims they cannot endorse Today's New International Version (TNIV) Bible translation that is produced by Zondervan publishers and the International Bible Society."[2]

What is all the fuss about? Vern Poythress and Wayne Grudem put it this way:

> The Bible is God's own Word to us. We depend on it for instructing us about the crucial issue of salvation: "What must I do to be saved?" (Acts 16:30). We depend on it to guide us in the right way to live: "Your word is a lamp to my feet and a light for my path" (Psalm 119:105). We depend on it for revealing Jesus Christ to us: "These things are written that you may believe that Jesus is the Christ, the Son of God, and that by believing you may have life in his name" (John 20:31). So it is surpassingly important that *the Bible be translated accurately.*[3]

Dallas Theological Seminary professor Darrell Bock understandably asked, "Is the current dispute much ado about nothing, much ado about something, or much ado about Bible translation gone astray?"[4]

He then observed that "those who object most strongly to gender sensitive types of translations…tend to prefer 'formal' equivalence translation theory. The non-gender approach argues that such gender sensitive renderings should not call themselves translations at all, but paraphrases."[5]

In these gender-inclusive translations, virtually hundreds of biblical references to "father," "son," "brother," and "man" have been converted to generalized terms inclusive of women. In many cases, in the place of such words can be found English words whose meaning does not appear in the original languages. One New Testament professor commented, "The question is, where do you draw the line? In translation, you have to be faithful."[6]

Some counter that in modern Western culture, 18- to 34-year-olds misinterpret male language about 90 percent of the time. This means that Bibles that are not gender-inclusive are not communicating to these people. Others rebut, "We're sympathetic to the concerns, but the Bible is not ours to renegotiate. When it comes to the Bible, we want it to be accurate."[7]

Though the debate has become more civil in tone, it nevertheless continues in full force to the present day. In this chapter, my goal is to provide only the briefest of overviews of the primary arguments of both sides. The reader should be aware that hefty volumes have been written on this subject, and hence this chapter represents only an introduction. Hopefully, though, this chapter will provide at least enough information so that you can weigh the matter yourself and come to an informed conclusion. I begin by setting forth the arguments *against* gender-inclusive language.

Representative Arguments *Against* Gender-Inclusive Language

Among the gender-inclusive translations today are the New Revised Standard Version, the Revised English Bible, the New International Reader's Version, the Contemporary English Version, GOD'S WORD, the Good News Bible, the New Century Version, the New Jerusalem Bible, and the New American Bible. Scholar Ron Minton points out that "some of these translations are more extreme than others. For example, the 1989 NRSV, one of the first major gender-inclusive translations, has altered the text more than 4,000 times to make it gender-neutral."[8]

Following are the more common arguments offered against gender-inclusive language in Bible translation:

There could be a loss of elegance in gender-inclusive translations. In other words, too many uses of such terms as *persons* and *people* within a relatively short space becomes inelegant very quickly.[9]

Changing singular references to "he" or "him" in the Bible to the third person "they" or "them" can obscure God's personal dealings with individuals. For example, Jesus' endearing promise, "I will come in and eat with him," is changed in the Good News Bible to "eat with them," a phrase that clearly loses the personal connection of Christ with individual believers (see Revelation 3:20). Readers might wrongly conclude that such verses are talking about a group of believers (like the church) instead of an individual believer. Theologian Wayne Grudem comments, "This systematic change from singulars to plurals is a substantial alteration in the flavor and tone of the entire Bible, with a significant loss in the Bible's emphasis on God relating directly to a specific, individual person." Significantly, he notes that the words *they, them, their,* and *those* occur 1,732 more times in the gender-inclusive NRSV than in the non-gender-inclusive RSV.[10]

Gender-inclusive translations are simply not as accurate in rendering Bible verses from the Hebrew and Greek. Consider a comparison between the New Revised Standard Version and the Revised Standard Version:

- The word *father* occurs 601 fewer times in the NRSV than in the RSV.
- The word *son* occurs 181 fewer times.

- The word *brother* occurs 71 fewer times.
- The words *he, him,* and *his* are either dropped or changed to *you, we,* or *they* over 3,400 times.
- The word *man* is changed to human, mortal, or mortals over 300 times.[11]

God Himself chose the words of Scripture, and human beings do not have the prerogative to change them. All Scripture is inspired or "God-breathed" (2 Timothy 3:16). Every word of God proves true (Proverbs 30:5). The inspired words that came from God included "he" and "him," and we are not free to change them to "they" and "them." God "breathed out" singular pronouns to be used in these various verses, and finite human beings do not have the prerogative to change God's words.

There are no new historical or archeological discoveries that warrant people changing the text of the Bible. The Bible ought to be translated as literally as possible, and then—via proper hermeneutics—interpret the generic use of words like *man* to include women, as intended by the biblical authors.

Well-loved phrases deeply entrenched in the minds of Bible believers can be lost. An example would be Jesus' intention to make His followers "fishers of men," an endearing phrase that many love.

Patriarchalism was part and parcel of the biblical culture, and to obscure it by removing a great deal of male-oriented language could lead people astray regarding this aspect of the Bible. The question is, what if these "patriarchal" elements in Scripture are part of what the Holy Spirit intended to be there by divine inspiration? If we hold to the absolute divine authority of every word of Scripture (Proverbs 30:5), then we should not seek to change or mute any content that the Holy Spirit caused to be there.

Sometimes gender-inclusive translations betray a theological bias against the use of man. The Greek term *anthropos* can be translated as either "man" or "person," depending upon the context. In the NRSV, the translators often refused to translate the word as "man" or "men" *even when the context called for that translation.* For example, where the RSV says the Old Testament high priest was chosen "from among men" (Hebrews 5:1), the NRSV changes it to "from among mortals." The fact is, no woman could be a high priest. The word should quite clearly be translated as "men."

Contrary to the claims of gender-inclusive theorists, the English language has not changed so much that the use of such terms as he, him, *and* his *is no longer proper.* Indeed, national publications such as *Newsweek, U.S. News and World Report,* and the *Chicago Tribune* continue to use *he* in a generic sense and *man* as a name for the human race. *The Associated Press Stylebook and Libel Manual* (1994) instructs one to "use the pronoun *his* when an indefinite antecedent may be male or female."[12] Moreover, the definitions of "man" in *Webster's New Twentieth Century Dictionary,* unabridged second edition, include: "1. a human being; a person, whether male or female. 2. the human race; mankind."[13]

It is not morally wrong to not use gender-inclusive language. As Professor E. Calvin Beisner puts it, "If it is morally wrong not to use gender-inclusive language today, then it was morally wrong for the Old and New Testaments to be written as they were. But if it was morally permissible for the Old and New Testaments to be written as they were, then it is not morally imperative to use gender-inclusive language today."[14]

The meaning of many Bible verses is subtly changed in gender-inclusive translations. Following are some notable examples. (Note that in a number of the following verses I contrast the RSV and NRSV, because one is traditional, and the other is both gender-inclusive and a revision of the other. In other cases I contrast the NIV with the NLT, or I contrast other translations. In each case I compare at least one traditional translation and one gender-inclusive translation. *Relevant words are italicized.*)

Psalm 1:1. In the RSV we read, "Blessed is the *man* who walks not in the counsel of the wicked, nor stands in the way of sinners...but *his* delight is in the law of the LORD." The Hebrew word translated "man" is *ish,* which normally refers to a male in distinction from a female. "Man" is the default meaning of the term. So, naturally and plainly understood, this verse speaks of a single individual man who is righteous and who stands against (plural) sinners, wherever they may be found.[15]

The NRSV, however, renders this verse, "Happy are *those* who do not follow the advice of the wicked…but *their* delight is in the law of the LORD." Everyone knows there is strength in numbers. This translation tends to take away from the spiritual resolve of the single, individual Christian taking a stand against multiple sinners. "Those" is much more generalized, portraying a group standing against evil. Clearly the meaning of the text is subtly changed.

Psalm 34:20. The RSV renders this, "He keeps all *his* bones; not one of them is broken." This is clearly a messianic prediction that was fulfilled in Christ, when none of His bones were broken at the crucifixion (see John 19:36). And yet the NRSV (as well as other gender-inclusive translations) masks the reference to a single man by translating in the plural: "He keeps all *their* bones; not one of them will be broken." One would never know this is a messianic reference.

Proverbs 16:9. In the RSV we read, "A *man's* mind plans *his* way, but the LORD directs *his* steps." The verse clearly refers to God's providential guidance of an individual person's life. The NRSV puts it this way: "The *human* mind plans *the* way, but the LORD directs *the* steps." Aside from making the verse gender-inclusive, the NRSV renders it in a particularly wooden and strange way. It also takes away from the individual connection between the LORD and a person. The New Living Translation renders it, "*We* can make *our* plans, but the LORD determines *our* steps." The New Century Version renders it, "*People* may make plans in *their* minds, but the LORD decides what *they* will do."

Notice how these various renderings subtly change the meaning of the verse. Indeed, they mask the Lord's connection with an individual person. Instead, a group is in view.

John 6:44. In the NIV we read, "No one can come to me unless the Father who sent me draws *him,* and I will raise *him* up at the last day." By contrast, notice how the gender-inclusive New Living Translation renders it: "For no one can come to me unless the Father who sent me draws *them* to me, and at the last day I will raise *them* up." A group is the main focus in the NLT, whereas the individual person is the main focus in the NIV. Does the NLT mean to communicate crowds of people coming to Jesus? The theological idea that God sovereignly elects and draws *individual sinners* to Christ is lost in the NLT translation.

John 6:56. In the NIV we read, *"Whoever* eats my flesh and drinks my blood remains in me, and I in *him."* In the NIVI (New International Version Inclusive), we read, *"Those* who eat my flesh and drink my blood remain in me, and I in *them."* Again, the emphasis on the individual is lost in favor of a group, perhaps a church or Bible study group or people in an evangelistic tent. Instead of the Lord's Supper picturing the Lord's spiritual communion with an individual, the Lord's communion is with the group. Individual intimacy is thereby masked.

John 14:23. In the RSV we read, "Jesus answered him, 'If a *man* loves me, *he* will keep my word, and my Father will love *him,* and we will come to *him* and make our home with *him.*'" To avoid use of *man, he,* and *him,* the NRSV renders the verse, *"Those* who love me will keep my word, and my Father will love *them* and we will come to *them* and make our home with *them."* By using plurals, the intimate connection of the Father and Son with the individual believer is completely lost. The use of the plurals could easily be wrongly interpreted as referring to believers in a church setting. *Personal* application has been masked in favor of a *group* application.

John 15:5. The RSV renders this verse, *"He* who abides in me, and I in *him, he* it is that bears much fruit, for apart from me you can do nothing." The NRSV, seeking to avoid *he* and *him,* renders it, *"Those* who abide in me and I in *them* bear much fruit, because apart from me you can do nothing." No longer is Christ viewed as individually dwelling with each disciple but rather the church seems to be in view.

1 Corinthians 14:28. The NIV renders this verse, "If there is no interpreter, the *speaker* should keep quiet in the church and speak to *himself* and God." The NIVI renders it, "If there is no interpreter, the *speakers* should keep quiet in the church and speak to *themselves* and God." The gender-inclusive rendering may easily be misinterpreted. Does this mean that tongues-speakers should go off by themselves in a separate room and speak to each other and to God in tongues? This ambiguous rendering results from the gender-inclusive translation.

1 Corinthians 15:21. The RSV renders this verse, "As by a *man* came death, by a *man* has come also the resurrection of the dead." The NRSV, seeking to avoid the use of *man,* renders it, "Since death came through a *human being,* the resurrection of the dead has also come through a *human being.*" This gender-inclusive rendering masks Adam's representative headship of the human race as well as the manhood of Christ.

Galatians 6:7. The RSV renders this verse, "Whatever a *man* sows, that will *he* also reap." The NRSV translates it, "*You* reap whatever *you* sow." This changes a universal teaching true of *people in general* to a narrow teaching dealing *with Christians alone.* Readers may wrongly conclude that Paul is speaking of something true only of Christians ("you"), but in fact, Paul is making a much more general statement about human conduct and about people generally. Such changes essentially amount to rewriting the Bible.

Colossians 3:18-19. The NIV renders this verse, "Wives, submit to your husbands, as is fitting in the Lord." However, in some of the gender-inclusive translations being published today, one gets an entirely different teaching. The Contemporary English Version, for example, renders it: "A wife must put her husband first. This is her duty as a follower of the Lord." What, specifically, does it mean for a wife to put her husband "first"? One can easily interpret this in a way that does not involve submission. One scholar thus pointed out, "The CEV's 'translation' harmonizes well with what many modern people might wish that the Apostle Paul said. But it does not do justice to what he actually said."[16]

Now, in pointing out such errors in translation, one should not conclude that those who participated in gender-inclusive translations intended evil. In fact, there is no question that they intended well. Their goal has been to communicate more effectively God's Word in a way that does not offend. However, those who are against gender-inclusive language believe such changes often result in subtle changes of meaning in the text of the Bible.

If such alterations constitute changing the Word of God, even minimally, then all of this becomes a quite serious matter. Throughout the Old Testament we find the phrase uttered by the prophets, "Thus saith the Lord." God informed Moses that He would send another prophet like Moses, affirming, *"I will put my words in his mouth,* and he will tell them everything I command him. *If anyone does not listen to my words* that the prophet speaks in my name, I myself will call him to account" (Deuteronomy 18:18-19; see also Numbers 22:38; Jeremiah 1:9; 14:14; 23:16-22; 29:31-32; Ezekiel 2:7; 13:1-16). Throughout the Bible God is often said to speak "through" the prophet (1 Kings 14:18; 16:12,34; 2 Kings 9:36; 14:25; Jeremiah 37:2; Zechariah 7:7,12). For this reason, ignoring anything a prophet said amounted to ignoring God Himself (Deuteronomy 18:19; 1 Samuel 10:8; 13:13-14; 15:3,19,23; 1 Kings 20:35,36). The apostle Paul in the New Testament affirmed that *all* Scripture is inspired or God-breathed (2 Timothy 3:16). Some conservative Christian scholars believe such verses have serious implications for changing biblical texts to include gender-inclusive language.

Representative Arguments
For Gender-Inclusive Language

Scholars who are in favor of gender-inclusive language in Bible translation offer a number of key arguments:

Many say that such language makes our English Bibles clearer and more accurate in terms of the biblical authors' intended meaning. It is suggested that even though masculine-oriented language was heavily used in the Bible, such terminology *today* can mislead people into thinking that men are the primary focus of God's words. But this is not so. Paul and the other biblical writers intended their letters to be read by the whole church, both men and women. It is therefore more accurate to refer to them as "brothers and sisters" rather than just "brothers." Today many female readers feel excluded by exclusively male terminology, and since the Bible writers intended to include women, it makes sense to reflect this in the translation.

Gender-inclusivity is in keeping with the dynamic equivalence philosophy of translation, which is sensitive to the issue "How would the biblical author communicate his ideas today?" In the ancient world, it was common to say *man* or *he* when speaking of all people. A basic principle of translation theory is to express the *ancient* text in the thoughts and idioms of *modern* language. It is suggested that translations should not be done strictly based on individual Hebrew or Greek words, but based on how those words are used *in the context.* If the context indicates inclusivity, then the translation should reflect this.

It is an accepted practice to substitute they *and* them *in place of* he *and* him. Indeed, as scholar Grant Osborn points out, the *Webster's Dictionary of English Usage* (1989) states, "The common solution (to the lack of a common-gender pronoun in English) has been to substitute the plural 'they'; even Chaucer used this dodge." The dictionary also notes, "The plural pronouns have been pressed into use to supply the missing form since Middle English." Osborn thus concludes, "In other words, *they* has been used for *he,* without distortion of meaning, for centuries."[17]

It is highly revealing that even the Bible translates itself in a dynamic fashion. For example, in Psalm 68:18 we read, "When you ascended on high, you led captives in your train." In Ephesians 4:8 the apostle Paul cites this verse: "This is why it says, 'When he ascended on high, he led captives in his train'." Paul here felt free to change pronouns without fear of doing injustice to the Word of God. Likewise in Psalm 104:4 we read, "He makes winds his messengers, flames of fire his servants." In Hebrews 1:7, this verse is cited: "In speaking of the angels he says, 'He makes his angels winds, his servants flames of fire.'" Here *messengers* is changed to *angels* and word order is changed, thereby giving credence to the dynamic equivalence theory of translation so popular today.[18]

Changing he *to* you *or* they *does not change the essential meaning of the text, and is therefore an acceptable practice.* Osborn comments, "There is more potential for misunderstanding when *man* or *he* is used where the text refers to both men and women. In that situation, *you* or *they* is more accurate, especially for those in our society who are not used to the generic masculine singular."[19]

There are also a variety of excellent words that can be used in place of less common words that refer to males, as the following chart demonstrates:

Bible Word	Gender-Inclusive Substitute
Workmen	workers
Craftsmen	craft workers or skilled workers
Herdsmen	herders
Foremen	slave drivers
Kinsmen	relatives
fellow countrymen	kindred
Watchmen	guards or lookouts
Bowmen	archers
Horsemen	riders[20]

Church history reveals that gender-inclusive language has been used in early translations, such as that by William Tyndale and even the King James Version. For example, Tyndale, whose translation of the New Testament was published in 1526, translated Matthew 5:9 this way: "Blessed are the peacemakers, for they shall be called *the children* [in the original Greek this term is *sons*] of God." As well, the King James Version translates the Hebrew phrase "sons of Israel" 644 times in the English as "children of Israel." Only four times in the Bible does the KJV translate the phrase as "sons of Israel" when the phrase is quite obviously referring to men. New Testament scholar Darrell Bock notes that "in the OT, the seventeenth century KJV rendered [the Hebrew word] *ben* (or its plural) 'son' or 'sons' 2,822 times, and as 'child' or 'children' 1,533 times, or right at 35 percent."[21]

There are innumerable cases in which gender-inclusive language makes the intended meaning of the biblical author much clearer. Following are some examples:

Hosea 2:4. This verse speaks of Gomer's three children (two sons and one daughter), and reads literally from the Hebrew, "Upon her sons also I will have no pity, because they are sons of whoredom." Many Bibles opt for "children" as a better contextual translation.

Romans 3:28. The NIV renders this verse, "For we maintain that *a man* is justified by faith." The TNIV, a gender-inclusive translation, renders it, "For we maintain that *a person* is justified by faith" (relevant words italicized). In this verse the apostle Paul is quite clearly referring to all people and not just to men, and so "person" is much more appropriate. Scholars point out that the Greek word translated "man" in the NIV is *anthropos,* which can also mean "person," and is the word from which we get the word "anthropology" (the study of human beings). This does not mean the NIV was necessarily incorrect in translating the word as "man" since in this context the word was intended to be taken generically as referring to both men and women. But the TNIV rendering is considered to be more contextually accurate.

1 Timothy 2:5. The NIV renders this verse, "For there is one God and one mediator between God and *men,* the *man* Christ Jesus." The TNIV, by contrast, renders it, "For there is one God and one mediator between God and *human beings,* Christ Jesus, himself *human*" (relevant words italicized). This is more accurate because, quite clearly, Jesus came to save not just men but all human beings, including women.

Luke 14:27. The NIV renders the important part of this verse, "*Anyone* who does not carry *his* cross...cannot be my disciple." The word *his* might be taken by some to mean that only males can become disciples. To correct this wrong idea, gender-inclusive translations render the verse in different ways. The NLT puts it this way: "If *you* do not carry *your* cross, *you* cannot be my disciple." The NIVI renders it, "And *those* who do not carry *their* cross...cannot be my disciple" (relevant words italicized).

Psalm 1:1. The NIV renders this verse, "Blessed is *the man* who does not walk in the counsel of the wicked or stand in the way of sinners or sit in the seat of mockers." Many argue that this verse is not referring to males alone but is also intended to include females. The New Living Translation thus renders it, "Oh, the joys of *those* who do not follow the advice of the wicked" (relevant words italicized).

Acts 20:30. The NIV renders this verse, "Even from your own number *men* will arise and distort the truth in order to draw away disciples after them." The NIVI renders it, "Even from your own number *some* will arise and distort the truth" (relevant words italicized). The latter is believed by many to be more accurate because false teachers are not just limited to men. Indeed, Revelation 2:20 speaks of a cultic group with false theology led by a woman named Jezebel. Hence, the warning in Acts 20:30 was no doubt intended to include both male and female false teachers.

Mark 8:36. The NIV renders this verse, "What good is it for a *man* to gain the whole world, yet forfeit *his* soul?" Obviously the intent of this verse is to refer to both men and women. Hence, the NIVI renders it, "What good is it for *you* to gain the whole world, yet forfeit *your* soul?" (relevant words italicized).

John 6:44. The NIV renders this verse, "No one can come to me unless the Father who sent me draws *him,* and I will raise *him* up at the last day." This verse is surely not limited to males, and hence the NLT renders it: "For no one can come to me unless the Father who sent me draws *them* to me" (relevant words italicized).

John 8:51. The NIV renders this verse, "If anyone keeps my word, *he* will never see death." Obviously the "anyone" in this verse is not restricted to males. Hence, the NLT puts it this way: "I assure you, anyone who obeys my teaching will never die." Such a rendering is inclusive of both males and females.

Seeking Balance

We have examined strong arguments both *for* and *against* gender-inclusive translations. The debate will no doubt continue in the years to come. As I close this chapter, my goal is to provide some closing perspectives on the matter that can help us keep a balance.

First, let us resolve never to forget that both sides in this debate have good intentions, each desiring to render the Bible as clearly as possible to English-speaking audiences. Each side is seeking to give proper high respect to the Word of God.[22] Therefore, it is inappropriate to question the integrity or the motives of those who hold to an opposing point of view on the issue.

Second, let us recognize that, despite the substantial differences between the two opposing points of view, there is nevertheless much that is held in common.[23] For example:

- All agree that the Bible is inspired by God and is therefore authoritative.

- While there is disagreement on *how* to transfer the meaning of a text from the source (or donor) language to the receptor (or target) language, all share the *goal* of transferring the meaning of a text from the source (or donor) language to the receptor (or target) language.

- All agree that because of the differences that exist among languages, an absolutely unbending word-for-word translation is impossible. All therefore agree that at least some interpretation must enter the process of translating text from one language to another.

- All agree that languages are constantly changing and it is therefore necessary to periodically update already-existing translations and even produce new translations so that people in each new generation can understand the Word of God.

- All agree that individual words do not just carry a single meaning but often can carry a range of nuances of meaning depending on the textual context (this is called the "semantic range"). An accurate translation is one in which the translator determines the correct nuance of meaning of the word or words in the source language and then chooses an appropriate word or phrase in the receptor language to capture that sense.

- Many agree that it is incorrect to use gender-inclusive language when the original author of Scripture intended an obvious gender-specific sense.

- All agree that the Greek term *anthropos* can be accurately translated "person" or "human being" when the author intended to refer to either a man or a woman.

- All conservatives agree (so far) that gender-inclusive language should not be used of the person of God.[24] Gordon Fee and Mark Strauss elaborate:

> Two points must be kept in mind concerning God-language. (1) God is neither male nor female. He is pure spirit (John 1:18; 4:24). Numbers 23:19 reads, "God is not a man [i.e., a human being], that he should lie, nor a son of man, that he should change his mind" (NIV; cf. Hos. 11:9; Job 9:32). (2) Although some of the biblical images related to God are feminine (e.g., God is like a mother who comforts her children: Ps. 131:2; Isa. 46:3; 49:15; 66:13; Hos. 11:3-4), most are masculine. God is King of the universe, sovereign Lord of all, and Father to his people as their Creator and Redeemer (Deut.

32:18; Ps. 103:13; Hos. 11:1). Jesus calls God his Father
(Mark 14:36) and invites his disciples to pray to him
as "our Father in heaven" (Matt. 6:9). It is appropriate, then, to refer to God as "he"—not because God
is a male, but because he is a person, and because a
masculine pronoun more accurately reflects the biblical
metaphors like "Father" used to describe God.[25]

Now, the points above are presented with a view to emphasizing
that such agreements ought to temper the way we view our brothers
and sisters who hold to a different overall viewpoint on the issue of
gender-inclusive language. Let's all choose to show a little grace!

*Third, a balanced viewpoint that many today are subscribing to is that
our goal should not be to eliminate gender distinctions in Scripture, but
rather to clarify them.* In other words, verses that refer exclusively to
males should remain masculine, while verses referring exclusively to
females should remain feminine. When the context indicates that both
males and females are in view, however, inclusive terms such as "persons" and "brothers and sisters" are more precise and more accurate.[26]

To be fair, others would rather deal with the problem *not* by removing
male language from Scripture but rather by emphasizing that such male
language does not carry an "exclusive" sense. In this line of thought,
it is better to retain a fully accurate translation and then address the
generic use of terms like "man" at the level of hermeneutics.

*Fourth, it may be wise to recognize that there is room for both literal
translations and dynamic equivalence translations.* As one scholar puts
it:

> For those who do not know the biblical languages, literal
> translations are a necessity for serious Bible study. For those
> who want to understand the message of the text clearly,
> a dynamic translation is indispensable. There is room for
> both the *retention* and the *replacement* of male pronouns
> and terms in various versions. Neither is wrong; both have

distinctive purposes. One lets the reader know exactly how the ancient author worded his message; the other tells the reader exactly what he meant.[27]

Keeping such points in mind will help us to remain balanced as the debate continues.

The King James Version

THE KING JAMES VERSION (KJV) is a word-for-word (formal equivalence) translation that was first published in A.D. 1611. The translation was "authorized" by King James I in England, and is thus known as the Authorized Version.[1] The overall goal was to produce a better translation than any other in existence at the time, a translation that could be understood by common people. Contrary to many modern translations, the KJV does not utilize gender-inclusive language. It has an approximate twelfth-grade reading level.

The KJV is unquestionably the most widely printed and distributed Bible in human history. It was "appointed to be read in churches." Given the support and endorsement of King James I, this version of the Bible was virtually destined for success and wide dissemination. It has been a classic and a standard for almost four centuries now.

The Story Behind the Translation

James VI of Scotland took over the English throne from the Tudors in A.D. 1603. He was promptly crowned King James I of England.

At that time, the number of English translations of the Bible caused disunity in the kingdom.

In January of 1604, James I called a conference of theologians and churchmen at Hampton Court in order to hear and then resolve things that were amiss in the church. He sought to deal with ecclesiastical grievances of all sorts. A number of those present pressed the new king for a new translation—one that would take the place of both the Geneva Bible and the Bishops' Bible (so named because a group of Anglican bishops revised it), as well as thwart the Catholic challenge symbolized by the Douay-Rheims Bible. The actual proposal for a new translation came from a Puritan, Dr. John Reynolds, president of Corpus Christi College, Oxford. King James I was agreeable to the proposal.

Not everyone was initially open to the new translation, however. There were some from more conservative expressions of the Christian faith who initially resisted publication of the KJV. These were unwilling to accept *anything* rooted in the official Church of England, or produced under the auspices of the king.[2]

Translation Philosophy and Procedure

The KJV is a word-for-word translation—though, many would say, not unbendingly so. In producing this translation, there were six panels of translators appointed by King James I, two meeting at Oxford, two at Cambridge, and two at Westminster. A total of 54 translators were involved in the project, and began their work in 1604. Of these six panels, two oversaw the translation of the New Testament, three oversaw the translation of the Old Testament, and one oversaw the translation of the Apocrypha.* The six groups worked separately, and once their work was complete, it was sent to the other panels for

---

* The Apocrypha refers to 14 or 15 books of doubtful authenticity and authority that the Roman Catholics decided belonged in the Bible sometime following the Protestant Reformation. The Catholic Council of Trent (1545–1563) canonized these books. See Appendix C—"Does the Apocrypha Belong in the Bible?"

comment and revision. The chief members of the six panels then met to make final decisions on all suggested revisions.[3]

The translation procedure was based upon 15 rules that were given to the team of 54 translators. For instance, the first rule states, "The ordinary Bible read in the Church, commonly called the Bishops' Bible, [was] to be followed, and as little altered as the truth of the original will permit." The sixth rule stipulates that no marginal notes be affixed "but only for the explanation of the Hebrew or Greek words, which cannot without some circumlocution, so briefly and fitly be express'd in the text." All 54 translators adhered to all 15 rules.

The original preface of the KJV tells us that the goal of the translation team was not to make "a new translation, nor yet to make of a bad one a good one...but to make a good one better, or out of many good ones one principal good one." So, dependence on the work of previous translators is acknowledged. The original title page of the KJV even states that it was made "with the former translations diligently compared and revised."[4]

Even though various preexisting translations contributed to the King James Version, it is primarily William Tyndale's work that is most pervasive. A 1998 scholarly analysis concluded that Tyndale's words account for 84 percent of the New Testament and 75 percent of the Old Testament books he translated. As one scholar put it, "His genius as a translator shines through in page after page and phrase after phrase."[5] Scholars agree that the KJV is at its very best when it keeps its wording close to that of Tyndale. It is at its worst when it does not. One linguistic critic lamented that in the KJV, "portions of those parts of the Old Testament that Tyndale did not translate, particularly in the prophetic books, are close to unintelligible."[6] (Job and parts of Isaiah are poorly translated.)

The King James translators avoided including interpretive marginal notes, but did include marginal notes with alternative translations of Greek words that have a range of possible meanings. Some today find this significant, especially in regard to the debate with KJV-only proponents, some of whom not only believe the King James Version is the only legitimate Bible but that its wording was directed by the very hand of God. The fact that the KJV translators acknowledged possible alternative translations would seem to undermine this position.

The KJV generally renders God's Old Testament name, YHWH (or Yahweh), as "Lord," using small capital letters. Interestingly, however, the KJV uses the term *Jehovah* for YHWH four times: Exodus 6:3, Psalm 83:18, Isaiah 12:2, and Isaiah 26:4. When the term *Adonai Yahweh* occurs in the Old Testament, it is rendered as "Lord God."

The KJV translators began each verse on a new line. The beginning of each paragraph was marked with a pilcrow (¶) in the 1611 publication. Interestingly, however, these pilcrow marks disappeared after Acts 20:36. (One wonders if the printer just ran out of pilcrows.)

Since its initial publication, the King James Version has undergone three revisions, incorporating more than 100,000 changes. The most careful and comprehensive revision was published in 1769. The KJV is well known for its archaic language, using such terms as *thee, thou,* and *ye,* and verbs often ending in "-eth" and "-est" (*loveth* and *doest*). This is one reason some love the KJV. The language seems so elegant.

Sampling the King James Version

We gain insight into the translation style of the KJV by considering its rendering of some famous Bible passages:

Genesis 1:1-3: "In the beginning God created the Heaven and the earth. And the earth was without form, and void; and darkness was upon the face of the deep. And the Spirit of God moved upon the face of the waters. And God said, Let there be light: and there was light."

Psalm 23:1-3: "The Lord is my shepherd; I shall not want. He maketh me to lie down in green pastures: he leadeth me beside the still waters. He restoreth my soul: he leadeth me in the paths of righteousness for his name's sake."

Proverbs 3:5-6: "Trust in the Lord with all thine heart; and lean not unto thine own understanding. In all thy ways acknowledge him, and he shall direct thy paths."

Matthew 6:9-13: "After this manner therefore pray ye: Our Father which art in heaven, Hallowed be thy name. Thy kingdom come. Thy will be done in earth, as it is in heaven. Give us this day our daily bread. And forgive us our debts, as we forgive our debtors. And lead us not into temptation, but deliver us from evil: For thine is the kingdom, and the power, and the glory, for ever. Amen."

John 3:16-17: "For God so loved the world, that he gave his only begotten Son, that whosoever believeth in him should not perish, but have everlasting life. For God sent not his Son into the world to condemn the world; but that the world through him might be saved."

Ephesians 2:8-9: "For by grace are ye saved through faith; and that not of yourselves: it is the gift of God: Not of works, lest any man should boast."

Philippians 4:13: "I can do all things through Christ which strengtheneth me."

Hebrews 11:1,6: "Now faith is the substance of things hoped for, the evidence of things not seen...But without faith it is impossible to please him: for he that cometh to God must believe that he is, and that he is a rewarder of them that diligently seek him."

Benefits

A notable benefit of the King James Version is that it is virtually unsurpassed in poetic beauty. In fact, no other version comes near the literary beauty and elegance of the KJV. Yet, despite such modern sentiments, the truth is that the KJV was written in the *everyday language of 1611* and was engineered to be understood by the common people. Of course, back in those days, the majority of people could not read or write, and hence most people came to love the KJV through its public readings.

Many of the translational phrases in the KJV are highly recognizable and highly memorable. Consider this representative selection:

- "And God said, Let there be light, and there was light" (Genesis 1:3).
- "Ye are the salt of the earth" (Matthew 5:13).
- "Ask, and it shall be given you; seek, and ye shall find; knock, and it shall be opened unto you" (Matthew 7:7).
- "Behold, I stand at the door and knock" (Revelation 3:20).
- "God shall wipe away all tears from their eyes" (Revelation 7:17).

It is also interesting to observe that a number of current English idioms are actually rooted in the King James Version. For example, in the KJV we find reference to the following:

- "fell flat on his face" (Numbers 22:31)
- "escaped with the skin of my teeth" (Job 19:20)
- "flies [in] the ointment" (Ecclesiastes 10:1)
- "pride goeth before...a fall" (Proverbs 16:18)
- "sour grapes" (Ezekiel 18:2)
- "pour out your heart" (Psalm 62:8)[7]

It has well been said that the combination of the King James Version and Shakespeare's writings together are responsible for over half of all our language's clichés and stock phrases.[8]

Cautions

Despite all the good things about the KJV, there are also some cautions to be aware of. Following are some of the more pertinent concerns cited by modern scholars.

Changes in Word Meaning

Word usage has changed since the KJV was initially translated in

1611. Some words are now obsolete, and others (over 300) have changed meaning. For example, in James 5:11 we are told that "the Lord is very pitiful." In current usage, the word *pitiful* means "lamentable," "deplorable," "woeful," or "pathetic." Back in King James' days, the word meant "one who has pity on others." Clearly, then, a modern reader encountering this verse might misunderstand its intended meaning.

Another example is the KJV rendering of James 2:3, where we find reference to a man wearing "gay" clothing being given a good seat in the church. Today this might be interpreted as having some kind of homosexual meaning, whereas in King James' days, "gay clothes" meant "fine clothes."[9] Again, then, a modern reader encountering this verse might misunderstand its intended meaning.

Yet another example is 1 Samuel 18:4, where we read that "Jonathan stripped...to his girdle." This would confuse many readers today, perhaps even causing some to raise their eyebrows. In King James' days, however, "girdle" simply meant "belt."

Late Manuscripts

Another caution relates to the fact that the King James Version was based on manuscripts which many scholars believe are not as accurate as some earlier-dated manuscripts more recently discovered. I know that KJV enthusiasts do not like to hear this, but it is wise to consider that many of today's top biblical scholars have provided substantive proof. One scholar notes that "the Hebrew and Greek texts available in the sixteenth and early seventeenth century were much inferior to what is available today, and at many points the words rendered by the King James' translators are not what is now agreed to be the original text.... The discovery of earlier texts and the advances in textual criticism mean that there are now serious textual questions to be set against the undoubted literary qualities of the KJV."[10]

Daniel Wallace, well-known professor of New Testament Greek at Dallas Theological Seminary (and whose textbooks are used at seminaries worldwide), adds the following:

The Greek text that stands behind the King James Bible is demonstrably inferior in certain places. The man who edited the text was a Roman Catholic priest and humanist named Erasmus. He was under pressure to get it to the press as soon as possible since (a) no edition of the Greek New Testament had yet been published, and (b) he had heard that Cardinal Ximenes and his associates were just about to publish an edition of the Greek New Testament and he was in a race to beat them. Consequently, his edition has been called the most poorly edited volume in all of literature! It is filled with hundreds of typographical errors that even Erasmus would acknowledge.[11]

Wallace proceeds to give one such example from Erasmus's Greek text:

In the last six verses of Revelation, Erasmus had no Greek manuscript (he only used half a dozen, very late manuscripts for the whole New Testament anyway). He was therefore forced to "back-translate" the Latin into Greek and by so doing he created seventeen variants* that have never been found in any other Greek manuscript of Revelation! He merely guessed at what the Greek might have been.[12]

An illustration of the difference this can make between the KJV and modern Bible versions relates to 1 John 5:7 and the doctrine of the Trinity. In most translations, there is no evidence for the Trinity in this verse. However, the KJV reads: "For there are three that bear record in heaven, the Father, the Word, and the Holy Ghost: and these three are one." The English Standard Version (a highly respected modern translation), by contrast, translates verses 7-8: "For there are

---

* A literary "variant" is a reading that differs from the standard form.

three that testify: the Spirit and the water and the blood; and these three agree."

Scholars today affirm that the words in the KJV rendering of 1 John 5:7 are not in the earliest Greek manuscripts. The words are found, however, in some Latin manuscripts. Its appearance in late Greek manuscripts is explained by the fact that Erasmus was placed under pressure by church authorities to include it in his Greek New Testament of A.D. 1522. (He had omitted it in his two earlier editions of 1516 and 1519 because he could not find any Greek manuscripts that contained it.) The inclusion of the verse in the Latin Bible was probably due to a scribe incorporating a marginal comment into the text as he copied the manuscript of 1 John.

This issue, if nothing else, points to the wisdom of using more recent translations of the Bible. Even if the KJV is preferred as one's general Bible, it ought to be supplemented by other, more modern translations to minimize possible wrong conclusions one might draw from reading the KJV alone.

Incorrect Renderings

It is also noteworthy that some translational errors in the KJV have never been corrected. For example, the name "Jesus" appears in both Acts 7:45 and Hebrews 4:8 when "Joshua" is actually the correct rendering. Moreover, Matthew 23:24 is rendered, "Ye blind guides, which strain at a gnat, and swallow a camel." The Greek text actually means "strain *out* a gnat," not "*at* a gnat."[13] The average reader, of course, is completely unaware of mistranslations such as these.

Better Understanding of the Languages Today

Aside from the fact that defective manuscripts were used in producing the KJV, and aside from the fact that the KJV has archaic language with words that have changed in meaning since 1611, it is also true that our understanding of the Hebrew, Aramaic, and Greek languages today is much improved.[14] The discovery of papyri in the twentieth century* has shed much light on the meaning of biblical words.[15] This means we are better equipped to translate the Bible than scholars were back in 1611.

Costly Printing Errors

I cannot close this chapter without noting an infamous misprint that made its way into the 1631 edition of the KJV. In this edition, the word *not* was omitted in the seventh commandment so that it read: "Thou shalt commit adultery." For this, the printers were fined three hundred pounds, which was "big money" back in those days. This Bible became known as the "Wicked Bible." All copies were ordered to be burned.

Later, in the 1653 edition, the word *not* was omitted from 1 Corinthians 6:9 so that it read, "The unrighteous shall inherit the kingdom of God." This Bible became known as the "Unrighteous Bible."

---

* In ancient times, a papyrus plant was made into strips and pressed into a material upon which one could write. In the twentieth century, papyri were discovered containing nonbiblical, nonliterary Greek and Latin ancient texts that shed light on the social, cultural, and religious setting in which the New Testament was written.

The Revised Standard Version

THE REVISED STANDARD VERSION (RSV) is not actually a new translation but an authorized revision of the 1901 American Standard Version (ASV), itself a revision of the KJV.* The goals of the RSV translation team were to (1) preserve the qualities of the King James Version that made it so great, (2) accurately reflect the meaning of the original languages, and (3) effectively render it in readable English.[1] The New Testament was completed in 1946, with the complete Bible following in 1952.

The RSV is a formal equivalence translation, seeking to be word-for-word where possible. Like many other such translations, the RSV does not use gender-inclusive language. It has an approximate middle school reading level.

The RSV aimed at being an ecumenical Bible, uniting Christians from various theological and denominational persuasions. Ironically, however, the translation ended up being both unifying *and* divisive at the same time (more on this below).

---

* I do not address the 1901 American Standard Version in detail in this book because it is not presently in wide circulation.

The new translation was recognized by many as one that accurately rendered the original Hebrew, Aramaic, and Greek. On the first day of its publication in 1952, it sold over a million copies. In many churches across America, it quickly replaced the Authorized Version as the Bible of choice.

By 1974, sales of the RSV had reached 30 million copies. And by the time the New Revised Standard Version (see chapter 11) was published in 1990, 55 million copies of the RSV had been sold.

The Story Behind the Translation

The stylistic qualities of the American Standard Version, published in 1901, were viewed by many as lacking in significant ways. The International Council of Religious Education (now the National Council of Churches)—a body linking together some 40 denominations in the United States and Canada—therefore recommended a revision of the ASV. The need for this revision was heightened by the discovery of several important biblical manuscripts in the 1930s and 1940s.[2] The work toward this revision began in 1937, involving a committee of 32 American scholars. Scholar Robert Thomas tells us these scholars "came from several backgrounds. Their expertise was in academic areas related to the original languages and in English, and in experience with conducting public worship."[3] The revision was produced with widespread denominational support.

Ideally, the intention was to include British scholars alongside American scholars in the work of revision. This would have made the RSV a truly international effort. The war years (1939–1945), however, made this infeasible. Besides, in the later stages of the translation work for the RSV, British scholars were already engaged in translating a new Bible—the New English Bible. Nevertheless, when the RSV was finally published, it received a generally positive welcome among the British.

Funding for the revision project was difficult to come by. Funds were not available at all until the worst years of the Depression had passed. In 1937, however, a special arrangement was made with the publisher Thomas Nelson and Sons. In exchange for advance royalties to the translators/revisers, Nelson obtained exclusive rights for publishing the Bible for ten years after the revision work was completed. After this ten-year period, the translation was to be made available to other publishers, under specific conditions.

Translation Philosophy and Procedure

The RSV sought to be word-for-word whenever possible (much like the ASV). However, the RSV translation committee also sought to modernize the language of the text. *Thee* and *thou* were changed to *you*, except when referring to deity. Archaic renderings such as *goeth* and *saith* were changed to *goes* and *says*. As well, the common KJV phrase, "And it came to pass," was removed. Moreover, in a major departure from the ASV, which rendered the divine name (YHWH) as "Jehovah," the RSV rendered it as "LORD," printed in small capitals, just like the KJV had done earlier.

An oddity of this translation is that Jesus is addressed as "you" during His incarnate state—that is, during the Gospels—but is referred to as "thou" following His ascension into heaven. The translators justified this practice by arguing that even though Jesus retained His deity during the Incarnation, He was not *thought of* as such until after His resurrection.[4]

There was much excitement when the work of the translators was finally done. After all, there had been over 80 meetings and some 450 12-hour working days among the translators/revisers. Once the translation was complete, a huge publicity campaign was inaugurated, with over 3,000 celebratory events being held throughout the United States and Canada, attended by an estimated 1.5 million people.[5]

The RSV was revised in 1971, almost 20 years after its initial publication. This revision took into account textual and linguistic studies that had been completed since the initial publication of the RSV. It is noteworthy that two Gospel passages disputed as belonging in the

Bible—the longer ending of Mark (Mark 16:9-20) and the story of the woman caught in adultery (John 7:53–8:11)—were restored to the text (the previous edition had omitted these passages). These passages, however, are separated from the context by a blank space with explanatory notes to indicate that they are not in the earliest Greek manuscripts.

An Expanded Edition of the RSV was published in 1977. It included not only the books considered "deuterocanonical" by Roman Catholics (that is, the Apocrypha[6]), but also 3 and 4 Maccabees and Psalm 151 (from the Septuagint[7]), thus making the Bible also acceptable to Eastern Orthodox churches.[8] This was in keeping with the ecumenical goals of the translation.

Sampling the Revised Standard Version

We gain insight into the translation style of the RSV by considering its rendering of some famous Bible passages:

Genesis 1:1-3: "In the beginning God created the heavens and the earth. The earth was without form and void, and darkness was upon the face of the deep; and the Spirit of God was moving over the face of the waters. And God said, 'Let there be light'; and there was light."

Psalm 23:1-3: "The LORD is my shepherd, I shall not want; he makes me lie down in green pastures. He leads me beside still waters; he restores my soul. He leads me in paths of righteousness for his name's sake."

Proverbs 3:5-6: "Trust in the LORD with all your heart, and do not rely on your own insight. In all your ways acknowledge him, and he will make straight your paths."

Matthew 6:9-13: "Pray then like this: Our Father who art in heaven, hallowed be thy name. Thy kingdom come. Thy will be done, on earth as it is in heaven. Give us this day our daily bread; and forgive us our debts, as we also have forgiven our debtors; and lead us not into temptation, but deliver us from evil."

John 3:16-17: "For God so loved the world that he gave his only

Son, that whoever believes in him should not perish but have eternal life. For God sent the Son into the world, not to condemn the world, but that the world might be saved through him."

Ephesians 2:8-9: "For by grace you have been saved through faith; and this is not your own doing, it is the gift of God—not because of works, lest any man should boast."

Philippians 4:13: "I can do all things in him who strengthens me."

Hebrews 11:1,6: "Now faith is the assurance of things hoped for, the conviction of things not seen…And without faith it is impossible to please him. For whoever would draw near to God must believe that he exists and that he rewards those who seek him."

Benefits

A major benefit of the Revised Standard Version is that it is easier to read than the KJV as well as the ASV. It modernized the biblical texts according to current English usage, which was appealing to many people. It is for this reason that the RSV quickly replaced the KJV in so many churches across America. For many, it accomplished the dual goal of accuracy and readability.

Cautions

Though the RSV sold a staggering number of copies, not everyone was pleased with it. Reactions against it came from a number of different sectors in American society. On the political front, one must keep in mind that during the years the RSV first emerged on the scene, the cold war with communism was in full swing. People were extraordinarily sensitive about possible communist intrusions. More to the point, Senator Joseph McCarthy of Wisconsin seemed to smell a communist rat just about everywhere he turned his attention. Because the RSV makes reference to the word *comrade* in three verses (Judges 7:13,14; Hebrews 1:9), and because communists call their friends "comrades," McCarthy reasoned that the RSV involved a communist plot. Some said it was inspired by "reds under the beds."

It was not long before the RSV became banned from use at Air Force bases across America. (A 1960s edition of the U.S. Air Force Training Manual warned recruits against the communist-tainted RSV.) Eventually, a thorough investigation conducted by nonpartisan authorities in Washington revealed that this entirely unsupported charge was nothing more than "venomous nonsense," and the Air Force Training Manual in question was withdrawn.

Meanwhile, on the religious front, conservative Christians were busy doing battle with secularists—something that became known as the fundamentalist-modernist controversy.* This came to a head in the 1925 Scopes Monkey Trial when a high school biology teacher went on trial in Tennessee for teaching Darwinian evolution in the classroom. As a result of this, fundamentalist Christians were sensitive toward any intrusion of modernistic influences in churches, seminaries, and even Bibles.

With that in mind, one must recall that the RSV was sponsored by the National Council of Churches, which includes several denominations, and whose doctrinal commitments were viewed as having some modernist leanings. As a result of this, fundamentalist Christians were biased against the RSV before it was even published. When it finally came into print, however, a veritable firestorm erupted over the RSV translation of Isaiah 7:14. Whereas other translations rendered this verse as a prophecy that Christ would be born of a *virgin,* the RSV rendering said Christ would be born of a *young woman.* This generated an immense controversy, igniting an explosion of fundamentalist wrath.

Conservative Christians have long believed the virgin birth of Christ is not only implied in the Old Testament—it is actually *predicted* there—in Isaiah 7:14. Many have argued that the Hebrew word *almah* in Isaiah 7:14 should be translated "virgin," and not merely

---

* Fundamentalism is a modern, conservative Christian movement that emphasizes adherence to certain "fundamentals" or basic doctrines of Christianity.

"young woman," since there are no examples in the Old Testament where it means anything but a young unmarried girl. Moreover, the Greek Old Testament (Septuagint), which predates the time of Christ, translated the Hebrew word *almah* with the unambiguous Greek word *parthenos,* which always means "virgin." Hence, the translators of the Greek Old Testament evidently believed this was a prediction of the virgin birth of the Messiah. The inspired New Testament text sanctioned the Septuagint translation of *almah* as "virgin" when it quoted the Septuagint rendering of Isaiah 7:14 to show that this prophecy was fulfilled in the virgin birth of Christ (see Matthew 1:23). [9]

Because of the RSV's rendering of this verse, it came under prolonged and bitter attack.[10] Conservative Christians accused the RSV translators of deliberately tampering with Scripture to deny the virgin birth of Jesus. Pamphlets were published with titles like *The Bible of Antichrist, The New Blasphemous Bible,* and *Whose Unclean Fingers Have Been Tampering With the Holy Bible—God's Pure, Infallible, Verbally Inspired Word?* Copies of the translation were publicly burned. One preacher even sent the ashes of a burnt RSV to the senior editor of the RSV.[11] Clearly, the RSV—while popular among many—at the same time became one of the most hated translations of all time. Dr. Bruce Metzger, of Princeton University, commented with a grin on his face, "I am grateful to be a Bible translator in the 20th century. Nowadays, they only burn the translations rather than the translators!" He also noted, however, how shameful it was to treat a Bible in this way.[12]

Some conservative evangelicals had other gripes with the RSV. For example, "expiation" was put in place of the earlier ASV's "propitiation" (Romans 3:25; Hebrews 2:17; 1 John 2:2; 4:10). In the eyes of some, this served to weaken the doctrine of the atonement.

Because of the strong negative reaction against the RSV, the King James Only movement (the members of which believe the KJV is the only legitimate Bible)—particularly within Independent Baptist and Pentecostal churches—found renewed vigor in its defense of the KJV. Further, this strong reaction against the RSV is one reason for the plethora of new translations that emerged in the latter twentieth century. Still further, since the time of the RSV, many Christians have used Isaiah 7:14 as a "litmus test" to judge new translations— that is, they check how a new translation renders Isaiah 7:14 before pronouncing it okay.[13] For many people, the translation of this single verse became a determining factor for orthodoxy.

As a footnote, it is interesting to observe that the chairman of the RSV translation committee, Luther Weigle, has been approached more than once about the possibility of producing an edition of the RSV that is more acceptable to the conservative Christians. Such requests have always been declined. When a Catholic edition of the RSV was published, the rift between the RSV and conservative Christians became seemingly insurmountable. In more recent days, however, a conservative revision has indeed been accomplished—the English Standard Version (see chapter 17).

6

The Amplified Bible

THE AMPLIFIED BIBLE is an expanded or amplified translation produced jointly by the Zondervan Corporation and the Lockman Foundation. The overall goal of the translation was to provide insights from the original Hebrew and Greek languages for English readers who do not know Hebrew or Greek. It does not utilize gender-inclusive language, and has an approximate eleventh-grade reading level.

The Amplified Bible is not intended to replace other, more traditional translations. Rather, it is intended to supplement them. The publisher tells us, "The genius of the Amplified Bible lies in its rigorous attempt to go beyond the traditional 'word-for-word' translation to bring out the richness of the Hebrew and Greek languages. The purpose of the Amplified Bible is to reveal any other clarifying meanings from the original languages that may be concealed by the traditional translation method."[1]

The Amplified Bible was published progressively in five editions. The Gospel of John was published in 1954, the New Testament in 1958, Job–Malachi in 1962, Genesis–Esther in 1964, and the complete Bible in 1965.

The Story Behind the Translation

The Amplified Bible is unique in that a single person "compiled" it. It is even more unique because that person was a woman, Frances E. Siewart (Litt.B., B.D., M.A., Litt.D.; 1881–1967). Mrs. Siewart dedicated her life to an intensive study of Scripture as well as to the cultural and archaeological background of biblical times.[2]

Without going into excessive detail, Mrs. Siewart was a hymn-lover, studied the Bible at the university and seminary level (Princeton Seminary), assisted many Christians in preparing Bible studies, married a minister who was a brilliant Greek student, assisted various ministers in their public written work, wrote articles for religious periodicals, and spoke often at various venues. Upon becoming a widow, she devoted her full time to doing biblical research for ministers and religious writers.

This prepared Mrs. Siewart and led up to her work on the Amplified Bible—which was based on 20,000 hours of research and prayerful study.[3] Her desire was to produce a Bible that would enable English readers to grasp the many rich insights in the original Hebrew and Greek of the Bible.

Translation Philosophy and Procedure

The Amplified Bible is actually based on the American Standard Version (ASV), published in 1901, with reference also made to various texts in the original languages. Much of the information in the Amplified Bible is actually derived from commentaries and exegetical works. Following Siewart's primary work, the Lockman foundation wisely appointed a committee of Hebrew and Greek scholars to carefully review her work to ensure accuracy. As well, multiple other translations of the Bible were examined to ensure the accuracy of the Amplified Bible.

Unlike traditional formal equivalence translations, the Amplified Bible seeks to provide not just a single-word English equivalent for each Hebrew or Greek word, but also adds phrases that provide clarifying shades of meaning from the original languages. It seeks to bring out the full nuanced meaning of the original languages. The Amplified Bible, by using synonyms and definitions, both "explains and expands the meaning of words in the text by placing amplification in parentheses and brackets and after key words or phrases."[4] Through amplification, "the reader gains a better understanding of what the Hebrew and Greek listener instinctively understood (as a matter of course)."[5]

The Amplified Bible has a unique format. Parentheses () in the text indicate additional nuances of meaning included in the original word, phrase, or clause in the original language. Brackets [ ] in the text contain clarifying words or comments that are not in the original text, as well as definitions of Hebrew and Greek names. Words in italics point to familiar passages now recognized as inadequately supported by the original Hebrew or Greek manuscripts. (Such italicized portions are often accompanied by an explanatory footnote.) The Old Testament divine name, YHWH, is rendered "Lord" (title case). Pronouns referring to deity are capitalized.

The Amplified Bible also contains helpful cross-references. These cross-references are contained within the text itself, making them easy to access. Scripture references are placed within brackets at the end of a verse, and are intended to cover any part of the preceding verse to which they apply.

Sampling the Amplified Bible

We gain insight into the translation style of the Amplified Bible by considering its rendering of some famous Bible passages. Pay special attention to words in parentheses and brackets.

Genesis 1:1-3: "In the beginning God (prepared, formed, fashioned, and) created the heavens and the earth. The earth was without form and an empty waste, and darkness was upon the face of the very great deep. The Spirit of God was moving (hovering, brooding) over the face of the waters. And God said, Let there be light; and there was light."

Psalm 23:1-3: "The Lord is my Shepherd [to feed, guide, and shield me], I shall not lack. He makes me lie down in [fresh, tender], green pastures; He leads me beside the still and restful waters. He refreshes and restores my life (my self); He leads me in the paths of righteousness [uprightness and right standing with Him—not for my earning it, but] for His name's sake."

Proverbs 3:5-6: "Lean on, trust in, and be confident in the Lord with all your heart and mind and do not rely on your own insight or understanding. In all your ways know, recognize, and acknowledge Him, and He will direct and make straight and plain your paths."

Matthew 6:9-13: "Pray, therefore, like this: Our Father Who is in heaven, hallowed (kept holy) be Your name. Your kingdom come, Your will be done on earth as it is in heaven. Give us this day our daily bread. And forgive us our debts, as we also have forgiven (left, remitted, and let go of the debts, and have given up resentment against) our debtors. And lead (bring) us not into temptation, but deliver us from the evil one. For Yours is the kingdom and the power and the glory forever. Amen."

John 3:16-17: "For God so greatly loved and dearly prized the world that He [even] gave up His only-begotten (unique) Son, so that whoever believes in (trusts, clings to, relies on) Him shall not perish (come to destruction, be lost) but have eternal (everlasting) life. For God did not send the Son into the world in order to judge (to reject, to condemn, to pass sentence on) the world, but that the world might find salvation and be made safe and sound through Him."

Ephesians 2:8-9: "For it is by free grace (God's unmerited favor) that you are saved (delivered from judgment and made partakers of Christ's salvation) through [your] faith. And this [salvation] is not of yourselves [of your own doing, it came not through your own striving], but it is the gift of God; Not because of works [not the fulfillment of the Law's demands], lest any man should boast. [It is not the result of what anyone can possibly do, so no one can pride himself in it or take glory to himself.]"

Philippians 4:13: "I have strength for all things in Christ Who empowers me [I am ready for anything and equal to anything through Him Who infuses inner strength into me; I am self-sufficient in Christ's sufficiency]."

Hebrews 11:1,6: "Now faith is the assurance (the confirmation, the title deed) of the things [we] hope for, being the proof of things [we] do not see and the conviction of their reality [faith perceiving as real fact what is not revealed to the senses]. ...But without faith it is impossible to please and be satisfactory to Him. For whoever would come near to God must [necessarily] believe that God exists and that He is the rewarder of those who earnestly and diligently seek Him [out]."

Benefits

The primary benefit of the Amplified Bible is that it is essentially a commentary on the original languages of the biblical text. Some biblical scholars suggest that "the strength of this version is that it acknowledges that no single English word or phrase can capture precisely the meaning of the Hebrew or Greek."[6] Many view the Amplified Bible as a helpful tool to use in conjunction with one's main Bible.

Cautions

A caution regarding the Amplified Bible is that with all the "amplified" material that is added, the text is sometimes hard to follow. Verses may sound awkward and even fragmented when read aloud. One reviewer I came across suggested that with all the synonyms inserted into the text, reading the Amplified Bible is almost like swallowing a thesaurus. Hebrews 1:2 is offered as an example: "[But] in the last of these days He has spoken to us in [the person of a] Son, Whom He appointed Heir and lawful Owner of all things, also by and through Whom He created the worlds and the reaches of space and the ages of time [He made, produced, built, operated, and arranged them in order]."[7]

Another caution noted by some is that the very process of adding "amplified" material into the text involves a level of interpretation on the part of the translator, despite the publisher's claim that it is "free of personal interpretation."[8] In fairness, one should keep in mind that Siewart's work was scrutinized by a team of Hebrew and Greek scholars to ensure accuracy.

Yet another caution, noted by some scholars, is that readers may wrongly assume that the Hebrew or Greek word in question carries the full range of meaning in each and every biblical context. Thus, scholar Alan Duthie warns that the Amplified Bible (and other such "expanded" translations) tend to "heap up words to cover the full range of meaning of every word, including the meanings irrelevant to the particular context."[9] Gordon Fee and Mark Strauss likewise warn that the Amplified Bible may give readers "the false impression that Hebrew and Greek words are 'packed' with theological content and can mean many things at once." This might lead some readers to believe that they can simply "pick whichever meaning they like instead of discerning the single correct meaning that fits the context."[10] David Dewey similarly warns, "While it is true that a word in Hebrew or Greek will have a range of meaning not always covered by just one word in English, it is wrong to assume the Hebrew or Greek word in question will carry that full range of meaning in every context. Generally, a writer has one specific meaning in mind when using a particular word."[11] Again, though, one should in fairness keep in mind that the translation was checked by a team of Hebrew and Greek scholars.

One final caution seems warranted. Though the Amplified Bible cites many good resources that have proven reliable over the years, it is unfortunate that appeal is also occasionally made to the work of George Lamsa, whose work has now proven to be unreliable by recent scholarly studies.[12]

Despite such cautions, I am glad to have a copy of the Amplified Bible in my collection. I should note, however, that some scholars have suggested that one way of getting insights on the original Hebrew and Greek languages *without using* the Amplified Bible is to compare a number of English translations and see how various translators render the verse in question. This sounds like wise counsel!

The New American Standard Bible

THE NEW AMERICAN STANDARD BIBLE (NASB) is a word-for-word, formal equivalence translation that does not use gender-inclusive language. It is a revision of the 1901 American Standard Version (ASV), which is not presently in wide distribution. Sometimes considered an evangelical counterpart to the Revised Standard Version, which itself was a revision of the ASV, the NASB was produced by the Lockman foundation.

The NASB took ten years to complete and was published in stages. The Gospel of John was published in 1960, the other Gospels in 1962, the entire New Testament in 1963, with the whole Bible following in 1971.[1] It has an eleventh-grade reading level.

The Story Behind the Translation

The Lockman Foundation is a California nonprofit Christian corporation whose goal is to promote Christian education, evangelism, and Bible translation in a number of languages. In 1959, Lockman launched a new translation project that was to be based on the 1901 ASV. Lockman was free to modify the ASV text since its copyright had expired.

Great care and reverence was given to this project. As we read in the NASB preface, "The New American Standard Bible has been produced with the conviction that the words of Scripture as originally penned in the Hebrew, Aramaic, and Greek were inspired by God."[2]

The translation project involved the work of 58 then-anonymous translators from a wide variety of denominational backgrounds—including Presbyterian, Methodist, American Baptist, Disciples, Southern Baptist, Nazarene, General Association of Regular Baptist, Congregational, Independent Baptist, and Free Methodist—a fact that helped the team avoid denominational or sectarian biases. These theologically conservative translators are now acknowledged, and a small sampling includes such well-known biblical scholars as Gleason Archer, Kenneth Barker, Charles Feinberg, E.F. Harrison, J. Barton Payne, Merrill Tenney, Bruce Waltke, Kenneth Wuest, Paul Enns, and Harold Hoehner. All the translators are conservative Bible scholars who have doctorates in biblical languages, theology, or other advanced degrees.

Translation Philosophy and Procedure

The NASB translation team sought to produce a literal yet readable translation of the Bible that would bring the contemporary reader as close as possible to the actual wording and grammatical structure of the original writers—including the distinctions in Greek tenses. The translators also sought to incorporate recent discoveries of Hebrew and Greek textual sources.

The translators are careful to distinguish their work from dynamic equivalence translations of the Bible. "Instead of telling the reader what to think, the NASB provides the most precise translation with which to conduct a personal journey through the Word of God."[3] It is the Holy Spirit's task to illumine the literally translated Word so that believers who read it understand it.

As alluded to previously, even though the NASB is a literal, word-for-word translation, the goal was also to make it readable. The NASB preface tells us, "The attempt has been made to render the grammar and terminology in contemporary English. When it was felt that the word-for-word literalness was unacceptable to the modern reader, a change was made in the direction of a more current English idiom. In the instances where this has been done, the more literal rendering has been indicated in the notes."[4]

The NASB translation team was guided by a fourfold aim:

1. These publications shall be true to the original Hebrew, Aramaic, and Greek.
2. They shall be grammatically correct.
3. They shall be understandable.
4. They shall give the Lord Jesus Christ His proper place, the place which the Word gives Him.[5]

Unlike the ASV, the NASB translators chose not to use the term *Jehovah* for the Old Testament personal name of God, YHWH. Instead, they chose to use "Lord" (printed with small capital letters), like many other modern translations do. The only exception is when YHWH appears in close proximity or right next to another Hebrew word for Lord, *Adonai,* in which case the rendering is "God."

A unique feature of the NASB is that quotations of the Old Testament in the New Testament are printed in small capital letters. Quotation marks are utilized for dialogue and for other quoted material. Such formatting enhances readability.

Though each verse starts on a new line in the NASB, paragraphs are designated via boldface numbers or letters. Words not in the original Hebrew or Greek languages, but added because they are implied, are italicized in the NASB.

In the 1971 edition (first edition) of the NASB, the King James-ish *Thou, Thee,* and *Thy* are used in prayer to God. Moreover, all pronouns referring to God, Jesus Christ, and the Holy Spirit are capitalized.

One of the most attractive features of the NASB is its excellent cross-reference system. It is among the best ever published. Also of great benefit are the alternate translations provided in the marginal notes on each page.

The NASB was, for a time, the best-selling modern Bible in America (mid-1970s). However, it was overtaken—indeed, *left in the dust*—by the New International Version (NIV) when it was published in 1978. Still, the NASB has maintained high respect and steady sales through the years, especially among conservative Christians.

In 1995, 20 biblical scholars took three years in producing an updated edition of the New American Standard Bible that further enhanced clarity and readability without reducing accuracy. "Vocabulary, grammar, and sentence structure were carefully reviewed for greater understanding and smoother reading."[6] More specifically, *Thees* and *Thous* were changed to *You,* other antiquated vocabulary was updated, sentences containing awkward English were smoothed out, difficult word order was fixed, and fewer sentences begin with *And.* Moreover, the updated edition is available in two formats—one (like the previous edition) where each verse begins on a new line, and one formatted with full paragraphing.[7]

Sampling the New American Standard Bible

We gain insight into the translation style of the New American Standard Bible by considering its rendering of some famous Bible passages:

Genesis 1:1-3: "In the beginning God created the heavens and the earth. The earth was formless and void, and darkness was over the surface of the deep, and the Spirit of God was moving over the surface of the waters. Then God said, 'Let there be light'; and there was light."

Psalm 23:1-3: "The LORD is my shepherd, I shall not want. He makes me lie down in green pastures; He leads me beside quiet waters. He restores my soul; He guides me in the paths of righteousness for His name's sake."

Proverbs 3:5-6: "Trust in the LORD with all your heart and do not lean on your own understanding. In all your ways acknowledge Him, and He will make your paths straight."

Matthew 6:9-13: "Pray, then, in this way: 'Our Father who is in heaven, hallowed be Your name. Your kingdom come Your will be done, on earth as it is in heaven. Give us this day our daily bread. And forgive us our debts, as we also have forgiven our debtors. And do not lead us into temptation, but deliver us from evil. [For Yours is the kingdom and the power and the glory forever. Amen.]'"

John 3:16-17: "For God so loved the world, that He gave His only begotten Son, that whoever believes in Him shall not perish, but have eternal life. For God did not send the Son into the world to judge the world, but that the world might be saved through Him."

Ephesians 2:8-9: "For by grace you have been saved through faith; and that not of yourselves, it is the gift of God; not as a result of works, so that no one may boast."

Philippians 4:13: "I can do all things through Him who strengthens me."

Hebrews 11:1,6: "Now faith is the assurance of things hoped for, the conviction of things not seen…And without faith it is impossible to please Him, for he who comes to God must believe that He is and that He is a rewarder of those who seek Him."

Benefits

The NASB has a number of benefits. First and foremost, because it is a highly literal translation, it is an excellent choice for detailed Bible study. The alternate translations in marginal notes, along with an excellent cross-reference system, make it all the better for Bible study.

Because each verse begins on a new line (in some editions), the verse numbers are more easily (and more quickly) seen by the human eye, making it easier to navigate to the verses one is looking for.

Because all Old Testament quotes are in capital letters, this makes it easy to distinguish between Old Testament quotes and the words of the New Testament writer.

All in all, the NASB is considered by many to be a great translation for Bible study.

Cautions

One caution regarding the New American Standard Bible is that it is not as easy to read and understand as some of the dynamic equivalence translations. Some claim this translation is somewhat stilted and wooden.[8] They say its language is not contemporary and its English is not idiomatic. Others say it does not flow as well as, say, the NIV. As one scholar put it, "Many times it is simply Greek put in English dress."[9] For this reason, some believe it is not as suitable for public reading or use from the pulpit. (Of course, others strongly disagree and believe it is the *best* Bible for the pulpit because it *is* so literal in its rendering.)

Some have claimed that beginning each verse on a new line (in some editions) makes it more difficult to follow the flow of thought of the biblical authors. Such is not a problem with Bibles that use full-paragraph formatting. Moreover, with each verse on a new line, some complain that the text often appears fragmented. Of course, since the publication of the updated edition in 1995, a full-paragraph edition of the NASB is available.

Another caution involves the claim by some that the NASB translators were too rigid in their understanding of the original Greek and Hebrew. Though this may seem somewhat technical, Professor Daniel Wallace explains it in a way that most will grasp:

> [The NASB translators] often translate the Greek perfect as though it were an English perfect. But the two do not mean the same thing. The Greek perfect should often be translated like an English present tense. In Ephesians 2:8, for example, the KJV has "for by grace ye *are* saved" while

the NASB has "for by grace you *have been* saved." But "you *have been* saved" in English offers no comfort to the present time since it says nothing about the continuation of salvation. The Greek perfect actually has the force of both: you have been saved *in the past* and you are *still* saved. In this instance, the KJV translators did a better job than the NASB largely because they understood English better than the NASB translators.[10]

Of course, if this is going to be a criticism of the NASB, then, in fairness, it must also be a criticism of quite a number of other Bible translations today that render the verse essentially the same way as the NASB, including the popular NIV and the more recent ESV.

Today both the 1995 updated edition and the original 1971 edition remain in print. I own both editions, and often use the 1995 edition for detailed Bible study.

The Good News Translation

THE GOOD NEWS TRANSLATION—formerly published as the Good News Bible, and Today's English Version—was published in 1976 by the American Bible Society. This was the first English Bible to intentionally adopt the dynamic equivalence (thought-for-thought) philosophy of translation. The principles behind this translation were directly derived from the work of Eugene Nida and his experience in mission-field translation for first-time Bible readers.[1] The Good News Translation has a sixth-grade reading level, suitable for ten-year-olds. More recent editions have revised passages in which the English style was unnecessarily "exclusive" and "inattentive to gender concerns" (though actual changes in the text were moderate).

This Bible has been widely endorsed by a number of denominations, from the Southern Baptist Convention, to the Presbyterian Church USA, to the Lutheran Church-Missouri Synod, to the Roman Catholic Church (with a special edition that includes the Apocrypha*).

---

* The Apocrypha refers to 14 or 15 books of doubtful authenticity and authority that the Roman Catholics decided belonged in the Bible sometime following the Protestant Reformation. The Catholic Council of Trent (1545–1563) canonized these books. See Appendix C—"Does the Apocrypha Belong in the Bible?"

This partially accounts for the astronomical sales this translation has enjoyed.

The Story Behind the Translation

The impetus for this new translation is rooted in requests to the American Bible Society from Africa and the Far East for a Bible translation specially designed for those who speak English as an *acquired* language. In other words, these countries needed an exceedingly easy-to-read English Bible for people for whom English was not their first language. There was also interest in the United States for a Bible that would be suitable for new literates (people who had just learned to read). Responding to such concerns, the American Bible Society agreed that the time had come for a common-language translation of the Scriptures in English.

While the Society's initial goal was to produce a Bible that would benefit readers for whom English was a *second* language, the Bible also ended up becoming extremely popular among those for whom English is their *first* language. In fact, this became the main "market niche" for this new translation. The appeal was that this Bible used standard, everyday, natural, clear, unambiguous English.

Translation Philosophy and Procedure

The translation of the New Testament was primarily the work of one Robert Bratcher, a former Southern Baptist missionary commissioned by the American Bible Society for the task. Bratcher worked with a consulting committee of theologians and biblical scholars appointed by the Society. To ensure accuracy, drafts were sent to a number of English-speaking Bible Societies throughout the world. Based on comments and suggestions that were received, Bratcher made a number of modifications in his rendering of the New Testament.

In 1966 this New Testament was published under the title *Good News for Modern Man: The New Testament in Today's English Version.* Subsequent editions were published in 1967 and 1973 as a direct result of further comments and suggestions that came in from readers all over the world. This New Testament sold many millions of copies.

The Old Testament was translated by a seven-man team, all members of different denominations—a fact that aided the team in avoiding sectarian bias. The Old Testament was published with a revised New Testament in 1976 as the Good News Bible. This version was renamed the Good News Translation (GNT) in 2001. This was done primarily because of misconceptions that the Good News Bible was merely a paraphrase and not a genuine translation.

The language of the GNT was intended to be natural, clear, simple, and unambiguous. It is said to be a "common language" translation. "Common language" is defined as the language that is common to both educated *and* uneducated people (including children). The GNT preface tells us, "The translators have tried to avoid words and forms not in current or widespread use; but no artificial limit has been set to the range of the vocabulary employed."[2]

Cultural words, such as *centurion,* and theological words, such as *justification,* have been modernized. Archaic language has been updated. For example, in 2 Samuel 7:16, instead of the literal "Thy throne shall be established for ever," the Good News Translation reads, "Your dynasty will never end." In Romans 12:20, "Heap coals of fire on his head" becomes "Make him burn with shame."[3] Ancient customs not known to today's readers have also been reworded; thus, "anointed my head with oil" (Psalm 23:5) becomes "welcomed me as an honored guest." As well, modern equivalents are used in place of the biblical terms for the hours of the day and measures of weight.

The Old Testament name for God, YHWH, is rendered as "Lord." However, when *Adonai,* another word meaning "Lord," is followed by YHWH, the combination is rendered by the phrase "Sovereign Lord."

The biblical text in the GNT has been divided into sections, and headings are provided throughout which indicate the contents of the section. The translation also features explanatory footnotes that contain cultural and historical information, textual information, alternative readings, and references to other passages. There are short introductions to each book of the Bible.

A Roman Catholic edition of the GNT, which includes the Apocrypha, was published in 1979. The GNT has also been anglicized into British English by the British and Foreign Bible Society.

Sampling the Good News Translation

We gain insight into the translation style of the Good News Translation by considering its rendering of some famous Bible passages:

Genesis 1:1-3: "In the beginning, when God created the universe, the earth was formless and desolate. The raging ocean that covered everything was engulfed in total darkness, and the Spirit of God was moving over the water. Then God commanded, 'Let there be light'— and light appeared."

Psalm 23:1-3: "The LORD is my shepherd; I have everything I need. He lets me rest in fields of green grass and leads me to quiet pools of fresh water. He gives me new strength. He guides me in the right paths, as he has promised."

Proverbs 3:5-6: "Trust in the LORD with all your heart. Never rely on what you think you know. Remember the LORD in everything you do, and he will show you the right way."

Matthew 6:9-13: "This, then, is how you should pray: 'Our Father in heaven: May your holy name be honored; may your Kingdom come; may your will be done on earth as it is in heaven. Give us today the food we need. Forgive us the wrongs we have done, as we forgive the wrongs that others have done to us. Do not bring us to hard testing, but keep us safe from the Evil One.'"

John 3:16-17: "For God loved the world so much that he gave his only Son, so that everyone who believes in him may not die but have eternal life. For God did not send his Son into the world to be its judge, but to be its savior."

Ephesians 2:8-9: "For it is by God's grace that you have been saved through faith. It is not the result of your own efforts, but God's gift, so that no one can boast about it."

Philippians 4:13: "I have the strength to face all conditions by the power that Christ gives me."

Hebrews 11:1,6: "To have faith is to be sure of the things we hope for, to be certain of the things we cannot see.... No one can please God without faith, for whoever comes to God must have faith that God exists and rewards those who seek him."

Benefits

The primary benefit of the Good News Translation is its easy readability, which makes it ideal for (1) those reading the Bible for the first time, (2) those for whom English is a second language, and (3) young people and even children. Some have used it as secondary dynamic equivalence (thought-for-thought) translation that is used alongside their formal equivalence (word-for-word) translation. (Comparing Bible translations is always a good idea!)

Another benefit is that simple line drawings by Swiss artist Annie Vallotton have been sprinkled throughout the text. This serves to make the layout more visually appealing.

Cautions

There are a number of cautions scholars have suggested in regard to the Good News Translation. Foundationally, because the GNT is a dynamic equivalence translation, it is not as suitable for serious Bible study as a literal word-for-word translation. Some have criticized the GNT for including too much interpretation from the translators—and even some paraphrase. Still others have suggested that this translation utilizes a far-too-limited vocabulary, thereby reducing the elegance of the Bible.

Some conservative Christians have criticized this translation for avoiding use of the common biblical word *blood* when referring to Christ's death (see Matthew 27:4,24,25; Acts 5:28; Colossians 1:20;

Hebrews 10:19; 1 Peter 1:19; Revelation 1:5; 5:9). "Blood" is sometimes replaced by "sacrificial death." For this reason, some have dubbed this Bible the "bloodless Bible"—something taken very seriously by many, for, as Scripture itself indicates, "without the shedding of blood there is no forgiveness of sins" (Hebrews 9:22 ESV).

Another concern among some conservative Christians relates to the GNT rendering of Isaiah 7:14: "A young woman who is pregnant will have a son." One might recall that following the widespread conservative condemnation of the Revised Standard Version for using the words *young woman* instead of *virgin,* the translation of Isaiah 7:14 (fairly or unfairly) became a litmus test to judge the orthodoxy of Bible translations. For many, the GNT fails the test.

Of similar concern is the GNT's treatment of Luke 1:27. While traditional translations such as the NASB and the NIV indicate that the angel Gabriel appeared "to a virgin" (Mary) to reveal that she would give birth to the Messiah, the GNT says Gabriel had a "message for a young woman promised in marriage to a man named Joseph." (A young woman promised in marriage is *not necessarily* a virgin.)

Unfortunately, in the early 1980s it came out that Robert Bratcher, translator of the GNT New Testament, had little respect for conservative Christians and their teachings. In 1981 he publicly scoffed at the teaching of conservative evangelicals that the words of the Bible were divinely inspired and authoritative. He even said, "Only willful ignorance or intellectual dishonesty can account for the claim that the Bible is inerrant and infallible…No one seriously claims that all the words of the Bible are the very words of God."[4] This resulted in a dramatic decline in donations to the American Bible Society, thus leading to a financial crisis for the organization. Soon enough, the Society asked for Bratcher's resignation and publicly and completely disassociated itself from his unorthodox comments.

There are also some who criticize this translation because in some verses it is not as clear as others in regard to the absolute deity of Jesus Christ. To illustrate this, consider the NIV rendering of Acts 20:28:

"Keep watch over yourselves and all the flock of which the Holy Spirit has made you overseers. Be shepherds of the church of God, *which he bought with his own blood*" (emphasis added; see also the NASB and KJV renderings). The GNT, by contrast, renders the verse this way: "So keep watch over yourselves and over all the flock which the Holy Spirit has placed in your care. Be shepherds of the church of God, which he made his own through the *blood of his Son.*" Many conservative Christians have voiced great concern over this, for they believe this translation undermines the deity of Jesus. To be fair, however, Greek scholars have noted that such a translation is viable from the original Greek, and there are other translations that render the verse this way.

Finally, some have criticized the ecumenism of the Good News Translation—that is, they have criticized the publishing of an edition that contains the Apocrypha for use by Roman Catholics. Inasmuch as many do not believe these books belong in the Bible, this is viewed as somewhat of a compromise. To be fair, however, there are certainly other translations that have published editions with the Apocrypha, such as the NRSV and the REB, not to mention the KJV. A translation of the Apocrypha is presently in the works for the NET Bible.

The New International Version

THE NEW INTERNATIONAL VERSION (NIV) falls somewhere between dynamic equivalence (thought-for-thought) and formal equivalence (word-for-word) translations. It does not use gender inclusive language, and has about a seventh-grade reading level.

A "sampler" featuring the Gospel of John was first published in 1969. The New Testament was released in 1973. In subsequent years several Old Testament "samplers" were published, with the whole Bible following in 1978. A minor revision was released in 1984, entailing 930 minor amendments.

One of the most popular translations, the NIV began to outsell the King James Version in the mid-1980s. To date, more than 110 million NIV Bibles have been sold or distributed. One reason for the NIV's popularity is that, on the one hand, it is clear and readable, and yet, on the other hand, is close enough to the "rhythm and cadence" of the King James Version that it still sounds like a real Bible.[1]

The Story Behind the Translation

Some conservative Christians strongly reacted against some of the tendencies in the Revised Standard Version, published in 1952. This was especially in regard to messianic verses pointing to Jesus Christ, such as Isaiah 7:14. As early as 1953, there were inquiries about publishing an evangelical edition of the RSV that would remove such elements, but such inquiries met with no success. Other Bibles, including the New American Standard Bible, were subsequently published seeking to meet the needs of conservatives. These met with some success, but there was still a felt need for a Bible that would become a true standard among evangelicals.

The NIV preface tells us that the NIV had its beginning in 1965 when, after several years of exploratory study by committees from the Christian Reformed Church and the National Association of Evangelicals, a group of conservative biblical scholars met at Palos Heights, Illinois, and agreed on the need for a new translation of the Bible in contemporary English.[2] The new translation was underwritten by the New York Bible Society (now the Colorado Springs-based International Bible Society) and Zondervan Bible Publishers. Work on the new translation began in 1968. Before it was all over, the total editorial cost of translating this Bible reached approximately eight million dollars.

The NIV was translated by over 100 evangelical scholars from America, England, Canada, Australia, South Africa, and New Zealand. It was thus an "international" effort, though, in reality, the majority of scholars were American. This group of scholars represents over 20 denominations—including Baptists, Assemblies of God, Christian Reformed, Methodists, Lutherans, Mennonites, Nazarenes, and Anglicans—thereby safeguarding against incorporating denominational traditions or sectarian bias into the translation.

Virtually all the translators, though from different countries and a variety of Christian denominations, subscribed to the authority and infallibility of the Bible as God's Word in written form. The NIV was a conservative translation produced for conservative Christian readers.

Translation Philosophy and Procedure

The goal of the NIV translators was to produce an accurate and readable translation of the Bible that would fall somewhere between formal equivalence (word-for-word) and dynamic equivalence (thought-for-thought) translations. They sought a balance between accuracy, beauty, clarity, and dignity. The translators believed that by using just the right words, it was possible to be faithful to the original Hebrew, Aramaic, and Greek texts while at the same time render the translation using clear and idiomatic English.

The NIV translators were broken into 20 teams. Each of these teams had two co-translators, two consultants, and an English stylist. Once each team completed the initial translation, it was sent to an intermediate editorial committee (either of the Old Testament or the New Testament). Following this, it was sent to the general editorial committee for further evaluation. Finally, it was sent to the 15-member committee on Bible translation.[3] There were lots of linguistic and stylistic eyes that scrutinized each verse in the NIV.

In this way, the entire Bible went through three revisions, during each of which the translation was thoroughly examined for (1) its faithfulness to the original Hebrew, Aramaic, or Greek, and (2) its English style. The result of the collective efforts of the translation team was a highly readable and accurate Bible.

The NIV is expressly a Protestant translation—that is, it does not include the so-called "deuterocanonical" books (the Apocrypha) found in Catholic versions of the Bible. Moreover, the contested issues related to the RSV were all changed in the NIV—including restoring the word *virgin* to Isaiah 7:14. The new translation avoided use of *thee* and *thou*, and was translated directly from the original Hebrew, Aramaic, and Greek as opposed to being a revision of a previous Bible translation.

The NIV renders the Old Testament divine name, YHWH, as "LORD" (using small capital letters). *Adonai,* another Hebrew term used of God in the Old Testament, is rendered "Lord" (using small letters). Wherever the two names stand together in the Old Testament as a compound name of God, they are rendered "Sovereign LORD."

Other highlights of the NIV include formatting poetical passages as poetry, inserting sectional descriptive headings throughout the biblical books, and providing footnotes with helpful information on alternative translations and manuscript discrepancies.

Sampling the New International Version

We gain insight into the translation style of the New International Version by considering its rendering of some famous Bible passages:

Genesis 1:1-3: "In the beginning God created the heavens and the earth. Now the earth was formless and empty, darkness was over the surface of the deep, and the Spirit of God was hovering over the waters. And God said, 'Let there be light,' and there was light."

Psalm 23:1-3: "The LORD is my shepherd, I shall not be in want. He makes me lie down in green pastures, he leads me beside quiet waters, he restores my soul. He guides me in paths of righteousness for his name's sake."

Proverbs 3:5-6: "Trust in the LORD with all your heart and lean not on your own understanding; in all your ways acknowledge him, and he will make your paths straight."

Matthew 6:9-13: "This, then, is how you should pray: 'Our Father in heaven, hallowed be your name, your kingdom come, your will be done on earth as it is in heaven. Give us today our daily bread. Forgive us our debts, as we also have forgiven our debtors. And lead us not into temptation, but deliver us from the evil one.'"

John 3:16-17: "For God so loved the world that he gave his one and only Son, that whoever believes in him shall not perish but have eternal life. For God did not send his Son into the world to condemn the world, but to save the world through him."

Ephesians 2:8-9: "For it is by grace you have been saved, through faith—and this not from yourselves, it is the gift of God—not by works, so that no one can boast."

Philippians 4:13: "I can do everything through him who gives me strength."

Hebrews 11:1,6: "Now faith is being sure of what we hope for and certain of what we do not see…. And without faith it is impossible to please God, because anyone who comes to him must believe that he exists and that he rewards those who earnestly seek him."

Benefits

The primary benefit of the New International Version is that it is an extremely readable translation with good clarity and decent literary quality. It has overall succeeded in its effort to fall between a dynamic equivalence translation and a formal equivalence translation. One scholar thus noted, "For many, the NIV is the ideal, all-around translation, suitable for devotional use, study purposes, and public reading."[4] Such factors no doubt account for the NIV's astronomical sales.

Cautions

Because of its staggering popularity, it is not surprising that the NIV has been targeted for criticism more so than most other translations. One must be careful to keep all this in perspective. (A translation can have some "cautions" and still be an overall good translation.)

One caution sometimes raised is that even though the NIV is highly readable, it is not as elegant as some other Bible translations. As one critic put it, "It is so readable that it has no memorable expressions, nothing that lingers in the mind."[5]

Others caution that because the NIV leans toward being a thought-for-thought translation (or at least falls somewhere between a thought-for-thought and word-for-word translation), it is not as accurate as a *strict* word-for-word translation, and hence may not be as suitable for detailed Bible study.[6] NIV enthusiasts, however, have disputed this claim.

Some scholars have noted that in the process of keeping the NIV translation simple, sentences are shortened and connecting conjunctions (*for, but, therefore,* and the like) are often removed, thereby blurring the continuity of thought. As one scholar put it, the translators "tended to leave out many of the 'connecting signals' (especially conjunctions) that teachers and preachers find useful to show students and congregations how one sentence is related to another."[7]

An example might be 1 Peter 5:6-7: "Humble yourselves, therefore, under God's mighty hand, that he may lift you up in due time. Cast all your anxiety on him because he cares for you." Some scholars note that the word *cast* in verse 7 is a participle that explains *how* we are to humble ourselves—that is, we humble ourselves *by* casting our cares upon the Lord. Hence, verses 6 and 7 are connected, but the connection—the logical cohesion—is lost in the NIV translation.[8] Of course, to be fair, if this is going to be a criticism of the NIV, it must also be a criticism of other translations that do not note this connection—including the New Living Translation, the New Revised Standard Version, and the Good News Translation.

The NIV translators have responded that, generally speaking, the frequent repetition of connective words makes for awkward and unnatural English. They believe the connection between clauses is generally clear from the context itself. Moreover, they point out that whereas the Greek often resorts to long sentences, English readers much prefer shorter sentences.

Some scholars have criticized certain renderings in the NIV. For example, the NIV rendering of Psalm 1:1, "Blessed is the man who does not...stand in the way of sinners," almost sounds as if the blessed man is one who steps *out of the way of* sinners so that they can have their evil way. To "stand" in someone's way is normally thought of as hindering that person from doing something. To *not* "stand" in their way involves allowing them unhindered to do something.

Other scholars criticize the NIV for not using the biblical terms "Lord of hosts" and "God of hosts." The NIV translators felt that such terms would make no sense to modern readers, and hence they rendered such phrases as "the Lord Almighty" and "God Almighty." They suggest that these alternative phrases "convey the sense of the Hebrew, namely, 'he who is sovereign over all the "hosts" (powers) in heaven and on earth, especially over the "hosts" (armies) of Israel.'"[9] Critics have argued, however, that without specific mention of the "hosts" (or armies), the term *almighty* seems to point more to God's omnipotence than His sovereignty. Critics thus say the translation subtly changes the meaning.[10]

Still other scholars have made note of some inconsistencies in the NIV. An example would be how it handles time of day. In the Gospels, for example, we find archaic renderings like "the third hour" (Matthew 20:3; Mark 15:25) and "the sixth hour" (Matthew 20:5; 27:45; Mark 15:33; Luke 23:44; John 4:6; 19:14). In the book of Acts, however, we find references to "nine in the morning" (2:15), "three in the afternoon" (3:1; 10:3,30), "about noon" (10:9), and "at nine tonight" (23:23).[11] Critics say the translation should be consistent.

In view of all the above, we must conclude that over the years, the NIV has had both proponents *and* opponents, but no one can deny its astounding success in terms of sales. If there is one thing we learn from this chapter (and other chapters in this book), it is that there is no such thing as a *perfect* translation. While not *perfect,* many still believe the NIV is a *good* translation. Indeed, many would say it is *excellent.*[12] I am glad to own one in my collection.

The New King James Version

THE NEW KING JAMES VERSION (NKJV) is a revision of the King James Version (KJV) in modern English. The overall goal was to render the text in such a way that archaic language was removed, with clarity increased, all the while retaining the original beauty of the KJV. The NKJV claims to be a "complete equivalence" translation, like the King James Version before it, and does not use gender inclusive language. It has an eighth-grade (middle school) reading level. The New Testament was published in 1979, the New Testament and Psalms in 1980, with the entire Bible following in 1982.[1] (More on the "complete equivalence" philosophy below.)

The Story Behind the Translation

The NKJV, sponsored by Thomas Nelson Publishers, was initiated by Arthur Farstad, a conservative Baptist and a former editor at Thomas Nelson.[2] Though Farstad conceived the idea, the NKJV was actually inaugurated in 1975 with meetings that took place in Nashville and Chicago involving 68 interested persons, mostly prominent

Baptists, but also some conservative Presbyterians. These men prepared the guidelines for translating the NKJV. All were interested in producing an accurate, readable translation that would retain the elegance and literary beauty of the KJV.

Over 130 evangelical scholars and church leaders worked over a seven-year period in producing the revision. All who participated in the project held firmly to the inspiration and inerrancy of Scripture: "In faithfulness to God and to our readers, it was deemed appropriate that all participating scholars sign a statement affirming their belief in the verbal and plenary inspiration of Scripture, and in the inerrancy of the original autographs."[3]

Translation Philosophy and Procedure

The NKJV claims to be a "complete equivalence" translation. In the NKJV preface we read: "This principle of complete equivalence seeks to preserve all of the information in the text, while presenting it in good literary form.... Complete equivalence translates fully, in order to provide an English text that is both accurate and readable."[4] Toward this end, the NKJV "follows the historic precedent of the Authorized Version in maintaining a literal approach to translation, except where the idiom of the original language cannot be translated directly into our tongue."[5]

To make for easier reading, obsolete words have been replaced with modern equivalents. As well, obsolete verb endings such as "-eth" (*loveth*) and "-est" (*doest*) have been removed. *Thee, Thou,* and *ye* have been replaced throughout with *you*. The NKJV significantly updates the KJV, making it a much more accurate translation. Many words and phrases that are italicized in the KJV—words designed to make the reading clear to an A.D. 1611 audience—are removed in the NKJV. The Old Testament divine name, YHWH, is rendered "LORD" (using small capital letters). Pronouns referring to deity are capitalized throughout. Additionally, subject headings are sprinkled throughout biblical books that guide the reader in understanding transitions in the biblical content. Oblique type in the New Testament indicates a quotation from the Old Testament. Poetry is structured as contemporary verse to reflect poetic form.

By making such changes, the translation committee was convinced it could produce a modern translation of Scripture, updating the style and grammar, and yet retain the purity and stylistic beauty of the original KJV. "The translators, the committees, and the editors of the present edition, while sensitive to the late-twentieth-century English idiom, and while adhering faithfully to the Hebrew, Aramaic, and Greek texts, have sought to maintain those lyrical and devotional qualities that are so highly regarded in the Authorized Version."[6]

The translation team felt there is historical precedence for building a new translation on the shoulders of previous translations. The NKJV preface tells us,

> In the preface to the 1611 edition, the translators of the Authorized Version, known popularly as the King James Bible, state that it was not their purpose "to make a new translation...but to make a good one better." Indebted to the earlier work of William Tyndale and others, they saw their best contribution to consist in revising and enhancing the excellence of the English versions that had sprung from the Reformation of the sixteenth century. In harmony with the purpose of the King James scholars, the translators and editors of the present work have not pursued a goal of innovation. They have perceived the Holy Bible, New King James Version, as a continuation of the labors of the earlier translators, thus unlocking for today's readers the spiritual treasures found especially in the Authorized Version of the Holy Scriptures.[7]

Sampling the New King James Version

We gain insight into the translation style of the New King James Version by considering its rendering of some famous Bible passages:

Genesis 1:1-3: "In the beginning God created the heavens and the earth. The earth was without form, and void; and darkness was on the face of the deep. And the Spirit of God was hovering over the face of the waters. Then God said, 'Let there be light'; and there was light."

Psalm 23:1-3: "The LORD is my shepherd; I shall not want. He makes me to lie down in green pastures; He leads me beside the still waters. He restores my soul; He leads me in the paths of righteousness for His name's sake."

Proverbs 3:5-6: "Trust in the LORD with all your heart, and lean not on your own understanding; in all your ways acknowledge Him, and He shall direct your paths."

Matthew 6:9-13: "In this manner, therefore, pray: Our Father in heaven, Hallowed be Your name. Your kingdom come. Your will be done on earth as it is in heaven. Give us this day our daily bread. And forgive us our debts, As we forgive our debtors. And do not lead us into temptation, But deliver us from the evil one. For Yours is the kingdom and the power and the glory forever. Amen."

John 3:16-17: "For God so loved the world that He gave His only begotten Son, that whoever believes in Him should not perish but have everlasting life. For God did not send His Son into the world to condemn the world, but that the world through Him might be saved."

Ephesians 2:8-9: "For by grace you have been saved through faith, and that not of yourselves; it is the gift of God, not of works, lest anyone should boast."

Hebrews 11:1,6: "Now faith is the substance of things hoped for, the evidence of things not seen.... But without faith it is impossible to please Him, for he who comes to God must believe that He is, and that He is a rewarder of those who diligently seek Him."

Benefits

The primary benefit of the New King James Version is that it is a great alternative for those who prefer the elegance and literary beauty of the King James Version but find the archaic language confusing.

The NKJV consciously seeks to retain the cadence, style, and idiom of the KJV, but uses more modern language. Many thus consider the NKJV to be a great alternative to the KJV. Even apart from the KJV connection, many find the NKJV to be a great formal equivalence (word-for-word) translation appropriate for detailed Bible study.

Cautions

Contrary to what is claimed, some scholars have suggested that the NKJV does not have near the literary beauty of the original KJV. Indeed, one critic suggests that "the translation is much more like the NASB than the KJV. And that means that the beauty of the original KJV has been sacrificed."[8]

Perhaps a more common caution is that, like its predecessor, the NKJV is based on manuscripts that many scholars believe are not as accurate as some earlier-dated manuscripts more recently discovered.[9] Some scholars charge that the editors of the NKJV recognized that the Greek *Textus Receptus** was wrong in nearly 2,000 places, and yet still chose to translate from it.[10] Other modern Bible translations use the "critical text" derived from older Greek manuscripts (so called because it is edited according to specific principles of textual criticism). Some scholars have leveled rather stinging criticisms against the NKJV translation team for using the *Textus Receptus*. For example:

> The KJV translators had little choice but to use the majority or "received" text in 1611; most of the earlier manuscripts lay as yet undiscovered. Given their academic excellence and deep reverence for the Bible, one would suppose that they would use the best text available, no matter what difficulties it posed. Any "reverence" for the text in the NKJV, however, seems to be for the English text of the KJV, rather than for the ancient texts of the Bible.[11]

---

* The *Textus Receptus* is the "Received Text"—the 1550 edition of the Greek New Testament behind the KJV New Testament. It is based on a relatively few available Greek manuscripts.

To be fair, however, there are extensive footnotes in the NKJV that alert the reader to alternate readings in the "critical text."[12] This would seem to deflect some of the criticism above.

Many today continue to believe that if one truly wants to understand the KJV better, the NKJV is the single best tool that will enable one to do so. Others view it as great for comparing with other translations. The debate rages on! In any event, I am glad to own one in my collection.

The New Revised Standard Version

INTENDED TO REPLACE THE Revised Standard Version (RSV), the New Revised Standard Version (NRSV) was first published in 1989, at which time the RSV was some 40 years old. The NRSV is a revision of the RSV authorized by the National Council of Churches. Preeminent New Testament scholar Bruce Metzger served as chairman of the translation committee.

The NRSV is considered a formal equivalence translation, though some have claimed it is on the borderline between formal equivalence and dynamic equivalence translations. Its guiding principle seems to have been: "As literal as possible, as free as necessary." It is a gender-inclusive translation that has a high school reading level, ranging between the eighth and tenth grades.

The Story Behind the Translation

The primary development that necessitated a revision of the RSV was that English usage had changed. One notable example involves the

RSV rendering of Psalm 50:9, which portrays God as saying, "I will accept no bull from your house." Back in the 1950s, people understood this to mean that God would not accept any animal sacrifices, including those of bulls. But the term eventually came to mean something decidedly different. Such changes in English usage urgently called for a revision to be made. Another reason a revision was in order was the growing sensitivity among many regarding the need for gender-inclusive language in the Bible.

The editorial committee consisted of 30 members of various Protestant denominations as well as the Roman Catholic Church. Eastern Orthodox and Jewish representatives also participated on the Old Testament. The committee took advantage of the latest manuscript discoveries, including the Dead Sea Scrolls, which were unknown to the translators of the RSV Old Testament.

Unlike most Bible translations, which are initially published by a single publisher, seven different publishers in the United States and in Great Britain were licensed to issue the NRSV. Within a few short years, the NRSV was available in over 70 different sizes, formats, and bindings.

From the very beginning, the NRSV was intended to be an ecumenical Bible. The NRSV standard edition contains only the Old and New Testaments. The NRSV Common Bible adds to this the Apocryphal/Deuterocanonical books. In addition to this are Anglicized editions, using British spelling, grammar, and punctuation; they also replace Americanisms with Britishisms in order to enhance readability.

Understandably, the NRSV is widely used among many denominations. Indeed, it is either accepted, commended, or used in the Episcopal Church, the Presbyterian Church (USA), the Evangelical Lutheran Church in America, Reformed Church in America, and the United Church of Canada. The NRSV Catholic Edition has the imprimatur of the National Conference of Catholic Bishops (USA) and the Canadian Conference of Catholic Bishops. The NRSV is also widely used in academic and scholarly circles. A number of American universities require this version for courses on Christianity or Christian doctrine.

Translation Philosophy and Procedure

The NRSV translation team followed four guiding mandates as they engaged in their work:

1. To improve paragraph structure and punctuation;
2. To eliminate archaisms, including all "thee/thou" language. (The RSV had eliminated these words from general usage, but retained them for references to deity.) In a prefatory essay in the NRSV Bible, the translation committee commented that "although some readers may regret this change, it should be pointed out that in the original languages neither the Old Testament nor the New makes any linguistic distinction between addressing a human being and addressing the Deity."[2]
3. To improve accuracy, clarity, and English style, especially when read aloud; and
4. To eliminate masculine-oriented language (though not with reference to God).[3]

The issue of eliminating masculine-oriented language is worthy of further comment. It is noteworthy that the NRSV was the first English translation to consistently utilize gender-inclusive language for masculine generic terms in Hebrew and Greek. The NRSV preface tells us, "Many in the churches have become sensitive to the danger of linguistic sexism arising from the inherent bias of the English language towards the masculine gender, a bias that in the case of the Bible has often restricted or obscured the meaning of the original text."[4] It is for this reason that gender-inclusive language is used in the NRSV.

The general philosophy that guided the NRSV team was that

masculine-oriented language should be replaced with gender-inclusive terminology when it can be done without altering verses that reflect the historical situation of ancient patriarchal culture. Sometimes, in accomplishing this goal, the NRSV expands gender-specific phrases—for example, translating *brothers* as "brothers and sisters." As well, the NRSV frequently substitutes *person* or *adult* when the literal text reads *man*. We find an example in 1 Corinthians 13:11, which in the RSV reads, "When I became a man, I gave up childish ways." The NRSV renders the verse, "When I became an adult, I put an end to childish ways."

Keeping the controversy alive, the NRSV retained the RSV decision to translate the Hebrew *almah* as "young woman" instead of "virgin" in Isaiah 7:14. A footnote, however, acknowledges that the Greek Septuagint reads "virgin," from the Greek word *parthenos*.

References to the Old Testament divine name, YHWH, are rendered as "Lord" (using small capitals).

Sampling the New Revised Standard Version

We gain insight into the translation style of the New Revised Standard Version by considering its rendering of some famous Bible passages:

Genesis 1:1-3: "In the beginning when God created the heavens and the earth, the earth was a formless void and darkness covered the face of the deep, while a wind from God swept over the face of the waters. Then God said, 'Let there be light'; and there was light."

Psalm 23:1-3: "The Lord is my shepherd; I shall not want. He makes me to lie down in green pastures; he leads me beside the still waters; he restores my soul. He leads me in right paths for his name's sake."

Proverbs 3:5-6: "Trust in the Lord with all your heart, and do not rely on your own insight. In all your ways acknowledge him, and he will make straight your paths."

Matthew 6:9-13: "Pray then in this way: Our Father in heaven, hallowed be your name. Your kingdom come. Your will be done, on earth as it is in heaven. Give us this day our daily bread. And forgive us our debts, as we also have forgiven our debtors. And do not bring us to the time of trial, but rescue us from the evil one."

John 3:16-17: "For God so loved the world that he gave his only Son, so that everyone who believes in him may not perish but may have eternal life. Indeed, God did not send the Son into the world to condemn the world, but in order that the world might be saved through him."

Ephesians 2:8-9: "For by grace you have been saved through faith, and this is not your own doing; it is the gift of God—not the result of works, so that no one may boast."

Philippians 4:13: "I can do all things through him who strengthens me."

Hebrews 11:1,6: "Now faith is the assurance of things hoped for, the conviction of things not seen.... And without faith it is impossible to please God, for whoever would approach him must believe that he exists and that he rewards those who seek him."

Benefits

The primary benefit of the New Revised Standard Version is that it is easier to read, is more accurate, and is based on more modern scholarship than the Revised Standard Version. Because it is essentially a formal equivalence (word-for-word) translation, many find it suitable for detailed Bible study. Many also like it for its gender-inclusive language.

Cautions

Many scholars believe the use of gender-inclusive language in the NRSV departs from the literal text, sometimes subtly changing its meaning. For example, in 2 Thessalonians 3:15, "Warn them as a brother" is changed to "Warn them as believers." The difference in meaning may be subtle, but it is a difference nonetheless (the former

has more of a familial sense). Related to this, some scholars criticize the
NRSV for occasions in which its translators employ gender-inclusive
language even in contexts where only males are intended.[5] An example
is the book of Proverbs, where we find a father giving advice to his son.
Throughout, however, the NRSV unnecessarily changes "my son" to
"my child."

We find another example in John 14:23, which the RSV renders
this way: "If a *man* loves me, *he* will keep my word, and my Father will
love *him,* and we will come to *him* and make our home with *him.*"
Seeking to avoid such gender-specific language, the NRSV renders
the verse this way: "*Those* who love me will keep my word, and my
Father will love *them,* and we will come to *them* and make our home
with *them*" (emphasis added in both citations). This subtly changes the
meaning of the text. The verse is intended to show the great intimacy
that the Father and Son can have *with the individual.* By changing it
to the plural ("them"), such one-on-one intimacy is lost.

Yet another example may be found in 1 Timothy 3:2. Instead of the
traditional translation indicating that an elder should be "husband of
one wife," the NRSV renders the verse as saying that the elder should
be "married only once." This translation masks the New Testament
requirement that an elder be a man.

Of course, things could have been worse. One (female) translator
on the NRSV committee suggested that God be treated as a woman,
a suggestion that was overruled by the majority. However, had this
suggestion been accepted, it would have the changed the Bible in a
major way. Professor Daniel Wallace notes that "Our Father who art
in heaven" would have become "Our Mother who art in heaven." In
the Great Commission Christ would have said, "Baptize them in the
name of the Mother, the Son, and the Holy Spirit." With apparent
glee, Wallace tells us what happened:

> Dr. Bruce Metzger, who was the chairman of the com-
> mittee, dealt with this issue swiftly and decisively. Now,

Dr. Metzger is a conservative Christian, and a diplomatic genius. He could sell ice cubes to Eskimos...So he responded to this woman translator: "Yes, I believe we should call God a 'she.'...And we should call the devil a she, too!" That was the end of the discussion.[6]

The Revised English Bible

THE REVISED ENGLISH BIBLE (REB) is a dynamic equivalence (thought-for-thought) translation that is essentially a major revision of the New English Bible (NEB), which had attained substantial popularity in British churches.* The REB was published in 1989. Its overall goal was to be an accurate translation in current English while at the same time reduce the highbrow literary style of the NEB. The REB is moderately committed to gender-inclusive language, and requires a high school level of reading ability.

The Story Behind the Translation

The New English Bible, officially commissioned by the majority of British churches, had been completed in 1970. Just three years later, however, the decision was made to revise it. The year the NEB was completed brought with it new forms of worship in the Church of England that moved away from the traditional language of the Prayer Book. Archaic language such as *Thee* and *Thou* used in the NEB for

---

* This book does not address the New English Bible because it is no longer in wide distribution.

addressing God, began to disappear from public worship.[1] As well, church services of the day were becoming increasingly informal. Such factors made the highbrow literary style of the NEB inappropriate. The need for a revision became acute.

Directing the revision was W.D. McHardy, who previously oversaw the translation of the NEB Apocrypha. Participating in the project were 19 translational revisers and 12 literary revisers. The translators themselves were chosen for their ability as scholars, without regard to any particular church affiliation. The multidenominational translation Joint Committee included representatives from the Baptist Union of Great Britain and Ireland, the Church of England, the Church of Scotland, the Congregational Church of England and Wales, the Council of Churches for Wales, the Irish Council of Churches, the London Yearly Meeting of the Religious Society of Friends, the Methodist Church of Great Britain, the Presbyterian Church of England, the Roman Catholic Church, the Moravian Churches, and even the Salvation Army. It is noteworthy that during the work on the NEB, the Roman Catholic representatives attended only as observers. Now, for work on the REB, they attended as full members.[2]

Translation Philosophy and Procedure

A primary goal of the translation team was to produce a Bible not only suitable for private use, but also for public liturgical use as well. The Revised English Bible preface tells us that "care has been taken to ensure that the style of English used is fluent and of appropriate dignity for liturgical use, while maintaining intelligibility for worshippers of a wide range of ages and backgrounds. The revisers have sought to avoid complex or technical terms where possible, and to provide sentence structure and word order, especially in the Psalms, which will facilitate congregational reading but will not misrepresent the meaning of the original texts."[3]

Quite a number of changes were introduced into the text. *Thees* and *Thous* were removed in favor of more current language. Technical theological terms were avoided where possible. The colloquial style was revised. The translators reduced the British idioms in order to give the REB more international appeal.[4] More section headings were introduced. And, overall, the wording was made clearer. For example, "She broke wind" in the NEB was changed to "She dismounted" in the REB (Joshua 15:18). "Have nothing to do with loose livers" in the NEB was changed to "Have nothing to do with those who are sexually immoral" in the REB (1 Corinthians 5:9). The divine name, YHWH, is rendered as "LORD," using small capital letters.

Minor concessions were made in favor of gender-inclusive language, to the extent that it is justified by the original language. "The use of male-oriented language, in passages of traditional versions of the Bible which evidently apply to both genders, has become a sensitive issue in recent years; the revisers [who produced the REB] have preferred more inclusive gender reference where that has been possible without compromising scholarly integrity or English style."[5] So, for example, references to "brothers" were changed to "brothers and sisters." The NEB rendering of Genesis 1:26, "Let us make man in our image," was changed in the REB to read, "Let us make human beings in our image." Broadly speaking, universal references to "man" (when referring to all human beings) are made to be gender-inclusive.

The REB also maintains greater consistency in the translation of individual words. For example, the Greek word *ekklesia* was rendered a variety of ways in the NEB, including "church," "congregation," "meeting," and "community." The REB consistently renders it "church."[6] Also, many punctuation errors in the NEB were cleaned up in the REB.

Sampling the Revised English Bible

We gain insight into the translation style of the Revised English Bible by considering its rendering of some famous Bible passages:

Genesis 1:1-3: "In the beginning God created the heavens and the earth. The earth was a vast waste, darkness covered the deep, and the spirit of God hovered over the surface of the water. God said, 'Let there be light,' and there was light."

Psalm 23:1-3: "The LORD is my shepherd; I lack for nothing. He makes me lie down in green pastures, he leads me to water where I may rest; he revives my spirit; for his name's sake he guides me in the right paths."

Proverbs 3:5-6: "Put all your trust in the LORD and do not rely on your own understanding. At every step you take keep him in mind, and he will direct your path."

Matthew 6:9-13: "This is how you should pray: Our Father in heaven, may your name be hallowed; your kingdom come, your will be done, on earth as in heaven. Give us today our daily bread. Forgive us the wrong we have done, as we have forgiven those who have wronged us. And do not put us to the test, but save us from the evil one."

John 3:16-17: "God so loved the world that he gave his only Son, that everyone who has faith in him may not perish but have eternal life. It was not to judge the world that God sent his Son into the world, but that through him the world might be saved."

Ephesians 2:8-9: "For it is by grace you are saved through faith, it is not your own doing. It is God's gift, not a reward for work done. There is nothing for any to boast of."

Philippians 4:13: "I am able to face anything through him who gives me strength."

Hebrews 11:1,6: "Faith gives substance to our hopes and convinces us of realities we do not see.... But without faith it is impossible to please him, for whoever comes to God must believe that he exists and rewards those who seek him."

Benefits

A primary benefit of the Revised English Bible is that it has a literary style that makes for interesting reading. From a literary standpoint, the REB has long been admired. Some believe it has the best overall literary quality of any modern English translation—at least since the publication of the King James Version. The REB has succeeded in its goal of suitability for both private use and public liturgical use.

Cautions

Some scholars have said that even though the Revised English Bible can be a delight to read, it is not the most reliable translation in terms of accuracy. They suggest that elegance versus accuracy should never be a trade-off. Others rebut that if alleged inaccuracies in the REB do exist, they are minor. Such people say the REB is not too wooden or too bland like some "accurate" translations are (such as the NASB). Still others note that the REB, as a dynamic equivalence translation, is not as suitable for detailed Bible study as a formal equivalence translation, such as the NASB. The NASB (and other literal translations), after all, retain technical theological words (which are often rich in meaning) whereas the REB does not. Those who do not like gender-inclusive language will not like this aspect of the REB.

One should be aware that the Revised English Bible appeals mainly to British readers, although it has some American users and admirers as well. It is viewed by many as a great Bible for people who appreciate literary beauty. "The Joint Committee commends the Revised English Bible to the Churches and to the English-speaking world with due humility, but with confidence that God has yet new light and truth to break forth from his word. The Committee prays that the new version will prove to be a means to that end."[7]

The New Century Version

THE NEW CENTURY VERSION (NCV) is a dynamic equivalence ("meaning-driven") translation published in 1991, originally by Word Publishers, and since 1992 by Thomas Nelson Publishers. The overall goal of this translation is to make the language of the Bible clear for any reader, at the same time maintaining faithfulness to the original Hebrew, Aramaic, and Greek manuscripts. It utilizes gender-inclusive language, and has an approximate reading grade level of 5.6.

The Story Behind the Translation

The New Century Version (NCV) and the International Children's Bible (ICB) both arose as revisions of a Bible that was originally designed for deaf people (or people who were hearing impaired) who were unfamiliar with many idioms of English as it is commonly spoken. This Bible project was overseen by the World Bible Translation Center of Fort Worth, Texas, founded in 1973, along with 50 additional Bible scholars. The translation was intended to be conservative and evangelical in tone. The translators were highly experienced, some of them having earlier participated in the translation of the New

International Version, the New American Standard Bible, and the New King James Version.

The New Testament English Version for the Deaf (EVD) was completed in 1978 and was published by Baker Book House. This may have been the simplest New Testament ever published, with a third-grade reading level. It featured easy words and short sentences. In 1980 it was republished by Baker under the title, *A New Easy-to-Read Version*, seeking to reach a wider audience (incidentally, no mention was made of its original intention of helping hearing-impaired readers). Over subsequent years, revisions were made, and Sweet Publications obtained the rights to publish it under two titles—the International Children's Bible, obviously designed for children, and the New Century Version, designed for more general readers.

Though these Bibles had different titles, there was no real difference between them until a substantial revision was done in 1991. Assisting in the 1991 revision were such eminent scholars as Dr. Harold W. Hoehner and Dr. Bruce M. Metzger. The NCV was edited so that it had a higher reading level than the ICB, incorporating longer sentences and a more sophisticated vocabulary. Today, the reading grade-level of the NCV is 5.6, suitable for a ten-year-old reader. A key difference between the NCV and the ICB is that the ICB does not utilize gender-inclusive language whereas the NCV does.

Word Publishers acquired Sweet Publications in 1988, and published the 1991 revision of the NCV. Thomas Nelson Publishers then acquired Word Publishers in 1992.

Translation Philosophy and Procedure

A primary goal of the NCV translation team was to make the language of the Bible clear for any reader. The basis of vocabulary is the Living Word vocabulary, designed by Dr. Edgar Dale and Dr. Joseph O'Rourke, which is the standard used by the *World Book Encyclopedia*.[1] This makes the Bible easier to comprehend.

The NCV preface tells us: "Two basic premises guided the

translation process of the New Century Version. The first concern was that the translation be faithful to the manuscripts in the original languages...The second concern was to make the language clear enough for anyone to read the Bible and understand it for himself."[2] So, *accuracy* and *readability* were the key concerns.

In an effort toward keeping things simple...

- Short, uncomplicated sentences are used throughout.

- Ancient customs, such as walking between the halves of a dead animal to seal a covenant agreement, are clarified either in the text or in footnotes.

- Rhetorical questions are couched in terms of their implied answers. For example, the psalmist's question, "What god is so great as our God?" has been restated more directly as, "No god is as great as our God."

- Figures of speech and ancient idioms are translated according to their intended meanings. For example, "he rested with his fathers" is rendered "he died."[3]

- Obscure biblical terms are made plain. Difficult words are replaced with easy, understandable terms: "justify" becomes "make right"; "genealogy" becomes "family history"; "high places" becomes "places where gods were worshiped."

- Modern equivalents are used for currency, weights, and measures (for words like "shekels," "cubits," "omer," and "hin").

- God's Old Testament name, YHWH, is indicated by the English word "LORD" (in small capitals).[4]

The gender-inclusive language used throughout reflects the intent of the biblical author. The NCV preface tells us, "To avoid the misconception that 'man' and 'mankind' and 'he' are exclusively masculine when they are being used in a generic sense, this translation has chosen to use less ambiguous language, such as 'people' and 'humans' and 'human beings,' and has prayerfully attempted throughout to choose gender language that would accurately convey the intent of the original writers. Specifically and exclusively masculine and feminine references in the text have been retained."[5]

Sampling the New Century Version

We gain insight into the translation style of the New Century Version by considering its rendering of some famous Bible passages:

Genesis 1:1-3: "In the beginning God created the sky and the earth. The earth was empty and had no form. Darkness covered the ocean, and God's Spirit was moving over the water. Then God said, 'Let there be light,' and there was light."

Psalm 23:1-3: "The LORD is my shepherd; I have everything I need. He lets me rest in green pastures. He leads me to calm water. He gives me new strength. He leads me on paths that are right for the good of his name."

Proverbs 3:5-6: "Trust the LORD with all your heart, and don't depend on your own understanding. Remember the Lord in all you do, and he will give you success."

Matthew 6:9-13: "So when you pray, you should pray like this: 'Our Father in heaven, may your name always be kept holy. May your kingdom come and what you want be done, here on earth as it is in heaven. Give us the food we need for each day. Forgive us for our sins, just as we have forgiven those who sinned against us. And do not cause us to be tempted, but save us from the Evil One.'"

John 3:16-17: "God loved the world so much that he gave his one and only Son so that whoever believes in him may not be lost, but have eternal life. God did not send his Son into the world to judge the world guilty, but to save the world through him."

Ephesians 2:8-9: "I mean that you have been saved by grace through believing. You did not save yourselves; it was a gift from God. It was not the result of your own efforts, so you cannot brag about it."

Philippians 4:13: "I can do all things through Christ, because he gives me strength."

Hebrews 11:1,6: "Faith means being sure of the things we hope for and knowing that something is real even if we do not see it.... Without faith no one can please God. Anyone who comes to God must believe that he is real and that he rewards those who truly want to find him."

Benefits

The primary benefit of the New Century Version is that it makes the Bible understandable, particularly for young people, or people with low reading skills, or people for whom English is a second language. With a 5.6-grade reading level, it is among the easiest-to-read translations.

Cautions

A caution regarding the New Century Version is that because it is a dynamic equivalence translation, and is couched in greatly simplified language, it is not appropriate for detailed Bible study. A more literal translation, such as the New American Standard Bible or the English Standard Version, would be more appropriate for detailed Bible study. Certainly the NCV would be a good translation to *compare* with a more literal translation.

Another caution is that because the New Century Version uses a greatly reduced and simplified vocabulary, it sometimes detracts from the beauty and elegance, as well as long-time familiarity, of certain Bible verses. For example, in Genesis 1:1 we read: "In the beginning God created the sky and the earth." Most translations render it something similar to the NIV: "In the beginning God created the heavens and the earth," and this is the rendering most people are familiar with.

Related to this, some readers may object to the lack of theological words in the NCV. An example is the word *justify* or *justification*. The word *justify* is typically translated as "made right" in the NCV. The truth is, though, that justification involves a far richer concept than just being "made right" with God. Negatively, the word means that one is once-and-for-all pronounced not guilty before God. Positively, the word means that one is once-and-for-all pronounced righteous. The very righteousness of Christ is imputed to the believer's life. So, the simpler language of the NCV may be easier to understand, but it can also mask some of the rich content of theological words.

Finally, those who object to gender-inclusive language in Bible translations will have problems with this aspect of the NCV. To be fair, of course, many translations today utilize gender-inclusive language.

Despite such cautions, many continue to believe that given the intended audience of the NCV—young people, people with minimal reading skills, and people for whom English is not their first language—the NCV remains a good option.[6]

GOD'S WORD

THE GOD'S WORD TRANSLATION is an easy-to-read Bible based on the "closest natural equivalence" philosophy (see below), with a reading grade level of 4.3. The overall goal of the translation team was to find equivalent English ways of expressing the meaning of the original text, also utilizing gender-neutral language. This translation was produced by God's Word to the Nations Bible Society, a Lutheran organization, and was initially published in 1995. While it is not as well known as many other translations, its acquisition by Baker Books in 2008 is likely to increase its market penetration in coming years.

The Story Behind the Translation

The Know the Truth Foundation was founded in 1983.[1] It was later renamed the Luther Bible Society, which eventually became the God's Word to the Nations Bible Society. This society is associated with the Missouri Synod of the Lutheran Church and has a primary concern for world missions. The purpose of the society was to revise *The New Testament in the Language of Today,* translated by Dr. William Beck and originally published in 1963. Beck died in 1966, and so the Old Testament was completed by a small group of Lutheran scholars. This led to the publication of the entire Bible in 1976 entitled *An American Translation*.

Under the leadership of Reverend Phillip Giessler, a pastor from Cleveland, Ohio, a committee was formed in 1978 to engage in updating the translation. He worked full-time on the effort, and was assisted by a full-time English stylist. This ultimately led to the publication of the *New Testament: God's Word to the Nations* in 1988. In 1990, it was renamed the New Evangelical Translation. For this new edition, comments and suggestions were provided by an editorial committee, in-house staff, and a small group of reviewers, but all final editorial decisions were made by Giessler alone.

Meanwhile, Dr. Eugene W. Bunkowske—a professor at Concordia Theological Seminary (a Lutheran seminary) as well as a missionary and translator—came on board as a translation consultant. Bunkowske's agreement to come on board, however, was contingent upon the translation project embracing the translation philosophy of "closest natural equivalence." I discuss this philosophy below, and how it led to the publication of the GOD'S WORD Bible in 1995.

Translation Philosophy and Procedure

The "closest natural equivalence" philosophy is neither the formal equivalence philosophy nor the dynamic equivalence philosophy. There are three primary considerations of this philosophy:

> The first consideration for the translators of GOD'S WORD was to find equivalent English ways of expressing the meaning of the original text. This procedure ensures that the translation is faithful to the meaning intended by the original writer. The next consideration was readability. The meaning is expressed in natural American English by using common English punctuation,

capitalization, grammar, and word choice. The third consideration was to choose the natural equivalent that most closely reflects the style of the Hebrew, Aramaic, or Greek text. This translation theory is designed to avoid the awkwardness and inaccuracy associated with form-equivalent translation, and it avoids the loss of meaning and oversimplification associated with function-equivalent translation.[2]

Toward the end of 1991, a team of five full-time Bible scholars and three English reviewers were assembled to work at the Society's facility in Cleveland. In 1992, leadership of the project passed to Reverend Michael Hackbardt. The translation work then sped forward at a fast pace. The work involved a number of critical stages:

- Translation (produced by biblical scholars)
- English Review (by an expert in English style)
- Peer Review (by other translators and English reviewers)
- Technical Review (by clergy, college professors, and seminary professors)
- Review by Book Editorial Committees (by members of the translation team)
- Review by Consultative Committee (by 50 Christian leaders from various denominations)
- Review by Old and New Testament Editorial Committees (who checked accuracy and readability)
- Review by Bible Editorial Committee (rendering a final review)
- Typesetting

The translation work was brought to completion in 1994, and the name of the translation was changed to GOD'S WORD. It was then published in 1995 by World Bible Publishers. In 2003, publishing rights passed to Green Key books. In 2008, publishing rights passed to Baker Books.

The translation generally features easy words, short sentences, and gender-inclusive language (or, more precisely, gender-neutral language) in passages referring to both males and females. Passages referring to an individual, however, retain gender-specific pronouns (such as *he, him,* and *his*).

Theological terms are often translated with easier equivalents. For example, "church" is sometimes changed to "community of believers"; "grace" becomes "good will" or "kindness"; "justification" becomes "God's approval"; and "the Law" becomes "Moses' Teachings."[3] Theological words that are retained are defined or explained in footnotes.

The translation employs a single column format, making it easy to read. It also formats poetry in an appealing, easy-to-follow layout (using layered indentions). The word LORD (small capital letters) is used for YHWH (the Old Testament name of God). Pronouns referring to deity *are not* capitalized.

Words in brackets [ ] contain translations of proper names or foreign words whose meanings are necessary for a proper understanding of the passage. For example, Genesis 3:20 says: "Adam named his wife Eve [Life] because she became the mother of every living person." Half brackets enclose words inserted by the translation team because the context of the passage contains implied meaning that is not explicitly stated in the original language.

Sampling GOD'S WORD

We gain insight into the translation style of GOD'S WORD by considering its rendering of some famous Bible passages:

Genesis 1:1-3: "In the beginning God created heaven and earth. The earth was formless and empty, and darkness covered the deep water. The Spirit of God was hovering over the water. Then God said, 'Let there be light!' So there was light."

Psalm 23:1-3: "The LORD is my shepherd. I am never in need. He makes me lie down in green pastures. He leads me beside peaceful waters. He renews my soul. He guides me along the paths of righteousness for the sake of his name."

Proverbs 3:5-6: "Trust the LORD with all your heart, and do not rely on your own understanding. In all your ways acknowledge him, and he will make your paths smooth."

Matthew 6:9-13: "This is how you should pray: Our Father in heaven, let your name be kept holy. Let your kingdom come. Let your will be done on earth as it is done in heaven. Give us our daily bread today. Forgive us as we forgive others. Don't allow us to be tempted. Instead, rescue us from the evil one."

John 3:16-17: "God loved the world this way: He gave his only Son so that everyone who believes in him will not die but will have eternal life. God sent his Son into the world, not to condemn the world, but to save the world."

Ephesians 2:8-9: "God saved you through faith as an act of kindness. You had nothing to do with it. Being saved is a gift from God. It's not the result of anything you've done, so no one can brag about it."

Philippians 4:13: "I can do everything through Christ who strengthens me."

Hebrews 11:1,6: "Faith assures us of things we expect and convinces us of the existence of things we cannot see.... No one can please God without faith. Whoever goes to God must believe that God exists and that he rewards those who seek him."

Benefits

This translation reads easier than many other translations on the market. It is therefore well suited to young readers, people with low reading skills, or people for whom English is a second language. It is also good to use alongside a more literal translation. Comparing Bible translations is always helpful to Bible study. We might also note that the bracketed and half-bracketed inserts help clarify the meaning of many Bible verses.

I should note that while claiming to subscribe to the "closest natural equivalent" philosophy, an objective examination of the translation by scholars not associated with the translation project claim it is more akin to the dynamic equivalence versions already on the market today. For example, Gordon Fee and Mark Strauss observe that despite the attempt to distinguish itself from other versions, the GOD'S WORD translation clearly fits into the genre of dynamic equivalence versions like the New Living Translation, Good News Translation, and New Century Version. "The version is generally accurate and readable, comparable to other functional equivalent versions in quality and style."[4]

Cautions

As is the case with many dynamic equivalence translations, some have criticized this translation for taking too much liberty in simplifying the original Hebrew, Aramaic, and Greek texts, thereby making it less suitable for detailed Bible study. Such translations, it is argued, involve too much interpretation on the part of the translator. The danger is that if the translator does not correctly understand the biblical author's intended meaning, then the translation could unintentionally communicate error.

Some have also commented that while the English is easy to read in this version, it is also a little bland and not as elegant as some of the more literal translations. This may bother some readers. Some also say the short sentences sometimes blur the connection between ideas in the text of Scripture. To be fair, however, while the GOD'S WORD translation does have many short sentences, not *all* are short.

Some may have problems with the way the GOD'S WORD translation simplifies theological terms. For example, the theological word *grace* means much more than just "kindness." Likewise, the word *justification* means more than just "God's approval."

One departure from most other Bible translations on the market today relates to the GOD'S WORD rendering of Galatians 5:16-18: "Let me explain further. Live your life as your *spiritual nature* directs you. Then you will never follow through on what your corrupt nature wants. What your corrupt nature wants is contrary to what your *spiritual nature* wants, and what your *spiritual nature* wants is contrary to what your corrupt nature wants. They are opposed to each other. As a result, you don't always do what you intend to do. If your *spiritual nature* is your guide, you are not subject to Moses' laws" (emphasis added).

By contrast, consider the NIV rendering of this passage: "So I say, live by *the Spirit,* and you will not gratify the desires of the sinful nature. For the sinful nature desires what is contrary to *the Spirit,* and *the Spirit* what is contrary to the sinful nature. They are in conflict with each other, so that you do not do what you want. But if you are led by *the Spirit,* you are not under law" (emphasis added).

The GOD'S WORD translation has "spiritual nature" where the NIV (and most other reliable translations today) have "Spirit," referring to the Holy Spirit. Obviously the GOD'S WORD translation means something entirely different than what is reflected in most other Bible translations. To be fair, there are some Greek exegetes who think the GOD'S WORD translation is *possible,* but the great majority of Greek exegetes disagree with that rendering.

It will be interesting to see if Baker Books makes any changes to the translation now that it has acquired the rights to it. Despite the cautions listed above, GOD'S WORD can no doubt be a benefit to young readers, people with low reading skills, and people for whom English is a second language.

The New Living Translation

THE NEW LIVING TRANSLATION (NLT) is a dynamic equivalence (meaning-driven) translation. The goal of the NLT is to have the same impact on modern readers as the original biblical books had on their audience. The NLT utilizes the vocabulary and language structures commonly used by the average person. It has sixth-grade (6.3) reading level, which means it can be read and understood by eleven-year-olds (junior high students). It utilizes gender-inclusive language where the biblical author clearly intended both males and females (see, for example, Genesis 1:27; Matthew 5:9; 25:45). It was published by Tyndale House Publishers in 1996.

The Story Behind the Translation

The NLT is a major revision of the over-40-million-selling Living Bible (LB). The differences between the two are notable. The LB was translated by a single individual, Kenneth Taylor, while the NLT was translated by a committee of 87 evangelical scholars from various denominations. While the LB is a simple paraphrase, the NLT is a dynamic equivalence translation. Whereas Taylor worked from the American Standard Version of 1901 to produce the LB, the revisers consulted the original Hebrew, Aramaic, and Greek as they did their work on the NLT.

The American-British translation team began their work in 1989 and took some seven years to complete the project in 1996. The NLT represents a vast improvement in accuracy over the LB.

Translation Philosophy and Procedure

The NLT translation team sought to take a balanced approach in their work. Their goal was to render the message of the original texts of Scripture into clear, contemporary English. As they engaged in their work, they were sensitive to the concerns of both the formal equivalence and dynamic equivalence philosophies. So, on the one hand, the translators "translated as simply and literally as possible when that approach yielded an accurate, clear, and natural English text. Many words and phrases were rendered literally and consistently into English, preserving essential literary and rhetorical devices, ancient metaphors, and word choices that give structure to the text and provide echoes of meaning from one passage to the next." On the other hand, however, they "rendered the message more dynamically when the literal rendering was hard to understand, was misleading, or yielded archaic or foreign wording. They clarified difficult metaphors and terms to aid in the reader's understanding."[1] As is common with many other translations, the NLT renders the Old Testament divine name, YHWH, as LORD (using small capitals).

Each portion of Scripture was assigned to scholars who had a recognized expertise in that part of Scripture. In fact, all of the translators have written books and/or scholarly articles in regard to the specific books of the Bible where they did their translation work. Their work was then checked by other scholars to ensure accuracy. English stylists were consulted for readability purposes.

It is instructive to consider how the Living Bible and the New

Living Translation are different in terms of actual translation. As an example, the Living Bible renders the first part of John 1:1, "Before anything else existed, there was Christ." The NLT renders the same phrase, "In the beginning the Word already existed." In this case, the NLT is much more faithful to the original Greek in retaining the Christological title of "the Word." This improved accuracy over the LB is characteristic of the NLT.

It is also instructive to observe how the NLT differs from a strict formal equivalence translation. Consider Romans 3:21 in the New American Standard Bible: "But now apart from the Law the righteousness of God has been manifested, being witnessed by the Law and the Prophets." The NLT renders the same verse: "But now God has shown us a way to be made right with him without keeping the requirements of the law, as was promised in the writings of Moses and the prophets long ago." One is a word-for-word translation, the other a thought-for-thought translation. One is more difficult to understand, the other easier.

Ecclesiastes 11:4 is another example. The NASB renders the verse, "He who watches the wind will not sow and he who looks at the clouds will not reap." The NLT renders the same verse, "Farmers who wait for perfect weather never plant. If they watch every cloud, they never harvest." Throughout the NLT, contemporary equivalents are used for ancient idioms, weights and measures, currency, the Hebrew calendar, weighty theological terms, and difficult wording.

Still another example is Amos 1:3. The NASB renders the verse: "Thus says the LORD, 'For three transgressions of Damascus and for four I will not revoke its punishment.'" The NLT renders it, "This is what the LORD says: 'The people of Damascus have sinned again and again, and I will not let them go unpunished!'" The dynamic equivalence translation of the NLT is clearly easier to understand than that of the formal equivalence translation of the NASB.

Regarding gender-inclusive language, the NLT preface tells us that "often the original language itself allows a rendering that is gender-inclusive. For example, the Greek word *anthropos*, traditionally rendered 'man,' really means 'human being' or 'person'."[2] So, when *anthropos* occurs in the NLT New Testament, gender-inclusive language is used. Gender-inclusive language is also used in the Old *and* New Testaments where the verse was obviously intended to include both males and females. So, for example, "brothers" is rendered "brothers and sisters."[3] However, all masculine nouns and pronouns used to represent God (such as "Father") have been maintained without exception.

Textual notes are added at the bottom of the page that provide several kinds of helpful information. For example, these notes include citations when the Old Testament is quoted in the New Testament, cultural and historical facts that may be obscure to modern readers, variant readings in ancient manuscripts, and alternative renderings from the Hebrew, Aramaic, or Greek.

There are a number of passages that are found in the KJV and NKJV that are based upon later-dated manuscripts of the Bible, but are excluded in the NLT. These include Matthew 17:21; 18:11; 23:14; 27:35b; Mark 7:16; 9:44,46; 11:26; 15:28; Luke 9:55b-56a; 17:36; 23:17; John 5:3b-4; Acts 8:37; 15:34; 24:6b-8a; 28:29; Romans 16:24; and 1 John 5:7b-8a. The NLT, however, includes a note about each such exclusion.

A revised edition of the NLT, incorporating substantial revisions related to accuracy and style, was published in 2004. One only need compare the original NLT with its latter revision to see the significance of the changes made. For example, the original NLT rendered Romans 12:1, "And so, dear brothers and sisters, I plead with you to give your bodies to God. Let them be a living and holy sacrifice—the kind he will accept. When you think of what he has done for you, is this too much to ask?" The revised edition of the NLT put it this way: "And so, dear brothers and sisters, I plead with you to give your bodies to God because of all he has done for you. Let them be a living and holy sacrifice—the kind he will find acceptable. This is truly the way to worship him." The 2004 edition increases the accuracy of the NLT.

Sampling the New Living Translation

We gain insight into the translation style of the New Living Translation by considering its rendering of some famous Bible passages:

Genesis 1:1-3: "In the beginning God created the heavens and the earth. The earth was formless and empty, and darkness covered the deep waters. And the Spirit of God was hovering over the surface of the waters. Then God said, 'Let there be light,' and there was light."

Psalm 23:1-3: "The Lord is my shepherd; I have all that I need. He lets me rest in green meadows; he leads me beside peaceful streams. He renews my strength. He guides me along right paths, bringing honor to his name."

Proverbs 3:5-6: "Trust in the Lord with all your heart; do not depend on your own understanding. Seek his will in all you do, and he will show you which path to take."

Matthew 6:9-13: "Pray like this: Our Father in heaven, may your name be kept holy. May your Kingdom come soon. May your will be done on earth, as it is in heaven. Give us today the food we need, and forgive us our sins, as we have forgiven those who sin against us. And don't let us yield to temptation, but rescue us from the evil one."

John 3:16-17: "For God loved the world so much that he gave his one and only Son, so that everyone who believes in him will not perish but have eternal life. God sent his Son into the world not to judge the world, but to save the world through him."

Ephesians 2:8-9: "God saved you by his grace when you believed. And you can't take credit for this; it is a gift from God. Salvation is not a reward for the good things we have done, so none of us can boast about it."

Philippians 4:13: "For I can do everything through Christ, who gives me strength."

Hebrews 11:1,6: "Faith is the confidence that what we hope for will actually happen; it gives us assurance about things we cannot see... And it is impossible to please God without faith. Anyone who wants to come to him must believe that God exists and that he rewards those who sincerely seek him."

Benefits

A primary benefit of the New Living Translation is that it makes the Bible understandable and even exciting to read.[4] As one reviewer put it, this translation is "accurate and idiomatically powerful." Another reviewer commented: "The language of the New Living Translation is clear and intelligible.... Its vastly improved accuracy over the Living Bible can be credited to the fine team of translators."[5] This accuracy and clarity is a primary reason for the strong sales this translation has enjoyed.[6]

While it is especially appropriate for young readers and readers for whom English is a second language, it is also a good translation for mature Christians. While some scholars may prefer a more word-for-word translation for detailed Bible study, it is noteworthy that there are several NLT study Bibles on the market—including the Life Application Study Bible and the NLT Study Bible.

Cautions

One caution regarding the New Living Translation is that because it is a thought-for-thought translation, it is not as accurate as a word-for-word translation, and hence may not be as suitable for *detailed* Bible study. For example, as is true with some other dynamic equivalence translations, the NLT does not use the rich, theological word *justification* in describing what Christ has done for believers at the cross. To illustrate this, note the NIV rendering of Romans 5:1: "Therefore, since we have been *justified* through faith, we have peace with God through our Lord Jesus Christ." The NLT, by contrast, renders it this way: "Therefore, since we have been *made right in God's sight* by faith, we have peace with God because of what Jesus Christ our Lord has done for us" (emphasis added in both renderings).

The NLT is certainly easier to understand. Many scholars, however, have noted that justification involves far more than just being "made right in God's sight." Justification involves a legal declaration by God. Negatively, this word means that a person is once-and-for-all pronounced *not guilty* before God. Positively, the word means that a person is once-and-for-all pronounced *righteous* before God. The very righteousness of Christ is legally imputed (or credited) to the believer's life. From the moment a person places faith in Christ the Savior, God sees that person through the lens of Christ's righteousness.[7] So, again, while "made right in God's sight" hints at what is meant by justification, the reality is that justification embraces a concept far richer than this. But the reader of the NLT will never realize this, for the term is never used. This is why it might be wise—even if the NLT is one's primary Bible—to at least compare the NLT with a formal equivalence translation.

Certainly there are those who are critical of the gender-inclusive language used in the NLT.[8] As noted elsewhere in the book, many believe that utilizing such language can subtly change the meaning of the inspired text. These would say it is better to translate literally, recognizing that male terms like "man" can generically refer to all humankind. Of course, in fairness, if this is going to be a criticism of the NLT, then it must also be a criticism of multiple other translations.

Despite the cautions listed above, many believe the NLT is a very good translation that can enable one to clearly understand the intended meaning of the biblical authors. I am glad to own a copy in my collection.

The New International Reader's Version

THE NEW INTERNATIONAL READER'S VERSION (NIrV) is a greatly simplified and highly readable revision of the New International Version (NIV) that features an easier vocabulary and shorter sentences.[1] Like the NIV, the NIrV is copyrighted by the International Bible Society (IBS) and was published by Zondervan Bible Publishers in 1996. This translation is aimed at children below the age of eight, adults for whom English is a second language, and adults who read at or below a fourth-grade reading level.[2] It has an approximate third-grade reading level. The original 1996 edition had moderate gender-inclusive language. After much controversy,[3] a new edition was published in 1998 that utilized traditional gender language.

The Story Behind the Translation

The NIrV was birthed when the board of the International Bible Society voted in 1992 to begin work on it. A committee promptly met in Colorado Springs to design some working guidelines for this new and easier-to-read translation, some of which focused on gender-inclusive language—a certain amount of which was to be allowed.

Following this, 40 translators and "simplifiers" were recruited, representing 14 denominations. Many of the translators had previously been involved in translating the NIV. These scholars were trained with the translation guidelines, and the translation process began. Once the work of translation was complete, it was submitted to a final review by an Old Testament scholar, a New Testament scholar, and an educator.

While these scholars consulted the original Hebrew, Aramaic, and Greek languages, they used the words of the NIV whenever possible. The team sometimes chose to use synonyms for some words, and in some cases explained words that might not be easily understood by a reader. A general guiding policy was to keep the sentences short and simple.

By early 1994, the initial process of simplification of the entire Bible was complete. The review and proofing stage then began. About two years later, in the fall of 1996, the Bible was published. Two years after that, in 1998, after a substantial wave of controversy, a revised edition was published which utilized more traditional gender language.

Translation Philosophy and Procedure

From the very beginning, the NIrV was intended to be easy to read. The translators explain, "We used the words of the NIV when we could. Sometimes we used shorter words. We explained words that might be hard to understand. We made the sentences shorter."[4] The target audience of the NIrV is children, adults for whom English is a second language, and adults who have reading difficulties. It has a reading age of 8.6 years (third grade)—the lowest of any mainline translation.

The NIrV translation intends to be distinguished by five fundamental characteristics—readability, understandability, compatibility with the NIV, reliability, and trustworthiness. To illustrate the ease of the NIrV, consider 1 Timothy 3:16 in the KJV, the NIV, and the NIrV:

KJV: "And without controversy great is the mystery of godliness: God was manifest in the flesh, justified in the Spirit, seen of angels, preached unto the Gentiles, believed on in the world, received up into glory."

NIV: "Beyond all question, the mystery of godliness is great: He appeared in a body, was vindicated by the Spirit, was seen by angels, was preached among the nations, was believed on in the world, was taken up in glory."

NIrV: "There is no doubt that godliness is a great mystery. Jesus appeared in a body. The Holy Spirit proved that he was the Son of God. He was seen by angels. He was preached among the nations. People in the world believed in him. He was taken up to heaven in glory."

A noteworthy policy of the NIrV translation team is that even though the Bible writers often used more than one name for the same person or place, the NIrV renders them the same way every time that person or place appears. Moreover, the translators tell us, "We also wanted to help our readers learn the names of people and places even in verses where those names don't actually appear. For example, when we knew that 'the River' meant 'the Euphrates River,' we used these words even in verses where only the words 'the River' are found."[5] The Old Testament divine name, YHWH, is rendered "LORD" (using small capitals).

There are other helpful features of the NIrV designed to make for easy reading. The translators tell us,

> Sometimes a Bible verse quotes from another place in the Bible. When that happens, we put the other Bible book's name, chapter, and verse right there. We separated each chapter into shorter sections. We gave a title to almost every chapter. Sometimes we even gave a title to the shorter

sections. That will help you understand what each chapter
or section is all about.[6]

The publishers have expressed the desire that the NIrV be used by
the Lord, like the NIV, to help people become stronger believers as a
result of reading it.[7] However, it has always been their intention that
when the time is right—that is, once the person's reading level becomes
a little more advanced—he or she can naturally graduate to the NIV.

Sampling the New International Reader's Version

We gain insight into the translation style of the New International
Reader's Version by considering its rendering of some famous Bible
passages:

Genesis 1:1-3: "In the beginning, God created the heavens and the
earth. The earth didn't have any shape. And it was empty. Darkness
was over the surface of the ocean. At that time, the ocean covered the
earth. The Spirit of God was hovering over the waters. God said, 'Let
there be light.' And there was light."

Psalm 23:1-3: "The LORD is my shepherd. He gives me everything
I need. He lets me lie down in fields of green grass. He leads me beside
quiet waters. He gives me new strength. He guides me in the right
paths for the honor of his name."

Proverbs 3:5-6: "Trust in the LORD with all your heart. Do not
depend on your own understanding. In all your ways remember him.
Then he will make your paths smooth and straight."

Matthew 6:9-13: "This is how you should pray. 'Our Father in
heaven, may your name be honored. May your kingdom come. May
what you want to happen be done on earth as it is done in heaven.
Give us today our daily bread. Forgive us our sins, just as we also have
forgiven those who sin against us. Keep us from falling into sin when
we are tempted. Save us from the evil one.'"

John 3:16-17: "God loved the world so much that he gave his one
and only Son. Anyone who believes in him will not die but will have

eternal life. God did not send his Son into the world to judge the world. He sent his Son to save the world through him."

Ephesians 2:8-9: "God's grace has saved you because of your faith in Christ. Your salvation doesn't come from anything you do. It is God's gift. It is not based on anything you have done. No one can brag about earning it."

Philippians 4:13: "I can do everything by the power of Christ. He gives me strength."

Hebrews 11:1,6: "Faith is being sure of what we hope for. It is being certain of what we do not see…Without faith it isn't possible to please God. Those who come to God must believe that he exists. And they must believe that he rewards those who look to him."

Benefits

Many would say the NIrV has succeeded as a translation that is appropriate for children, adults for whom English is a second language, and adults who have reading difficulties.[8] Many parents have commented publicly that their children truly like to read the NIrV. With its third-grade reading level, it has put the Bible within the grasp of millions of English readers with a low reading ability.

Cautions

The obvious caution with the NIrV is that even though it might help readers with low reading skills to understand the Bible, it is certainly not appropriate as a study Bible. One must not forget the general maxim that the easier the translation, the more interpretive elements have been inserted by the translation team. The NIrV is no exception to this rule.

Moreover, this is not a Bible one should *keep* using once one's reading skills begin to improve. This should be considered a "special needs" Bible for challenged readers. As noted previously, the publisher itself urges people to graduate to the NIV when the time is right.

Some have noted that the very process of simplifying the text by utilizing short sentences and standardized words has removed some of the elegance that is traditionally found in more literal renderings of Scripture. This may be bothersome to some. Furthermore, the short words and short sentences can sometimes make for choppy reading.

To be fair, however, I think the translators would probably say that for the sake of its intended audience (children and challenged readers), a tradeoff between these cautions and greater readability is probably tolerable.

The English Standard Version

THE ENGLISH STANDARD VERSION (ESV) was published in 2001 by Crossway Bibles, a division of Good News Publishers. It is a formal equivalence (literal, word-for-word) translation with an eighth-grade (middle school) reading level. On gender issues, when the biblical author intended gender-specific language, that language has been preserved in the ESV. When the biblical author was clearly intending to include more than males, words like *persons* or *people* are used.

A British edition of the ESV was published in 2002. A minor revision of the ESV was completed in 2007, entailing about 360 changes.[1]

The Story Behind the Translation

In the early 1990s, some theological conservatives were unhappy with some of the then-existing translations. For example, the Revised Standard Version was perceived as being theologically liberal. The New American Standard Bible was viewed as too woodenly literal. The New Revised Standard Version was perceived as having gone too far in its gender-inclusive language.[2] The gender issue had, by then, become a lightning rod of controversy.

A meeting was called in 1997 by James Dobson at Focus on the Family, the goal of which was to resolve the gender-neutral language debate.* The result was the "Colorado Springs Guidelines for Translation of Gender-Related Language in Scripture." Meeting attendees signed an agreement holding to these guidelines.

The night prior to the meeting, critics of gender-inclusive language in Bible translations gathered in a Colorado Springs hotel room to talk strategy. Among other things, some at the meeting spoke of the merits of the Revised Standard Version.

Not many months later, Trinity Evangelical Divinity School professor Wayne Grudem and Crossway President Lane Dennis negotiated with the National Council of Churches to obtain permission to use the 1971 Revised Standard Version as a basis for a new translation. This new translation would be the English Standard Version—a translation that would deliberately adhere to the guidelines agreed upon at the Dobson meeting.

It is rather significant that the National Council of Churches granted permission. One might recall that an earlier attempt at an evangelical revision of the RSV had failed in the 1960s. Perhaps the reason the National Council of Churches was more open this time around was because sales of the RSV had plummeted—understandable in view of the fact that the NRSV had been published in 1990.

Well-known theologian J.I. Packer became chief editor of the new project. A 14-member oversight committee was assisted by a translation review board of 60 scholars working on individual Bible books. An additional 60 scholars served on an advisory council. Both American and British scholars served on all three panels. All participating scholars shared a common commitment to the truth of God's Word and to historic Christian orthodoxy. Many denominations were represented

---

* The controversy had become acute because an inclusive version of the NIV had been published.

among the collective group. Their goal was to produce a modern, readable, and accurate translation in the tradition of the Tyndale Version of 1535 and the King James Version of 1611.

Translation Philosophy and Procedure

The English Standard Version is a formal equivalence translation with an eighth-grade (middle school) reading level. The translators made great efforts to capture the precise wording of the original languages. "The Bible says every word was 'breathed out by God' (2 Timothy 3:16). For this reason, the ESV seeks to translate the original Greek and Hebrew words with the greatest possible accuracy and precision."[3] Indeed, "each word and phrase in the ESV has been carefully weighed against the original Hebrew, Aramaic, and Greek, to ensure the fullest accuracy and clarity and to avoid under-translating or overlooking any nuance of the original text."[4]

The translators also paid close attention to—and sought to reflect—the personal writing style of each biblical author. More specifically, we see in the ESV the logical writing style of Paul, the simple writing style of John, the smooth style of Luke, the rich metaphors in poetic books, the flowing narratives of historical books, and much more.

The ESV seeks to be an "essentially literal" though readable translation.[5] The result was a translation that is more literal than the New International Version, but is more idiomatic and readable than the New American Standard Bible. The ESV preface observes that "every translation is at many points a trade-off between literal precision and readability, between 'formal equivalence' in expression and 'functional equivalence' in communication, and the ESV is no exception. Within this framework we have sought to be 'as literal as possible' while maintaining clarity of expression and literary excellence."[6] In the ESV, therefore, "faithfulness to the text and vigorous pursuit of accuracy were combined with simplicity, beauty, and dignity of expression."[7]

Unlike some dynamic equivalence translations, theological terminology is retained throughout the ESV. Words such as *grace, faith, justification, sanctification, redemption, regeneration, reconciliation,* and *propitiation* are utilized, for such words lie at the very heart of Christian doctrine. Even in New Testament times, the underlying Greek terms for these words were already becoming technical terms referring to key theological concepts. Hence, the ESV retains these important words.

The ESV renders God's Old Testament personal name, YHWH, as "Lord" (printed in small capitals). When the Hebrew word *Adonai* (Lord) appears together with YHWH, they are rendered together as "the Lord God." *Elohim* is normally translated as "God." In the New Testament, the Greek word *Christos* is consistently translated as "Christ."

Bible writers often used "connectives" between sentences, such as "and," "but," and "for." Obviously we do not speak that way today. Nevertheless, the ESV translates these connectives, though sometimes renders them using alternative words like *also, however, now, so, then,* or *thus.* Such alternatives make the flow of thought easier to follow for the English reader.

Unlike some dynamic equivalence translations, the ESV has usually retained the word *behold* to translate the Hebrew word *hinneh* and Greek word *idou.* This choice was made because alternatives like *Look* or *See* or *Listen* (words commonly used in dynamic equivalence translations) do not carry the same weight and dignity.

It might surprise some to learn that less than 10 percent of the RSV text was actually changed in the ESV, and many of the corrections relate to RSV renderings that conservative Protestants felt were tainted with theologically liberal views. For example, the ESV translation team changed "young woman" (Hebrew: *almah*) in Isaiah 7:14 to "virgin." As well, obsolete words were removed, and *thee* and *thou* were modernized. It is thus correct to call the ESV a "light revision" of the RSV.

There has been some interesting discussion regarding the ESV's policy on gender-inclusive language. Some have noted that some of the strongest criticism against Today's New International Version (which uses gender-inclusive language pervasively) has come from some translators who have introduced similar gender-inclusive language in the ESV. However, Wayne Grudem, one of the ESV translators, responded that while there are occasions in which the words *person* or *one* are used in place of "man," this is only in cases where the biblical author was clearly intending to include more than just males. Likewise, "'people' rather than 'men' is regularly used where the original languages refer to both men and women."[8]

Grudem emphasizes, however, that when the biblical author was intending *gender-specific* language, that language has been preserved in the ESV. "The words 'man' and 'men' are retained where a male meaning component is part of the original Greek or Hebrew."[9] The term "brothers" is consistently translated as "brothers" and not "brothers and sisters," for the term "brothers" was often used in Greek to refer to both men and women. (When the term "brothers" occurs in the ESV, there is an accompanying recurring note that makes this clear.) The word *sons* is also retained in specific instances "because of its meaning as a legal term in the adoption and inheritance laws of first-century Rome." This term was used by the apostle Paul of all Christians, men and women, "who, having been adopted into God's family, now enjoy all the privileges, obligations, and inheritance rights of God's children."[10] The inclusive use of the generic "he" has also regularly been retained.[11]

Sampling the English Standard Version

We gain insight into the translation style of the English Standard Version by considering its rendering of some famous Bible passages:

Genesis 1:1-3: "In the beginning, God created the heavens and the earth. The earth was without form and void, and darkness was over the face of the deep. And the Spirit of God was hovering over the face of the waters. And God said, 'Let there be light,' and there was light."

Psalm 23:1-3: "The LORD is my shepherd; I shall not want. He makes me lie down in green pastures. He leads me beside still waters. He restores my soul. He leads me in paths of righteousness for his name's sake."

Proverbs 3:5-6: "Trust in the LORD with all your heart, and do not lean on your own understanding. In all your ways acknowledge him, and he will make straight your paths."

Matthew 6:9-13: "Pray then like this: 'Our Father in heaven, hallowed be your name. Your kingdom come, your will be done, on earth as it is in heaven. Give us this day our daily bread, and forgive us our debts, as we also have forgiven our debtors. And lead us not into temptation, but deliver us from evil.'"

John 3:16-17: "For God so loved the world, that he gave his only Son, that whoever believes in him should not perish but have eternal life. For God did not send his Son into the world to condemn the world, but in order that the world might be saved through him."

Ephesians 2:8-9: "For by grace you have been saved through faith. And this is not your own doing; it is the gift of God, not a result of works, so that no one may boast."

Philippians 4:13: "I can do all things through him who strengthens me."

Hebrews 11:1,6: "Now faith is the assurance of things hoped for, the conviction of things not seen.... And without faith it is impossible to please him, for whoever would draw near to God must believe that he exists and that he rewards those who seek him."

Benefits

This is overall an excellent word-for-word and theologically conservative translation that is ideal for serious Bible study. It is highly accurate though also very readable. Many conservative Christian scholars have opted for this translation as their Bible of choice.[12]

There are additional benefits. Section headings are included throughout the text to help identify and locate important themes and topics throughout the Bible. Textual footnotes include alternative translations, explanations of Greek and Hebrew terms, information about the meanings of names in the original languages, information about grammatical points that might not come across in an English translation, information about English equivalents for weights, measures, and monetary values, and more. Among the study Bibles that have been published utilizing the ESV are the Scofield Study Bible, The Reformation Study Bible, and the highly acclaimed ESV Study Bible.

Cautions

Although the ESV is more literal and reliable than most English versions published in recent years, there are some scholars who believe it may need improvement in a few places. As one reviewer put it, "Not all will be convinced that its biblical scholarship is as up to date as it could be or its style as natural as might have been achieved even without compromise to its form-driven principles."[13]

It has also been suggested that some of the changes from the RSV to the ESV are not necessarily for the better. For example, a few scholars have expressed concern about how the ESV substitutes numerals for spelled-out words—that is, 16,000 in place of the RSV's "sixteen thousand" (Numbers 31:46). The words *sixteen thousand* seem to communicate *approximation,* which may have been the biblical author's intention. The numeral 16,000 seems to communicate *precision,* something probably not intended by the biblical author. (Personally, I think this criticism *may* involve splitting hairs.)

Another example might be how the Greek word *monogenes* is translated in the ESV. In the RSV (and other translations), the word is translated "only-begotten" in reference to Jesus being God's only-begotten Son (John 3:16). The ESV renders the word as "only," not "only-begotten." While this is an acceptable translation of the Greek word, there are some who believe it is an *under*-translation of an important theological term. It is suggested that perhaps a footnote should be included to clarify this.

Still, it is the general consensus of Christian scholars and church leaders that the English Standard Version is an excellent translation of the Bible. A look at the Crossway Bible website reveals a plethora of endorsements by famous theologians, linguistic scholars, and church leaders.

The NET Bible

THE NET BIBLE PRIMARILY EMPLOYS a dynamic equivalence method of translation, though some of its 60,000+ notes include a formal equivalence translation as well.[1] A goal of the translation team was to translate passages consistently and properly within their *grammatical, historical,* and *theological* context (see below). The translation seeks to be gender-accurate as opposed to being gender-inclusive. After a number of "beta editions," the final first edition was published in 2005 by the Biblical Studies Press.

The Story Behind the Translation

The origins of the NET Bible are rooted in an annual meeting of the Society of Biblical Literature held in Philadelphia in 1995. Long story short, a group of Old and New Testament scholars met over dinner at an Italian restaurant with a sponsor of the NET Bible project, who all later met again in the hotel lobby to discuss the possibility of producing a new translation of the Bible for electronic distribution over the Internet. Initially some tossed around the idea of using an already-existing translation, but subsequent discussions led everyone to conclude that a completely new translation was desirable.

The name, "NET Bible," carries two relevant meanings. On the one hand, it refers to the New English Translation. As well, however, the name reflects the goal of providing the Bible to an Internet audience in electronic format in addition to the more traditional print media. Internet users easily understand and relate to what is meant by "NET," so "NET Bible" is an appropriate way to describe the translation.

A team of more than 25 scholars—all experts in the biblical languages—were involved in the project. Most of them teach Hebrew or Greek exegesis at seminaries or graduate schools. Each book of the Old and New Testaments was assigned to a scholar with high expertise in that book. In most cases, the scholar has published various works on the biblical book to which he was assigned. Each such scholar produced an initial translation of the book, along with an initial suggested set of translator notes.

This work was then submitted to the New Testament or Old Testament Editorial Committee for extensive editing and revision. These revisions were then made in the manuscript either by the original translator or an editor.

Following this, the work was resubmitted to the appropriate committee for final approval. The task, however, was not yet finished. The work was then submitted to an English style consultant who reviewed the translation for smoothness, clarity, and elegance. Suggested style changes were then checked against the original manuscripts before incorporation into the translation. It was then meticulously proofread and field-tested in various settings.

It is important to note that the NET Bible is not funded by any particular denomination or publisher or special interest group. This has served to preserve the integrity of the biblical text. In other words, the translators and editors felt no compulsion from anyone regarding making the translation fit a particular doctrinal statement, or be absolutely faithful to some particular translation philosophy. "Translators and editors were left free to follow where the text leads and translate as they thought best."[2]

Of course, one must be cautious in making such assertions. Linguistic scholar Hall Harris suggests that the NET team's assertion that it is free from ecclesiastical control *could* be construed as implying that other translations in common use have been produced under the direct control of ecclesiastical officials. "But this is not true. Most of the versions currently in use among Protestants were produced by committees which were not subject to any regular church authority."[3]

In any event, the NET Bible was specially designed to be placed on the Internet, downloaded for free, and used around the world for ministry. The sentiment was that the Bible is God's *gift* to humanity, and gifts should be *free*. The NET Bible is available for download at www.bible.org, the Web site for the Biblical Studies Foundation. The NET team believes that "this approach helps us come closer to fulfilling the Great Commission of Matthew 28:19-20 by allowing all people of all nations on earth to learn what God has revealed in his Word for them to understand and obey." Indeed, "to a server on the Internet, distributing 6 billion copies—one for every person on earth!—costs almost nothing, unlike all previous methods of distributing Bibles. The Internet represents the single best opportunity for ministry in the history of the world."[4]

Though initially conceived as a study Bible, it is also designed to be useful for reading aloud, memorizing, teaching, and preaching. The present plans call for updating the translation every five years. For those who do not necessarily feel a need for the 60,000+ translator notes, a reader's edition is available without the notes.

Translation Philosophy and Procedure

The NET Bible is a completely new translation, not a revision or an update of a previous English version. It is unique in that it features over 60,000 translator notes. That is an average of two translator notes for each verse in the Bible. These notes document the translators' decisions and choices as they worked, providing a gold mine of insights rooted in the original languages. The notes are the cumulative result of hundreds of thousands of hours of biblical and linguistic research. The NET Bible preface tells us,

> The translators' notes make the original languages far more accessible, allowing you to look over the translator's shoulder at the very process of translation. This level of documentation is a first for a Bible translation, making transparent the textual basis and the rationale for key renderings (including major interpretive options and alternative translations). This unparalleled level of detail helps connect people to the Bible in the original languages in a way never before possible without years of study of Hebrew, Aramaic, and Greek. It unlocks the riches of the Bible's truth from entirely new perspectives.[5]

By consulting these translator notes, the reader can easily understand options for interpretation, the finer nuances of Hebrew and Greek words which are usually lost in translation, and facts about grammatical, lexical, historical, and textual data that most Bible readers are unaware of. As well, some of the notes include a formal equivalence translation of a verse rendered in the text using the dynamic equivalence translation philosophy. Thus, the actual text of the Bible in these instances is easy to read, but it is convenient to compare it with a literal rendering in the notes.

Romans 16:7 is illustrative of the benefit of these translator notes. The English Standard Version says that Andronicus and Junia are well-known "*to* the apostles." The New International Version, however, renders it as saying that Andronicus and Junia are outstanding "*among* the apostles." Is the correct translation "to" or "among"? The NET Bible says the best translation is that they are well-known "*to* the apostles," and then provides translator notes explaining *why* this is the best translation.

To ensure accuracy, the NET team translated every passage within its *grammatical, historical,* and *theological* context. All three are critically important. Grammatical context involves an accurate understanding of the language of the original biblical text (Hebrew, Aramaic, or Greek). Historical context involves an understanding of the peoples, cultures, customs, and history of the times in which the biblical authors wrote. Theological context involves an understanding of God and His work that a particular biblical author would have had at the time he wrote a particular passage of Scripture.

These three concepts form a contextual hierarchy, with the grammatical context most important, since it deals with the nuts and bolts of the language itself. However, the historical and theological context provide a reasonable system of checks and balances—that is, they help the translator decide what is the most *probable* meaning of the original text and how that meaning should be translated.

The Old Testament divine name, YHWH, is rendered in the NET Bible as "Lord" (using small capitals). The traditional "Lord of hosts" is rendered either as "the Lord who rules over all" or "the Lord who commands armies," depending on the context.

As an added help to Bible students, sectional headings in italics are scattered throughout the Old and New Testaments. These help the reader to understand the broad context of the section being read.

On the issue of gender sensitivity, the goal of the NET Bible is to be gender-*accurate* as opposed to being gender-*inclusive*. The translation team states, "We do not believe the Bible should be rewritten to incorporate gender-inclusive language foreign to the original." So, for example, male language is used in the case of Jesus being on the Sea of Galilee with His disciples, for it is almost certain that only males were present. Yet, the NET Bible is also sensitive to the reality that many verses are not limited to males. In contexts where it is clear that both men and women are present, more generic terms like "people" have been used. Moreover, the term "brothers" has been rendered "brothers and sisters" in New Testament epistles where the church is addressed at large.

A unique feature of the NET Bible is that it has been beta-tested on the Internet. The NET Bible preface tells us:

> In this beta-testing process all working drafts of the NET Bible were posted on www.bible.org for public review and comment. The significance of this is that the NET Bible team, from day one, has been listening to its readers. The purpose of the public review and comment was not to achieve a consensus translation, but to be accountable, to be transparent, and to request that millions of people provide feedback on the faithfulness and clarity of the translation as well as on the translators' notes. Countless valuable suggestions have been made by scholars, by junior high school students, by college professors, and by lay Christians who speak English as a second language. Because of the open approach of the NET Bible team, the resulting product has been enriched immeasurably.[6]

The idea here is that every person comes to the Bible from a different perspective, and therefore it makes good sense for scholars to listen to the person in the pew just as the person in the pew listens to the scholar. The NET Bible is said to be a symbiotic effort between the insights of biblical scholars and the needs of lay Christians. Indeed, "by creating a translation environment that is responsible both to the world's scholars and to lay readers, the NET Bible was read, studied, and checked by more eyes than any Bible translation in history."[7]

The first beta edition of the entire NET Bible was sent to the printer in September of 2001. The second beta went to the printer two years later in September of 2003. After two more years of use, in which changes were incorporated from users, the finalized first edition of the NET Bible was published in August of 2005.

Sampling the NET Bible

We gain insight into the translation style of the NET Bible by considering its rendering of some famous Bible passages:

Genesis 1:1-3: "In the beginning God created the heavens and the earth. Now the earth was without shape and empty, and darkness was over the surface of the watery deep, but the Spirit of God was moving over the surface of the water. God said, 'Let there be light.' And there was light!"

Psalm 23:1-3: "The LORD is my shepherd, I lack nothing. He takes me to lush pastures, he leads me to refreshing water. He restores my strength. He leads me down the right paths for the sake of his reputation."

Proverbs 3:5-6: "Trust in the LORD with all your heart, and do not rely on your own understanding. Acknowledge him in all your ways, and he will make your paths straight."

Matthew 6:9-13: "So pray this way: Our Father in heaven, may your name be honored, may your kingdom come, may your will be done on earth as it is in heaven. Give us today our daily bread, and forgive us our debts, as we ourselves have forgiven our debtors. And do not lead us into temptation, but deliver us from the evil one."

John 3:16-17: "For this is the way God loved the world: He gave his one and only Son, so that everyone who believes in him will not perish but have eternal life. For God did not send his Son into the world to condemn the world, but that the world should be saved through him."

Ephesians 2:8-9: "For by grace you are saved through faith, and this is not from yourselves, it is the gift of God; it is not from works, so that no one can boast."

Philippians 4:13: "I am able to do all things through the one who strengthens me."

Hebrews 11:1,6: "Now faith is being sure of what we hope for, being convinced of what we do not see.... Now without faith it is impossible to please him, for the one who approaches God must believe that he exists and that he rewards those who seek him."

Benefits

The primary benefit of the NET Bible is that it is a readable and yet accurate translation of the Bible, which makes it well suited for Bible study.[8] Further, the reader is privileged to "look over the shoulder" of the translators as they work by consulting the 60,000-plus notes. This in itself makes the NET Bible well worth owning. It is also reassuring to know that this Bible has undergone such extensive testing with both scholars and readers worldwide.

Cautions

There have been a few criticisms of the NET Bible. Some have claimed that it has an uneven translation quality, ranging from being moderately form-driven (that is, moderately word-for-word) to moderately meaning-driven. Others have claimed that the NET Bible may not be as accurate as some might initially think. Linguistic scholar W. Hall Harris tells us that "the translators have for the most part employed a dynamic equivalence method, in which they have tried to use expressions in 'common language.' This method gives the version a simple and contemporary English style, which may be appreciated by some readers; but it does tend to degrade the accuracy of the translation."[9]

Some laypersons have commented that many of the translator notes are so technical that they seem to require knowledge of Hebrew and Greek to even understand many of them. One scholar commented that the translator notes often seem "tiresome and tendentious."[10] To be fair, however, there are other kinds of notes besides translator notes (typically marked "sn"—short for "study note") that laypersons *can* understand without knowledge of Hebrew and Greek.

A warning to the wise: Students who use the NET Bible may get the idea that its notes provide *all one needs* in terms of exegetical information* about specific verses. However, as one scholar put it,

---

* *Exegetical* means "critically explanatory" or "interpretive." *Exegesis* literally means "drawing the meaning out of the text."

many of these notes "barely scratch the surface of the interpretive issues, and they are no substitute for a comprehensive exegetical commentary."[11]

One final caution relates only to the print version of the NET Bible. In order to cram 60,000-plus notes into the Bible, with the entire text of the Old and New Testaments, means that the font used for the notes is rather tiny—much too small for my 50-plus-year-old eyeballs. If they ever publish a giant-print edition, I will be the first in line to buy it. Despite the cautions listed above, I personally think the NET Bible is a very good translation, and I am glad to own a copy.

The Message

THE MESSAGE IS AN EASY-TO-UNDERSTAND paraphrase that makes heavy use of modern English idioms.[1] It was translated by Eugene H. Peterson, a former professor who has a background in the Semitic languages. This paraphrase is not meant to replace one's current Bible. Rather, it is designed as a reading Bible that can provide a fresh perspective. It has an approximate reading grade level of 4.3.

The New Testament appeared in 1993, the Psalms in 1994, Proverbs in 1995, the Wisdom books in 1998, the Prophets in 2000, the Pentateuch in 2001, and the Historical Books along with the whole Bible following in 2002, all published by NavPress. Just as the Living Bible struck a chord with people in the 1960s and 1970s, so The Message has struck a chord with modern readers.* It has been a steady huge seller.[2]

The Story Behind the Translation

Experts in Bible translation have often noted that translations accomplished by a single person are often more colorful and stylistically

---

* Many, however, would say that the Living Bible seems tame in comparison to The Message.

distinct that a translation done by a committee.[3] This is certainly true in the case of Eugene Peterson's The Message. Peterson's ability as a wordsmith, and his passion to communicate, are largely responsible for the success of The Message.

Peterson was once asked why he produced The Message. His response is noteworthy:

> While I was teaching a class on Galatians, I began to real-ize that the adults in my class weren't feeling the vitality and directness that I sensed as I read and studied the New Testament in its original Greek. Writing straight from the original text, I began to attempt to bring into English the rhythms and idioms of the original language. I knew that the early readers of the New Testament were captured and engaged by these writings and I wanted my congregation to be impacted in the same way. I hoped to bring the New Testament to life for two different types of people: those who hadn't read the Bible because it seemed too distant and irrelevant and those who had read the Bible so much that it had become "old hat."[4]

The rest is history! Peterson first translated the New Testament, and then step-by-step translated the Old Testament, all of it couched in modern idiom and phraseology.

Translation Philosophy and Procedure

The Message is essentially a paraphrase that is written in earthy, street language—the way people really talk today. The Message was intended "to convert the tone, rhythm, and ideas of the Bible into the way people think and speak today."[5] Peterson wanted to capture the conversational feel of the original languages in contemporary English.

The original Greek, Peterson says, was the street language of the day:

> In the Greek-speaking world of that day, there were two
> levels of language: formal and informal. Formal language
> was used to write philosophy and history, government
> decrees and epic poetry. If someone were to sit down and
> consciously write for posterity, it would of course be writ-
> ten in this formal language with its learned vocabulary and
> precise diction. But if the writing was routine—shopping
> lists, family letters, bills, and receipts—it was written in
> the common, informal idiom of everyday speech, street
> language. And this is the language used throughout the
> New Testament. Some people are taken aback by this,
> supposing that language dealing with a holy God and holy
> things should be elevated—stately and ceremonial. But
> one good look at Jesus—his preference for down-to-earth
> stories and easy association with common people—gets
> rid of that supposition.[6]

An example of the earthiness of The Message might be John 1:14, where we read: "The Word became flesh and blood, and moved into the neighborhood. We saw the glory with our own eyes, the one-of-a-kind glory, like Father, like Son, generous inside and out, true from start to finish." Describing the human birth of Jesus as *moving into the neighborhood* is highly imaginative and communicative, but it might be slightly stunning to folks more accustomed to traditional translations.

Another example of the earthiness of The Message might be Matthew 23:27. For comparison sake, the NIV renders this verse: "Woe to you, teachers of the law and Pharisees, you hypocrites! You are like whitewashed tombs, which look beautiful on the outside but on the inside are full of dead men's bones and everything unclean." By contrast, The Message renders the verse: "You're like manicured grave plots, grass clipped and the flowers bright, but six feet down it's all rotting bones and worm-eaten flesh." Peterson's skill as a wordsmith comes through loud and clear in this instance.

Though The Message was translated by one person, Eugene Peterson, a team of exegetical consultants from various well-known seminaries reviewed his work to ensure overall accuracy. This added a measure of academic accountability to his work.

There has been at least some revision through the years. In early versions of The Message, we find the divine name, YHWH, rendered as "Yahweh" throughout the Old Testament. In more recent editions, we find "Yahweh" replaced by "God." Moreover, the early editions had no verse numbers (as was true in the original Hebrew, Aramaic, and Greek manuscripts). Today one can purchase editions of The Message with or without verse numbers.

Sampling The Message

We gain insight into the translation style of The Message by considering its rendering of some famous Bible passages:

Genesis 1:1-3: "First this: God created the Heavens and Earth—all you see, all you don't see. Earth was a soup of nothingness, a bottomless emptiness, an inky blackness. God's Spirit brooded like a bird above the watery abyss. God spoke: 'Light!' And light appeared."

Psalm 23:1-3: "God, my shepherd! I don't need a thing. You have bedded me down in lush meadows, you find me quiet pools to drink from. True to your word, you let me catch my breath and send me in the right direction."

Proverbs 3:5-6: "Trust God from the bottom of your heart; don't try to figure out everything on your own. Listen for God's voice in everything you do, everywhere you go; he's the one who will keep you on track."

Matthew 6:9-13: "Like this: Our Father in heaven, reveal who you are. Set the world right; do what's best—as above, so below. Keep us alive with three square meals. Keep us forgiven with you and forgiving others. Keep us safe from ourselves and the Devil. You're in charge! You can do anything you want! You're ablaze in beauty! Yes. Yes. Yes."

John 3:16-17: "This is how much God loved the world: He gave his Son, his one and only Son. And this is why: so that no one need be destroyed; by believing in him, anyone can have a whole and lasting life. God didn't go to all the trouble of sending his Son merely to point an accusing finger, telling the world how bad it was. He came to help, to put the world right again."

Ephesians 2:8-9: "Saving is all his idea, and all his work. All we do is trust him enough to let him do it. It's God's gift from start to finish! We don't play the major role. If we did, we'd probably go around bragging that we'd done the whole thing! No, we neither make nor save ourselves."

Philippians 4:13: "I can make it through anything in the One who makes me who I am."

Hebrews 11:1,6: "The fundamental fact of existence is that this trust in God, this faith, is the firm foundation under everything that makes life worth living. It's our handle on what we can't see.... It's impossible to please God apart from faith. And why? Because anyone who wants to approach God must believe both that he exists and that he cares enough to respond to those who seek him."

Benefits

The obvious benefit of The Message is that it makes the Bible come alive in an exciting way. It is very easy to read, and communicates by using modern Western idioms and figures of speech. For this reason, The Message may be of some benefit to those seeking to read the Scriptures with "fresh eyes." It might also help modern readers grasp something of the impact the Scriptures may have had on its original audience so long ago. Further, it may aid those who have deficient reading skills in English, and those for whom English is a second language. And finally, it might be useful for evangelism purposes.[7]

Cautions

A primary caution regarding The Message is that it involves significant interpretive commentary from Peterson. Sometimes it is hard to know where the biblical text ends and the clarifying commentary begins. Some critics have commented that Peterson seems to make style more important than faithfully and accurately communicating the content of the original documents of Scripture.[8]

Some have pointed out that Peterson at times pads the biblical text with additional details with a view to heightening the vividness and drama of the text. To illustrate, Colossians 1:18-20, speaking of Jesus, is rendered this way in the NIV: "And he is the head of the body, the church; he is the beginning and the firstborn from among the dead, so that in everything he might have the supremacy. For God was pleased to have all his fullness dwell in him, and through him to reconcile to himself all things, whether things on earth or things in heaven, by making peace through his blood, shed on the cross." By contrast, The Message renders the passage this way: "He was supreme in the beginning and—leading the resurrection parade—he is supreme in the end. From beginning to end he's there, towering far above everything, everyone. So spacious is he, so roomy, that everything of God finds its proper place in him without crowding. Not only that, but all the broken and dislocated pieces of the universe—people and things, animals and atoms—get properly fixed and fit together in vibrant harmonies, all because of his death, his blood that poured down from the Cross." Some think a bit too much liberty is taken in such renderings.[9]

Some reviewers have commented that some of Peterson's renderings seem awkward. For example, in John 1:1 we read: "The Word was first, the Word present to God, God present to the Word." In John 1:18 we read: "This one-of-a-kind God-Expression, who exists at the very heart of the Father, has made him plain as day." Sometimes one may be hard-pressed to follow certain renderings in The Message.[10]

Others have pointed out that in the process of making the Scriptures palatable to modern Western ears, some of Peterson's renderings have stripped the Scriptures of their first-century Jewish context. Noted scholar Bruce Metzger is representative, noting that sometimes Peterson "goes beyond the acceptable bounds of dynamic equivalence in that he will often divest passages from their first-century Jewish context, so that Jesus, for example, sounds like a twentieth-century American."[11]

Still others have criticized The Message for not retaining enough specificity. To illustrate, 1 Corinthians 6:9-10 is rendered in the NIV: "Do you not know that the wicked will not inherit the kingdom of God? Do not be deceived: Neither the sexually immoral nor idolaters nor adulterers nor male prostitutes nor homosexual offenders nor thieves nor the greedy nor drunkards nor slanderers nor swindlers will inherit the kingdom of God." By contrast, this passage is rendered in The Message: "Don't you realize that this is not the way to live? Unjust people who don't care about God will not be joining in his kingdom. Those who use and abuse each other, use and abuse sex, use and abuse the earth and everything in it, don't qualify as citizens in God's kingdom." The Message speaks in generalities and fails to specify the sins that will keep one from inheriting God's kingdom.

In view of all of this, many believe The Message should not be used for Bible study. One should utilize a more literal translation for Bible study, and perhaps have a good dynamic equivalence translation with which to compare it. One should remember what Peterson himself said: This paraphrase *is not meant to replace one's current Bible.* Rather, it was designed as a reading Bible that can provide a fresh perspective.[12]

The Holman Christian Standard Bible

THE HOLMAN CHRISTIAN STANDARD BIBLE (HCSB) is an accurate and easy-to-read translation that has a 7.5 reading grade level (middle school), and is published by the Broadman and Holman Publishing Group. It is designed for Bible readers of all ages and is Protestant, evangelical, and conservative in orientation. The HCSB Gospels appeared in 1999, the New Testament in 2001, Psalms and Proverbs in 2003, with the whole Bible following in 2004. On gender issues, while the translation does not seek to overuse words like *man,* neither does it avoid use of such terms when the translation calls for it. Robert Thomas sums it up by saying, "The HCSB has sought to safeguard against liberal theology and gender-neutral language in its renderings."[1] However, though limited, there are at least some generic terms used in the HCSB.[2]

The Story Behind the Translation

The Holman Christian Standard Bible is ultimately a product of the Southern Baptist Convention. The backdrop is that the Southern

Baptist Convention Sunday School Board had been using the New International Version, under license, in its various programs (curriculum and ministry). But the Board became increasingly concerned over two matters: (1) the escalating controversy over gender-inclusive language (Paige Patterson, the Southern Baptist Convention Secretary, spoke out harshly against such language), and (2) the high cost of licensing the NIV for its programs.[3]

In 1998, Arthur Farstad—who had been the general editor of the New King James Version—reached an agreement with LifeWay Christian Resources, the publishing arm of the Southern Baptist Convention. This agreement stipulated that LifeWay would fund— to the tune of $10 million—and then publish a new translation that had already been well underway under Farstad's leadership since the mid-1980s. Farstad passed away, however, just a few months after the agreement was reached. Leadership of the editorial team was handed over to Dr. Edwin Blum, former professor at Dallas Theological Seminary and Farstad's assistant who had already been intimately involved in the project.

It is interesting to observe that Farstad's death resulted in the translation team making a change in the Greek texts to be used for the translation. Under Farstad, the New Testament was to be based upon the same Greek texts used for the original King James Version as well as the New King James Version. Following Farstad's death, the editorial team decided to go with the more modern Greek text established by modern scholars. However, though following the modern critical Greek text (so called because it is edited according to specific principles of textual criticism), the HCSB is unique in that it supplies alternative readings from the *Textus Receptus** and the Majority Text** in its footnotes, which served as the basis for the KJV and NKJV.[4]

---

* The *Textus Receptus* is a Latin term for "Received Text"—the 1550 edition of the Greek New Testament behind the KJV New Testament. It is based on a relatively few available Greek manuscripts.

** A term for the Byzantine text-type that underlies the *Textus Receptus* Greek text.

The translation team was made up of 100 scholars and proofreaders. Each member of the translation team affirmed belief in the inspiration and inerrancy of Scripture. The team represented some 20 different Protestant denominations—including Baptists, Plymouth Brethren, Presbyterians, Congregationalists, Church of England, Church of God, Evangelical Free Church, Methodists, Evangelical Mennonites, and Episcopalians—as well as several nondenominational churches. In view of this, the HCSB should not be considered a "Baptist Bible," but a Bible suitable to all English-speaking Christians and all Protestant denominations.

Translation Philosophy and Procedure

The Holman Christian Standard translation seeks to strike a balance between the two popular translation philosophies: the formal equivalence philosophy (form-for-form or word-for-word) and the dynamic equivalence philosophy (meaning-for-meaning or thought-for-thought). The translators chose to call this balanced approach "optimal equivalence." We are told: "Optimal equivalence recognizes that the form should not be changed unless comprehension demands it. The primary goal of optimal equivalence translations is to convey a sense of the original text with as much clarity as possible."[5]

What this ultimately means is that while the translators gave priority to a form-driven (word-for-word) approach, they felt free to use moderate meaning-driven methods when necessary for the sake of creating readable English. In cases where a meaning-driven rendering was necessary in the text, a more literal translation appears in the footnotes. Edwin Blum, the general editor of the project, explains it this way: "A conscientious translator has to render the meaning exactly, but present it in a form his readers find inviting and naturally expressive. We work using a word-for-word translation philosophy, but we always keep our contemporary American English reader in mind."[6]

In accomplishing its task, the translation team engaged in an exhaustive analysis of the ancient Hebrew, Aramaic, and Greek texts—

examining every word, phrase, clause, sentence, and discourse—to uncover the precise meaning. Biblical linguists then used the best translation tools available to modern scholars in order to translate these ancient texts into readable English. Using this translation philosophy, the HCSB ended up more literal than the NIV but less literal than the NASB or ESV.

The HCSB retains use of traditional theological words such as *grace* and *justification,* but provides concise word studies in the back of the Bible to help readers grasp their full meaning. Small lower corner brackets ⌞ ⌟ indicate words supplied for clarity by the translators. The term "Yahweh" is used of God in the Old Testament when a particular text emphasizes YHWH as a name (see, for example, Psalm 68:4).[7] Otherwise, the term is rendered "LORD" (with small capitals). Nouns and pronouns referring to deity are capitalized throughout. Old Testament citations in the New Testament are formatted in boldface type.

On gender-inclusive language, the translation team tells us, "While the Holman CSB avoids using 'man' or 'he' unnecessarily, the translation does not restructure sentences to avoid them when they are in the text. For example, the translators have not changed 'him' to 'you' or to 'them,' neither have they avoided other masculine words such as 'father' or 'son' by translating them in generic terms such as 'parent' or 'child.'"[8]

Sampling the Holman Christian Standard Bible

We gain insight into the translation style of the Holman Christian Standard Bible by considering its rendering of some famous Bible passages:

Genesis 1:1-3: "In the beginning God created the heavens and the earth. Now the earth was formless and empty, darkness covered the surface of the watery depths, and the Spirit of God was hovering over the surface of the waters. Then God said, 'Let there be light,' and there was light."

Psalm 23:1-3: "The LORD is my shepherd; there is nothing I lack.

He lets me lie down in green pastures; He leads me beside quiet waters. He renews my life; He leads me along the right paths for His name's sake."

Proverbs 3:5-6: "Trust in the LORD with all your heart, and do not rely on your own understanding; think about Him in all your ways, and He will guide you on the right paths."

Matthew 6:9-13: "Therefore, you should pray like this: Our Father in heaven, Your name be honored as holy. Your kingdom come. Your will be done on earth as it is in heaven. Give us today our daily bread. And forgive us our debts, as we also have forgiven our debtors. And do not bring us into temptation, but deliver us from the evil one. [For Yours is the kingdom and the power and the glory forever. Amen.]"

John 3:16-17: "For God loved the world in this way: He gave His One and Only Son, so that everyone who believes in Him will not perish but have eternal life. For God did not send His Son into the world that He might judge the world, but that the world might be saved through Him."

Ephesians 2:8-9: "For by grace you are saved through faith, and this is not from yourselves; it is God's gift—not from works, so that no one can boast."

Philippians 4:13: "I am able to do all things through Him who strengthens me."

Hebrews 11:1,6: "Now faith is the reality of what is hoped for, the proof of what is not seen…. Now without faith it is impossible to please God, for the one who draws near to Him must believe that He exists and rewards those who seek Him."

Benefits

The accurate translation, clear style, excellent footnotes, and helpful cross-references make the Holman Christian Standard Bible a good choice for serious Bible study. And its clear connection to the Southern Baptist Convention serves to guarantee its acceptability to many Christians across America. Keep in mind, however, that this is not intended to be a "Baptist Bible." It is suitable for Christians of all Protestant denominations. The translation has been endorsed by a number of major Christian leaders.

Cautions

Some reviewers have claimed that the HCSB is slightly wooden in its style, occasionally awkward, and sometimes choppy. For this reason, it is claimed, the HCSB may not be as suitable for public reading as some other versions. However, this is a minor criticism, and not all would agree with it.

Some reviewers have questioned a few of the word choices in the HCSB. For example, if the goal is to keep things simple and clear, why use the word "deluge" instead of the easier word "flood" in the Genesis account of Noah? This, too, is a minor criticism.

A few reviewers have commented that the small lower corner brackets that indicate "words supplied for clarity by the translators" can be a little distracting. The reviewers concede, however, that this is an improvement over the insertion of italicized words (as in the New American Standard Bible). Personally, I like the bracketed insertions.

Some have commented that the alternate translations provided in the notes may be slightly distracting. Personally, I don't see it that way, and very much appreciate having those notes.

Those who feel strongly about the need for gender-inclusive language may be less than satisfied with this Bible, since such language is minimal. On the other hand, those who feel gender-inclusive language mistranslates Scripture will be pleased.

Today's New
International Version

Today's New International Version (TNIV), a revision of the NIV, is intended to fall somewhere between a word-for-word (formal equivalence) translation and a thought-for-thought (dynamic equivalence) translation. It seeks to be gender-*accurate* rather than gender-*inclusive*. The TNIV New Testament was published in 2001, followed by the whole Bible in 2005. It has about a seventh-grade reading level.

The Story Behind the Translation

Cultural observers have noted that in our day some eight million 18-to-34-year-olds are on the verge of leaving the Christian church. Today's New International Version is intended to engage these people with the Word of God with a translation that reflects biblical scholarship, clarity, and gender accuracy.[1]

The backdrop to the TNIV is that the Committee on Bible Translation, which is the committee that oversees the New International Version, periodically updates the NIV so that it remains in keeping with current English usage as well as new advances in biblical scholarship. One assumed goal was the eventual introduction of "gender-accurate" language.

Significant controversy emerged in 1997, however, when a gender-inclusive version of the NIV was published by Hodder and Stoughton in Great Britain entitled the NIV Inclusive Language Edition. Conservative Christians, including James Dobson of Focus on the Family, made their feelings loudly known. Significant negative publicity was also generated by an article in *World* magazine, a publication widely read by Christians. A huge controversy erupted.

At this time, the International Bible Society (who holds the copyright to the NIV) and Zondervan Bible Publishers made the decision to "freeze" the 1984 edition of the NIV without gender-inclusive language. However, Zondervan also made the decision to publish Today's New International Version, which was intended to be a "revisable" edition of the NIV. The initial TNIV took some ten years to complete and was published in 2005. From henceforth, the TNIV will remain a revisable translation that will be periodically updated in light of advances in biblical scholarship and changes in the English language.

Translation Philosophy and Procedure

Each biblical book was revised by two evangelical scholars noted for their expertise on that particular book. All scholars working on the project were united in their commitment to the authority and infallibility of the Bible as God's Word in written form. A goal of the translators was to make the TNIV fall somewhere between the most literal translations and the most free translations. More specifically, they wanted it to fall somewhere between a word-for-word (formal equivalence) translation and a thought-for-thought (dynamic equivalence) translation. They sought it to be an accurate translation "that would have clarity and literary quality and so prove suitable for public and private reading, teaching, preaching, memorizing and liturgical use."[2]

Once the proposed revisions were complete, they were brought to the Committee on Bible Translation, where an 80 percent majority vote was required to make proposed changes. This committee has members from respected evangelical Christian colleges and seminaries, representing a variety of evangelical denominations.

In the end, approximately 7 percent of the NIV's text was altered in the TNIV. About one-third of these alterations relate to gender. Additionally, hundreds of changes have been made in the text to enhance exegetical* accuracy.[3] In an analysis conducted by Dr. Craig Blomberg, some 70 percent of the changes in the TNIV move in a "more literal direction three times more often than not." Moreover, Dr. Mark Strauss has affirmed that the majority of textual changes are "based on advances in biblical scholarship, linguistics, and archaeology."[4] Understandably, TNIV promotional literature claims it is "an uncompromisingly accurate Bible translation in today's language."[5]

Some of the changes more precisely render the intended contextual meaning of the original Hebrew, Aramaic, or Greek text. For example, there are cases when a reference to "the Jews" is rendered more specifically, based on the context, as "the Jewish leaders" or "the Jews there" (see John 1:19; 5:10,15,16; 7:1,11; 9:22; 18:14,28,36; 19:12,31,38; 20:19; Acts 13:50; 21:11; 25:2; 28:17). Sometimes the context indicates that a specific group of Jews, as opposed to Jews in general, is meant. The TNIV preface tells us, "To achieve clarity the translators have sometimes supplied words not in the original texts but required by the context. In a few instances, where some uncertainty about such material remained, it is enclosed in corner brackets."[6]

Other changes relate to increasing clarity for modern English readers. For example, to say that Mary is "with child" is not a way most people speak today. Hence, instead, Mary is said to be "pregnant." Likewise, the phrase "the third watch of the night" is meaningless to most English readers, and is hence changed to "shortly before dawn."

---

* *Exegetical* means "critically explanatory" or "interpretive." *Exegesis* literally means "drawing the meaning out of the text."

"Fellow workers" is rendered "co-workers." "Saints" is often rendered "God's people" or "believers." As John Kohlenberger notes, "the NIV has *saints* 45 times, while in the TNIV *saints* remains only 9 times (Rom. 1:7; 15:26; 1 Cor. 1:2; 2 Cor. 1:1; Eph. 1:1; Phil. 1:1; Col. 1:2; Rev. 8:4; 18:20)."[7]

We might point to John 1:18, a verse speaking of Jesus, to illustrate how the TNIV provides a clearer rendering than the NIV. The NIV makes reference to "God the One and Only, who is at the Father's side." By contrast, the TNIV makes reference to "the one and only [Son] who is himself God and is in closest relationship with the Father."

Interestingly, "Messiah" is often substituted for "Christ" in the TNIV. "Where the term is clearly used to designate the God-sent deliverer of Jewish expectations (primarily in the Gospels and Acts), it was judged more appropriate to use 'Messiah.' However, where this sense seems less prominent (primarily in the Epistles), the transliteration of the Greek word ('Christ') has been retained."[8] In point of fact, the TNIV has "Messiah" 68 times whereas the NIV has it only 2 times. Moreover, the TNIV has "Christ" 468 times whereas the NIV has it 530 times.[9] The Old Testament divine name, YHWH, is rendered as "Lord" (using small capitals).

For readability purposes, changes have also been made to paragraph structure, sentence structure, word order, punctuation, spelling, and capitalization. Every effort has been made to make the Bible more understandable for readers.

Regarding gender issues, the TNIV boasts of being gender-*accurate* rather than gender-*inclusive*. When it is clear from the original text that both men and women were intended, generic terminology is used. In such contexts, "sons of God" becomes "children of God," and "brothers" becomes "brothers and sisters."[10] In keeping with this, Genesis 1:27 reads, "So God created *human beings* in his own image" (emphasis added). Likewise, Matthew 5:9 reads, "Blessed are the peacemakers, for they will be called *children of God*" (emphasis added). Titus 2:11 reads, "For the grace of God has appeared that offers salvation *to all people*" (emphasis added). However, references originally intended to be masculine remain masculine in the TNIV. As well, masculine references to God ("Father" and "Son") are never changed.

Sampling Today's New International Version

We gain insight into the translation style of Today's New International Version by considering its rendering of some famous Bible passages:

Genesis 1:1-3: "In the beginning God created the heavens and the earth. Now the earth was formless and empty, darkness was over the surface of the deep, and the Spirit of God was hovering over the waters. And God said, 'Let there be light,' and there was light."

Psalm 23:1-3: "The LORD is my shepherd, I lack nothing. He makes me lie down in green pastures, he leads me beside quiet waters, he refreshes my soul. He guides me along the right paths for his name's sake."

Proverbs 3:5-6: "Trust in the LORD with all your heart and lean not on your own understanding; in all your ways submit to him, and he will make your paths straight."

Matthew 6:9-13: "This, then, is how you should pray: 'Our Father in heaven, hallowed be your name, your kingdom come, your will be done, on earth as it is in heaven. Give us today our daily bread. And forgive us our debts, as we also have forgiven our debtors. And lead us not into temptation, but deliver us from the evil one.'"

John 3:16-17: "For God so loved the world that he gave his one and only Son, that whoever believes in him shall not perish but have eternal life. For God did not send his Son into the world to condemn the world, but to save the world through him."

Ephesians 2:8-9: "For it is by grace you have been saved, through faith—and this is not from yourselves, it is the gift of God—not by works, so that no one can boast."

Philippians 4:13: "I can do all this through him who gives me strength."

Hebrews 11:1,6: "Now faith is being sure of what we hope for and certain of what we do not see.... And without faith it is impossible to please God, because anyone who comes to him must believe that he exists and that he rewards those who earnestly seek him."

Benefits

A number of scholars have gone on record as affirming that the TNIV is a translation that not only maintains and improves the readability of the NIV, but is also a more accurate rendering in terms of intended meaning.[11] It is thus claimed that more modern English readers will understand this version of the Bible than others.

Cautions

With interest, I read the following words in an article: "I would rather be torn in pieces by wild horses than permit any such translation to be forced upon poor churches. The new edition infuriates me. I require it to be burned."[12] Upon reading such words, it might be your initial impression that someone penned these words about the TNIV, in view of how this translation ignited a public storm of controversy upon its release.[13] In fact, the words were written centuries ago about the King James Version. This adds a bit of perspective to the current debate about Bible translations.

Frankly, I do not think I have ever seen a translation come under as much criticism—even *condemnation*—as Today's New International Version. It is not my purpose to provide a full accounting of the vitriolic language sometimes used in reference to this translation. In what follows, however, I provide a representative sampling of the kinds of concerns and cautions that various people have expressed about it. It is up to you—the reader—to weigh these considerations.

One caution is that there are some cases where the TNIV offers a different or nuanced understanding of a particular verse. An example is Psalm 26:3, where, in the NIV, we read: "For your love is ever before me, and *I walk continually in your truth.*" In the TNIV, we read: "For

I have always been mindful of your unfailing love and *have lived in reliance on your faithfulness*" (emphasis added in both renderings). These renderings are obviously quite different and communicate different meanings. It naturally causes the reader to wonder which rendering is correct.

Some critics have noted problems related to the so-called "gender-accuracy" of the TNIV.[14] An example is the TNIV rendering of Psalm 1:1: "Blessed are *those* who do not walk in step with the wicked or stand in the way that sinners take or sit in the company of mockers." The NIV reads, "Blessed is *the man* who does not walk in the counsel of the wicked or stand in the way of sinners or sit in the seat of mockers" (emphasis added in both renderings). Some criticize the TNIV because the original Hebrew (reflected in the NIV) highlights the struggle of *the individual* against the wicked masses.

Another example is Revelation 3:20. In the TNIV we read: "Here I am! I stand at the door and knock. If anyone hears my voice and opens the door, I will come in and eat with *them,* and *they* with me." In the NIV, by contrast, we read: "Here I am! I stand at the door and knock. If anyone hears my voice and opens the door, I will come in and eat with *him,* and *he* with me" (emphasis added in both renderings). The NIV rendering, more faithful to the Greek, portrays Christ fellowshipping *with the individual.* The TNIV blurs this focus on the individual.

A final example is John 6:44, which in the TNIV reads: "No one can come to me unless the Father who sent me draws *them,* and I will raise *them* up at the last day." In the NIV, by contrast, we read: "No one can come to me unless the Father who sent me draws *him,* and I will raise *him* up at the last day" (emphasis added in both renderings). The verse is supposed to highlight the Father and Son drawing and raising *the individual believer* as opposed to a group of people.

TNIV enthusiasts, however, continue to maintain that the heavy use of male language in the Bible is confusing to many modern English readers, and hence, for the sake of communication, such changes are justified. Moreover, linguistic scholar Craig Blomberg commented: "The TNIV has numerous places where it retains gender-exclusive language,* when a case could have been made for a more inclusive rendering. I counted about two dozen such places (Matt. 10:21,35; 12:29; 13:44,45; 15:38; 23:8; Lk. 17:7-9; Acts 3:25; 13:50; 22:1; 27:10,21,25; 28:17; Rom. 5:15-17; 8:15)."[15] Blomberg's point is that one must maintain balance in critiquing the TNIV in this regard.

One might also note that the TNIV is not the only gender-inclusive translation around today. In point of fact, gender-inclusive translations include the New Revised Standard Version, the New Living Translation, and the Catholic New Jerusalem Bible, among others. It may be that the TNIV has become the special target of such broad and vitriolic criticism because it is tied to the venerable and wildly popular New International Version.

Despite all the controversy, there are prominent Christian leaders and scholars who have gone on record as supporting the TNIV. This would include Lee Strobel, Bill Hybels, Philip Yancey, John R.W. Stott, Ronald F. Youngblood, Mark L. Strauss, John Ortberg, Kenneth L. Barker, Gordon Fee, Douglas Moo, Rob Bell, Bruce K. Waltke, Craig Blomberg, Darrell Bock, Don Carson, Erwin McManus, and Ben Witherington III. Denominational support includes the Christian Reformed Church, the Evangelical Covenant Church, and the Free Methodist Church of North America.

On the opposite side of the spectrum are numerous leaders and scholars that continue to oppose the TNIV. These would include J.I. Packer, James Dobson, Charles Colson, Nancy Leigh DeMoss, the late Jerry Falwell, Wayne Grudem, Howard Hendricks, Erwin Lutzer, Pat Robertson, Charles Swindoll, the late D. James Kennedy, Josh McDowell, Albert Mohler, John Piper, Dennis Rainey, R.C. Sproul, and Joni Eareckson Tada. Denominations have also taken a stand against it, including the Southern Baptist Convention.

---

* Language that maintains a distinction between males and females.

Blomberg feels that many churchgoers have not been provided accurate information on the TNIV: "Unfortunately, the new translation's critics have so politicized the issue, convincing bookstore owners not to carry the translation and persuading entire denominations to issue statements against it, that the average churchgoer simply has little access to accurate information about the TNIV."[16] Blomberg has personally documented quite a few verses where he feels the TNIV is more exegetically accurate than the NIV.[17]

We close with this statement in the TNIV preface:

> The Committee has again been reminded that every human effort is flawed—including this revision of the NIV. We trust, however, that many will find in it an improved representation of the Word of God, through which they hear his call to faith in our Lord Jesus Christ and to service in his kingdom. We offer this version of the Bible to him in whose name and for whose glory it has been made.[18]

The New Jerusalem Bible
(Catholic)

BOTH THE JERUSALEM BIBLE (JB), published in 1966, and the New Jerusalem Bible (NJB), published in 1985, have generally been popular among English-speaking Roman Catholics worldwide. As Catholic Bibles, they include the so-called deuterocanonical* books (also known as the Apocrypha**). The NJB has an approximate high school reading level. It seeks to be fairly literal in its approach, and introduces moderate use of gender-inclusive language.

The Story Behind the Translation

The original Jerusalem Bible, published in 1966, was heavily influenced by the French translation, the *Bible de Jérusalem,* prepared by the faculty of the Dominican Biblical School in Jerusalem (1961). This

---

* Deuterocanonical means "second canon."

**The Apocrypha refers to 14 or 15 books of doubtful authenticity and authority that the Roman Catholics decided belonged in the Bible sometime following the Protestant Reformation. The Catholic Council of Trent (1545–1563) canonized these books. See Appendix C—"Does the Apocrypha Belong in the Bible?"

French translation was then translated into English, though still, obviously, utilizing the Hebrew, Aramaic, and Greek manuscripts. This work was done by 20 members of the British Catholic Biblical Association, and was published as the Jerusalem Bible. Scholars note that "the significant influence of the French version cannot be overlooked. A few books, the preface admits, were translated from the French and only then compared to the Hebrew, Aramaic, and Greek. The study notes were translated directly from the French."[1]

It was after the French translation was later updated in 1973, incorporating widespread changes to both the biblical text and notes, that the English version of the Jerusalem Bible was revised as well, and then published as the New Jerusalem Bible in 1985. Henry Wansbrough of Ampleforth Abbey, Yorkshire, was the chief editor of the revision. The NJB foreword affirms that "the translation follows the original Hebrew, Aramaic, and Greek Texts," while also acknowledging the French editions.[2] Bruce Metzger notes that "the New Jerusalem Bible (1985) is not just a translation of the French, but an edition in its own right, with textual improvement and explanatory notes, under the direction of the new editor, Dom Henry Wansborough of Ampleforth Abbey in Yorkshire."[3]

The NJB is the most widely read Catholic Bible among English speakers *outside* of the United States. (Most Catholics in the United States seem to prefer the New American Bible—see chapter 23.) A "Reader's Edition" of the New Jerusalem Bible was published in 1990.

Translation Philosophy and Procedure

Editor Dom Henry Wansbrough affirmed that there were five main principles that guided his translation work: (1) to improve the accuracy of translation, introductions, and notes; (2) to remove elements which were narrowly Roman Catholic, such as references in the notes to passages used in the Roman Catholic liturgy; (3) where possible to use the same English word throughout for the same Hebrew concepts;

(4) in the Synoptic Gospels and other parallel sets of texts (for example, the Books of Kings and of Chronicles) to show the differences between the text, in order to make possible a study of the redactional changes made by the authors; and (5) where possible to go some way toward using inclusive language.[4]

The New Jerusalem Bible is more literal in its approach—more form-driven—than the Jerusalem Bible, but is somewhat freer than the New American Bible, another popular Catholic Bible.[5] The NJB introduces moderate use of gender-inclusive language, though much less than that of the New Revised Standard Version Catholic Edition. The primary goal of the NJB was a reduction of masculine-oriented language in passages that clearly involve both men and women. As we read in the NJB foreword, "Considerable efforts have been made, though not at all costs, to soften or avoid the inbuilt preference of the English language, a preference now found so offensive by some people, for the masculine; the word of the Lord concerns men and women equally."[6]

What kinds of gender changes were made? "Men of good omen" becomes "an omen of things to come" (Zechariah 3:8). "Rich men" becomes "the rich" (Micah 6:12). "Man" becomes "someone" (Zechariah 4:1). "The wicked man's oracle is sin" becomes "Sin is the oracle of the wicked" (Psalm 36:1).[7] Some more conservative Catholics reject the NJB because of its gender-inclusiveness.

One gets a sense of the differences between the Jerusalem Bible and the New Jerusalem Bible in how they render Hebrews 1:1-4. Consider:

The Jerusalem Bible rendering:

> At various times in the past and in various different ways, God spoke to our ancestors through the prophets; But in our own time, the last days, he has spoken to us through his Son, the Son that he has appointed to inherit everything and through whom he made everything there is. He is the

radiant light of God's glory and the perfect copy of his nature, sustaining the universe by his powerful command; and now that he has destroyed the defilement of sin, he has gone to take his place in heaven at the right hand of divine Majesty. So he is now as far above the angels as the title which he has inherited is higher than their own name.

The New Jerusalem Bible rendering:

At many moments in the past and by many means, God spoke to our ancestors through the prophets; but in our time, the final days, he has spoken to us in the person of his Son, whom he appointed heir of all things and through whom he made the ages. He is the reflection of God's glory and bears the impress of God's own being, sustaining all things by his powerful command; and now that he has purged sins away, he has taken his seat at the right hand of the divine Majesty on high. So he is now as far above the angels as the title which he has inherited is higher than their own name.

Unlike most other translations today, the New Jerusalem Bible renders the Old Testament name for God, YHWH, as "Yahweh," just as the Jerusalem Bible did. In place of "Lord of hosts" is "Yahweh Sabaoth." Where in the Beatitudes (Matthew 5:3-10) the original Jerusalem Bible had "Happy," the New Jerusalem Bible reverts to the more traditional "Blessed." Quotations from the Old Testament in the New Testament are formatted by italics.

Sampling the New Jerusalem Bible

We gain insight into the translation style of the New Jerusalem Bible by considering its rendering of some famous Bible passages:

Genesis 1:1-3: "In the beginning God created heaven and earth. Now the earth was a formless void, there was darkness over the deep, with a divine wind sweeping over the waters. God said, 'Let there be light,' and there was light."

Psalm 23:1-3: "Yahweh is my shepherd, I lack nothing. In grassy meadows he lets me lie. By tranquil streams he leads me to restore my spirit. He guides me in paths of saving justice as befits his name."

Proverbs 3:5-6: "Trust wholeheartedly in Yahweh, put no faith in your own perception; acknowledge him in every course you take, and he will see that your paths are smooth."

Matthew 6:9-13: "So you should pray like this: Our Father in heaven, may your name be held holy, your kingdom come, your will be done, on earth as in heaven. Give us today our daily bread. And forgive us our debts, as we have forgiven those who are in debt to us. And do not put us to the test, but save us from the Evil One."

John 3:16-17: "For this is how God loved the world: he gave his only Son, so that everyone who believes in him may not perish but may have eternal life. For God sent his Son into the world not to judge the world, but so that through him the world might be saved."

Ephesians 2:8-9: "Because it is by grace that you have been saved, through faith; not by anything of your own, but by a gift from God; not by anything that you have done, so that nobody can claim the credit."

Philippians 4:13: "There is nothing I cannot do in the One who strengthens me."

Hebrews 11:1,6: "Only faith can guarantee the blessings that we hope for, or prove the existence of realities that are unseen.... Now it is impossible to please God without faith, since anyone who comes to him must believe that he exists and rewards those who seek him."

Benefits

This Bible is designed for Roman Catholics, and many have found it to meet their needs for many years. It is more literal than the Jerusalem Bible, but less literal than the New American Bible. Those who prefer the rendering "Yahweh" as the name of God in the Old Testament will find this Bible appealing.

Cautions

While many Roman Catholics like this Bible, it is rejected by most Protestants because they reject the Apocrypha as belonging in the Word of God (See Appendix C—"Does the Apocrypha Belong in the Bible?"). Beyond this, one should beware that the introductions and notes contained in the New Jerusalem Bible presuppose the acceptance of skeptical views and modernistic theories concerning the authorship and authenticity of the biblical books. The doctrine of the inspiration and inerrancy of Scripture is thereby undermined. Hence, this is certainly not a Bible that conservative Christians would feel comfortable with. Some conservative reviewers have noted that the NJB fails the Isaiah 7:14 "litmus test"—that is, it has "young woman" instead of "virgin."[8]

Just as there are Protestants who do not like gender-inclusive language in Protestant Bibles, so there are Catholics who do not like gender-inclusive language in Catholic Bibles. While the NJB introduces only a moderate level of gender-inclusive language, it will not be to the liking of those who prefer a literal rendering from the Hebrew, Aramaic, and Greek languages.

Another caution relates to the NJB's handling of YHWH (the Old Testament divine name). Where most translations have "Lord," the NJB has "Yahweh." As well, compound names of deity in the Old Testament are transliterated from the Hebrew instead of using English translations of these names. Hence, where most translations have "God Most High," the NJB has "El Elyon." Where most translations have "God Almighty," the NJB has "El Shaddai." Where most translations have "Lord of Hosts," the NJB has "Yahweh Sabaoth." This will confuse many readers not familiar with such terms.

The New American Bible
(Catholic)

THE NEW AMERICAN BIBLE—not to be confused with the New American Standard Bible—is a Catholic Bible that includes the so-called deuterocanonical* books (also known as the Apocrypha**). It was published in 1970 and is among the most popular Catholic Bibles—especially for liberal Catholics. It is relatively word-for-word in its approach (formal equivalence), and has a 6.6 reading grade level (middle school).

The Story Behind the Translation

The New American Bible is the direct result of an encyclical by Pope Pius XII in 1943, in which he stated: "We ought to explain the original text which was written by the inspired author himself and

---

* Deuterocanonical means "second canon."

**The Apocrypha refers to 14 or 15 books of doubtful authenticity and authority that the Roman Catholics decided belonged in the Bible sometime following the Protestant Reformation. The Catholic Council of Trent (1545–1563) canonized these books. See Appendix C—"Does the Apocrypha Belong in the Bible?"

has more authority and greater weight than any, even the very best, translation whether ancient or modern. This can be done all the more easily and fruitfully if to the knowledge of languages be joined a real skill in literary criticism of the same text."[1] The following year, in 1944, the Catholic Biblical Association of America proceeded to translate the Scriptures from the original languages and "to present the sense of the biblical text in as correct a form as possible."[2]

Some 50 scholars were involved in the translation, most—though certainly not all—were Catholics. (In point of fact, 5 of the 15 members of its committee were Protestants.[3]) The editors-in-chief of the translation devoted 25 years to finishing the assigned task.

As to why non-Catholic scholars were included in the translation team, the New American Bible preface tells us: "The collaboration of scholars who are not Catholic fulfills the directive of the Second Vatican Council, not only that 'correct translations be made into different languages especially from the original texts of the sacred books,' but that, 'with the approval of the church authority, these translations be produced in cooperation with separated brothers' so that 'all Christians may be able to use them.'"[4]

Translation Philosophy and Procedure

The New American Bible is relatively word-for-word in its approach (formal equivalence). The translators sought to retain the thought and individual style of the biblical writers. Their goal was to accurately render the sense of what the sacred authors actually wrote. This task was more easily accomplished today than in former times because so many excellent resources in Hebrew, Aramaic, and Greek are available.

The translation seeks to be gender-neutral in many places.[5] The Old Testament name of God, YHWH, is rendered "LORD" in the New American Bible (small capitals). Headings are sprinkled throughout to guide the reader. Individual biblical books have short introductions. The translation passes the Isaiah 7:14 "litmus test," rendering the verse: "*The virgin* shall be with child, and bear a son, and shall name him

Immanuel" (emphasis added). At the end of the Bible there is a glossary of biblical theological terms with references.

Catholics and even some non-Catholics have had some positive things to say about this translation. Bruce Metzger, a non-Catholic New Testament scholar, commented, "This version represents capable and dedicated scholarship and provides a rendering of the Scriptures in modern American idiom."[6]

The translators realize that no translation is perfect. We are told:

> Conscious of their personal limitations for the task thus defined, those who have prepared this text cannot expect that it will be considered perfect; but they can hope that it may deepen in its readers "the right understanding of the divinely given Scriptures," and awaken in them "that piety by which it behooves us to be grateful to the God of all providence, who from the throne of his majesty has sent these books as so many personal letters to his own children."[7]

Parts of the Bible have been revised through the years. More specifically, the New Testament was revised with the goal of reducing instances of paraphrase (1986). This revision was more literal in its approach, but incorporated more gender-neutral language. The Psalms were revised in 1991.

Sampling the New American Bible

We gain insight into the translation style of the New American Bible by considering its rendering of some famous Bible passages:

Genesis 1:1-3: "In the beginning, when God created the heavens and the earth, the earth was a formless wasteland, and darkness covered the abyss, while a mighty wind swept over the waters. Then God said, 'Let there be light,' and there was light."

Psalm 23:1-3: "The LORD is my shepherd; there is nothing I lack. In green pastures you let me graze; to safe waters you lead me; you restore my strength. You guide me along the right path for the sake of your name."

Proverbs 3:5-6: "Trust in the LORD with all your heart, on your own intelligence rely not; In all your ways be mindful of him, and he will make straight your paths."

Matthew 6:9-13: "This is how you are to pray: Our Father in heaven, hallowed be your name, your kingdom come, your will be done, on earth as in heaven. Give us today our daily bread; and forgive us our debts, as we forgive our debtors; and do not subject us to the final test, but deliver us from the evil one."

John 3:16-17: "For God so loved the world that he gave his only Son, so that everyone who believes in him might not perish but might have eternal life. For God did not send his Son into the world to condemn the world, but that the world might be saved through him."

Ephesians 2:8-9: "For by grace you have been saved through faith, and this is not from you; it is the gift of God; it is not from works, so no one may boast."

Philippians 4:13: "I have the strength for everything through him who empowers me."

Hebrews 11:1,6: "Faith is the realization of what is hoped for and evidence of things not seen.... But without faith it is impossible to please him, for anyone who approaches God must believe that he exists and that he rewards those who seek him."

Benefits

This is a relatively word-for-word translation that includes the Apocrypha, thereby making it appealing to its primary audience: Roman Catholics. Headings are scattered throughout to help guide the reader. Some editions include helpful study notes and cross-references.

Cautions

While many Roman Catholics like this Bible, it is rejected by most Protestants because they reject the Apocrypha as belonging in the Word of God (See Appendix C—"Does the Apocrypha Belong in the Bible?"). Beyond this, a number of scholars have noted that even though some passages are translated well in the NAB, others are translated poorly[8] or inaccurately.[9] Some have noted that because a committee was involved in the translation, with different scholars working on different biblical books, the style of rendering among the various books does not have a consistent quality. (Some books are translated better than others.)

There are a few places in the NAB where the wording seems unnatural to the modern ear. This is illustrated in its rendering of Psalm 24:1: "The LORD's are the earth and its fullness." This is not the way modern Americans speak.

Scholars have also noted that this translation is not consistent in how it translates technical or quasi-technical words and phrases. An example is that the Greek word *makarios* is translated as "blest" in the beatitudes recorded in Matthew and Luke, but is translated as "happy" in the beatitudes recorded in the book of Revelation. Likewise, the Greek phrase *he basileia tou theou* is seemingly arbitrarily translated in different ways, including "The kingdom of God," "God's kingdom," "kingdom of heaven," and "the reign of God."[10]

Further, scholars have noted that there are places in the Old Testament in which the actual sequence of verses has been changed from that of other traditional translations. As Metzger put it, "sections of material have been rearranged where scholars have reason to think that lines were accidentally disordered in the transmission of the text."[11]

Finally, study notes are included in the New American Bible that betray openness to higher critical theories of the Bible. For example, in place of the traditional conservative view that Moses wrote the books of the Pentateuch is the liberal idea that various literary traditions—the so-called Yahwist, Elohist, Priestly, and Deuteronomic strands—were woven together by redactors (editors). We are thus told that "the reader is not held to undeviating literalness in interpreting the words, 'the

LORD said to Moses.'"[12] The traditional authorship of a number of biblical books is questioned in this Bible, including some books traditionally ascribed to the apostle Paul. Clearly, this Bible was designed for *liberal* Roman Catholics.

Choosing the Best Translation *and* the Best Bible

THE BIBLE TRANSLATION THAT IS BEST for you may not necessarily be the translation that is best for me. The best translation for reading aloud during a church service may not necessarily be the best translation for detailed Bible study or even personal devotions. The best translation for a mature Christian may not be the best translation for a new believer or seeker. The best translation for a person fluent in English may not be the best translation for a person for whom English is a second language. The best translation for an adult may not be the best translation for a child or young person.

For this reason, there is no single "right answer" when it comes to the question, "What Bible translation is right for you?" However, there are some guidelines to consider that will point you in the right direction.

If you are an adult, you are fluent in English, and your primary purpose is detailed study of the Scriptures, then a more literal translation (formal equivalence) would be an excellent choice. Two very good options here would be the New American Standard Bible and the more recent English Standard Version. These are my personal favorites when it comes to formal equivalence translations, with the edge going to the English Standard Version because of its great readability. However, do not just take my word for it. You should check out all the formal equivalence translations to determine which best fits your needs.

Middle-of-the-road translations (translations midway between formal equivalence and dynamic equivalence) might also suit you for personal Bible study. These include the New International Version, the Holman Christian Standard Bible, and the NET Bible. If you choose to use one of these Bibles for detailed study, however, it still might be a good idea to compare it with a formal equivalence translation.

If your purpose is to have personal devotionals, and you desire easy reading, then a dynamic equivalence translation might be a good choice. For example, you might choose to have personal devotions from the New Living Translation. Of course, this is not to say that a formal equivalence translation cannot be used for personal devotions. Certainly the New American Standard Bible and the English Standard Version are very good for devotions too, but they do require a higher reading level—they are not as easy to understand. Optionally, you may prefer to use a translation like the New International Version, or the Holman Christian Standard Bible, or the NET Bible, all of which are midway between a formal equivalence translation and a dynamic equivalence translation. You cannot go wrong with any of these Bibles for your personal devotions.

If English is your second language, or you feel your reading ability is lacking, then a dynamic equivalence translation is definitely the way to go. You might find the New Living Translation, GOD'S WORD, or the New Century Version helpful. (There are others as well.) As you grow in your knowledge of God's Word, and you increase in your natural reading ability, you may eventually graduate to a formal equivalence translation, or to one of the translations that fall somewhere between dynamic equivalence and formal equivalence.

If you love the poetic style of the King James Version, but you find that you cannot understand this version with its archaic language, then you might consider using the New King James Version. It retains much of the poetic feel of the KJV, but updates all of the language. (This is not intended to knock the King James Version; it is just not as easy to understand as other translations.)*

I encourage all readers to have at least one good formal equivalence translation and one good dynamic equivalence translation. As Augustine put it, "variety of translations is profitable for finding out the sense of the Scriptures." If you can afford it, it is beneficial to own a variety of dynamic equivalence and formal equivalence Bibles. I say this because by studying how different translations render specific verses, you can get a great sense of the different nuances of words in the original Hebrew and Greek.

Some Christians I know go through one biblical book at a time, incorporating several translations. For example, in a morning quiet time, they might read John 1 from a dynamic equivalence translation, such as the New Living Translation. In the evening before they go to bed, they read the same chapter from John's Gospel in a formal equivalence translation, such as the English Standard Version. By using two translations—one dynamic equivalence and one formal equivalence—they get the best of both worlds. *Not a bad idea!*

Of course, whichever version or versions you decide to use, a critically important factor is that *you must read it often!* There is no use in owning a Bible unless you are going to use it. Pick one Bible as your primary version, and feel free to mark it all up. Use other Bible translations to help you increase your understanding of Bible passages.

Suggestions for Choosing a Specific Bible

Having provided a few tips to guide you in choosing a translation,

---

* Keep in mind, however, that both the KJV and the NKJV are based on later manuscripts than the other translations. For this reason, I think it is a good idea to own an additional Bible based on the earliest (best) manuscripts. *Comparing Bibles is always a good thing!*

let us now consider a few tips for choosing an actual Bible. This can be a daunting task, for there are more Bibles in print today than ever before in human history. There are a number of variables to keep in mind, but I will try to be brief.

Calfskin Leather, Genuine Leather, Bonded Leather, Hardback, or Paperback?

One factor to consider is that many editions of the Bible are published in calfskin leather, genuine leather, bonded leather, hardback, or paperback. Personally, I would never consider purchasing a paperback Bible, only because it will not last as long. However, there is no doubt that you can get some good deals on paperback Bibles. (They are much cheaper.)

Of course, it is ultimately your choice as to which you buy. But durability ought to be a consideration. Both hardback and leather Bibles will last you many years.

Calfskin leather Bibles will cost you a lot—often between $100 and $250. The other Bibles get progressively cheaper, from the genuine leather, to the bonded leather, to the hardback, to the paperback. (Bonded leather is essentially *reconstituted* leather—a man-made material constructed from leather fibers, often from scraps in a leather shop.)

Bible Paper

Paper is an important consideration. Some Bible papers are thinner than others. Some are of a higher quality than others. Some tear easier than others. A problem that very often afflicts many Bibles is that there is far too much bleed-through of the ink from the other side of the page. Too much bleed-through can be distracting and can make it harder to read the words on the page. My recommendation is to not just pick up a Bible off the shelf at the bookstore and purchase it without examining it. My policy is that if there is significant bleed-through from the other side of the page, I simply will not buy it. *No exceptions!*

Number of Columns

Some Bibles are formatted with two columns of text on each page, often with cross references in the middle. Other Bibles are formatted with a single column of text, like a normal book, often with cross references in the outer margin. This is really a matter of choice for the reader. Some people think the narrow margins in the dual-column Bibles make it easier to read the text.

Binding

Another important consideration is the type of binding on your Bible. With some Bibles, the publisher just glues the pages in. In many cases this will be sufficient for most people. However, beware that with such Bibles it is possible that steady use of the Bible might cause some of the pages to start falling out. This has happened to some of the Bibles in my collection.

I personally prefer Bibles that are smyth-sewn. These are Bibles in which the pages are sewn together with threads. The quality is much better. I have never experienced pages falling out of a Bible with a smyth-sewn binding. Smyth-sewn Bibles will last, and it is worth any extra cost.

Size of Print

The size of the print of the Bible is an important consideration, for if the print is too small, the likelihood is that you will not read that Bible very much. Even with reading glasses, some Bibles are hard to read. Some Bible publishers have study Bibles that not only contain the entire text of the Bible, but also cross-references, a concordance, and lots of study notes. Believe me, when you cram all that in between two covers, the print must of necessity be small. If you have good eyes, then go for it. Otherwise, buy a Bible that is published in large print or even giant print. Even some study Bibles are published in large-print editions. Such Bibles are *much* easier to read.

Red-Letter Edition

Red-letter editions of the Bible are, of course, a human invention. Red letters for the words of Christ are not in the original Greek manuscripts. In fact, there were no red-letter editions of the Bible prior to 1899, when Louis Klopsch prepared a red-letter King James Version New Testament for publication in New York.[1] When you buy a Bible, you need to decide whether you want a red-letter edition or not.

Actually, this is an important matter to consider. Even apart from whether you want Christ's words to be in red is the publisher's success (or lack thereof) in printing the Bible *in high quality* with red letters. As a Bible collector, I can tell you that the great majority of red-letter Bibles published by major American publishers have less-than-satisfactory printing.

A primary consideration involves consistency. It is fairly typical that when you flip page-by-page through Matthew, Mark, Luke, and John, you will notice some pages printed in a darker red, some pages printed in medium red, and some pages printed in what looks like pink, sometimes even light pink. Some publishers have red-letter editions that look much more like burnt-orange ink. If none of this bothers you, then do not give it another thought. If, however, you prefer print consistency in your red-letter Bible, you will probably want to thoroughly examine your Bible *prior to purchase.*

There is also the issue of lining up the red letters with the black letters on the same page. Perhaps most people will not even notice this. But the careful eye will often see red letters that do not line up with the black letters on the page. Sometimes the red letters might be elevated slightly above the black letters; sometimes the red letters are slightly lower than the black letters.

Because of such factors, my preference is to buy non-red-letter Bibles. But if you like red-letter Bibles, then—as I said—be sure to inspect the Bible before you buy it.

As a footnote, let me add that some theologians have complaints about red-letter editions. For example, some have wondered whether

God the Father has been slighted with only Christ's words being in red. Gordon Fee and Mark Strauss, for example, say that one "wonders why God the Father has been left out here. Should not his words in the Old Testament and the New be printed in a distinct color?"[2] Bruce Metzger has a different complaint about red-letters for Christ's words: "Such a procedure not only destroys the unity of the text...but also implies a theological judgment that what Jesus said is more significant than what he did."[3]

Cross-references

Yet another important consideration involves whether or not the Bible has cross-references. I strongly recommend that you buy a Bible *with* cross-references, because this will be a tremendous aid to your Bible study. Cross-references can take you from one verse to another verse with similar key words, phrases, or ideas. This can make Bible study exciting.

Note that some Bibles put the cross-references in between two columns of text, some single-column Bibles put the cross-references on the outer margins of the page, some Bibles have a boxed-in grouping of cross-references in the lower part of the page, and some Bibles put the cross-references (though generally fewer) at the end of each paragraph. Moreover, some publishers cram all the cross-references close together on the page, thereby increasing the difficulty of finding the cross-references you are looking for, whereas other publishers spread them out more so it is easier to navigate.

Some Bibles have "chain references." In these types of Bibles, one can trace a particular theme or topic through the whole Bible, from Genesis to Revelation. Perhaps the most famous Bible that provides this is the Thompson Chain Reference Bible, available in several translations.

My recommendation: Open up the Bible in the bookstore and do a "test run" to see how easy it is to find the cross-references as you read.

Study Notes

A question you will need to ask yourself is whether or not you want a study Bible. Most study Bibles include cross-references, a concordance, book introductions (which include information about the author, readers, date, origin, and content of a book), outlines of biblical books, and study notes that provide historical background and commentary on the text. Some study Bibles include theological and historical studies at the back of the Bible.

If you do want a study Bible, do you want notes written primarily by one person (as is the case, for example, with the Ryrie Study Bible and the MacArthur Study Bible)? Or do you want notes written by a committee, with different scholars writing notes for different books (as is the case, for example, with the NIV Study Bible and the ESV Study Bible)?

If the notes are written by one person (such as Charles Ryrie or John MacArthur), you will probably notice more theological consistency throughout the Bible. Also, keep in mind that in the cases of Ryrie and MacArthur, both are first-rate scholars. If the notes are by a committee of scholars, by contrast, there may be *some* lack of theological consistency throughout the Bible, but the benefit is that the scholar that writes the notes for a particular Bible book is generally considered an expert in that one book. As well, keep in mind that the general editor of a study Bible produced by a committee will seek to keep things relatively consistent.

Some study Bibles advocate a particular theological system. For example, the Scofield Study Bible, the New Scofield Study Bible, and the Ryrie Study Bible are based on dispensational theology. The Full Life Study Bible and the Spirit-Filled Life Bible are based on Pentecostal or charismatic theology. The New Geneva Study Bible, the Spirit of the Reformation Study Bible, and the Reformation Study Bible are based on Reformed theology. Other, more general study Bibles that are conservative and evangelical are the NIV Study Bible, the Disciples Study Bible, The Quest Study Bible, the Open Bible, and the Life Application Study Bible.

If you decide on buying a study Bible, do you want one that is formatted in regular size print or large print? The NIV Study Bible, the MacArthur Study Bible, and the New Scofield Bible are available in large print editions. So far as I know, the Ryrie Study Bible and the ESV Study Bible are not yet available in large print editions. I recommend that you open up the Bible in the bookstore and take a look at the print.

Concordance

I recommend that you purchase a Bible with a concordance. A concordance is an alphabetical index of biblical words along with the most important verses containing those words. This is a great tool to use in Bible study. You will find yourself using it often.

Of course, if you purchase a Bible that does not have a concordance, or if your Bible has a concordance but you want a more detailed one, such tools are available at your local Christian bookstore. Concordances are a great way to find biblical information on specific topics.

Margins

One final issue worthy of consideration is whether or not you want substantive margins in your Bible. These days lots of Christians like to take notes in their Bibles. They often like the option of writing in the outer margins of the Bible. Some Bibles, however, have such small margins that this is difficult to do. So, my recommendation is that you open up a prospective Bible at the bookstore, and guesstimate whether you think the margin is big enough for your future note taking.

Conclusion

Once you find a Bible you really like, based on the considerations above, *read it daily!* To learn the importance of reading it daily, you might want to begin with Psalm 119.

Appendixes

The Textual Basis
of Modern Translations

A TECHNICAL ASPECT of the study of Bible translations that was not addressed in the main body of this book involves the *textual basis* for each translation. While this may not be of interest to everyone, it is an important consideration inasmuch as each translation can only be as accurate as the sources from which it is derived.

The following brief discussion is divided into three parts: (1) a brief description of the primary New Testament textual sources available for use by translation teams; (2) a brief description of the primary Old Testament textual sources available for use by translation teams; and (3) a listing of the primary textual sources actually used for each translation addressed in this book.

1. Primary New Testament Textual Sources

Textus Receptus

The *Textus Receptus* is a Latin term for "Received Text"—the 1550 edition of the Greek New Testament edited by a Roman Catholic priest and humanist named Erasmus in the sixteenth century. It is based on only about a half dozen Byzantine text-type manuscripts* that date from the twelfth to fourteenth centuries. (This means that Erasmus did not have access to early biblical manuscripts, which were discovered later.)

This is actually a rather sloppy piece of scholarship. Professor Daniel Wallace tells us that Erasmus "was under pressure to get it to the press as soon as possible since (a) no edition of the Greek New Testament had yet been published, and (b) he had heard that Cardinal Ximenes and his associates were just about to publish an edition of the Greek New Testament and he was in a race to beat them. Consequently, his edition has been called the most poorly edited volume in all of literature!"[1] The volume is filled with virtually hundreds of typographical errors that even Erasmus would acknowledge.

Wallace also notes that "in the last six verses of Revelation, Erasmus had no Greek manuscript (he only used half a dozen, very late manuscripts for the whole New Testament anyway). He was therefore forced to 'back-translate' the Latin into Greek and by so doing he created seventeen variants that have never been found in any other Greek manuscript of Revelation! He merely guessed at what the Greek might have been."[2]

Westcott-Hort Greek New Testament

This is a Greek text that is based on the Alexandrian text-type. (The Byzantine family of [late] manuscripts was not consulted.) The oldest manuscripts we currently possess are in the Alexandrian family. The best known among them are Codex Vaticanus (A.D. 325; containing most of the New Testament except Hebrews 9:14ff., the Pastoral Epistles, Philemon, and Revelation), Codex Sinaiticus (A.D. 350; containing the entire New Testament), and Codex Alexandrinus (A.D. 425;

---

* The majority of surviving biblical manuscripts fall into this category. Most manuscripts in the Byzantine family are dated relatively late. It may be that early manuscripts in the Byzantine family did not survive because of a humid climate, which may have caused many manuscripts to deteriorate. The Byzantine text-type derives from the Lucianic text, which apparently went through a bit of scribal editing to make the text smooth and harmonious.

containing most of the New Testament). It may be that the dry climate of Egypt helped preserve these manuscripts so that they survived to the present day. The Westcott-Hort Greek Text was the textual basis for the American Standard Version and the English Revised Version.

Nestle-Aland Novum Testamentum Graece

The Nestle-Aland Novum Testamentum Graece (27th edition) is the Greek textual basis for many of today's translations. The Greek text is based on what biblical textual critics refer to as the "critical text." This is an eclectic text that was compiled by a committee that examined numerous Greek manuscripts and weighed them to determine which was thought to be closest to the lost original. After scholars examined all the variants contained in various Greek manuscripts, they practiced textual criticism and made a judgment regarding which variant was likely the correct one—that is, the variant that was likely in the original autograph penned by the biblical author. The textual criticism they engaged in involved examining both the external evidence (date [earlier is better], source, geographical distribution, and its relationship to other manuscripts) and the internal evidence (the text itself, in which scholars watch for possible accidental or intentional corruptions).

The Nestle-Aland Novum Testamentum Graece includes some of the most recently discovered manuscripts, such as the Chester Beatty Papyri and the Bodmer Papyri. The Chester Beatty papyrus (P45)* dates to the third century A.D. and contains the four Gospels and the book of Acts (chapters 4–17). The Chester Beatty papyrus (P46) dates to about A.D. 200 and contains ten Pauline Epistles (all but the Pastorals) and the Book of Hebrews. The Chester Beatty papyrus (P47) dates to the third century A.D. and contains Revelation 9:10–17:2. The Bodmer Papyrus (P66) dates to about A.D. 200 and contains the Gospel of John. The Bodmer Papyrus (P75) dates to the early third century and contains Luke and John.

---

* P = papyrus.

The Nestle-Aland Novum Testamentum Graece, along with the United Bible Societies' Greek New Testament (see below), serves as the Greek textual basis for a number of Bibles, including the English Standard Version, the New American Standard Bible, the Amplified Bible, the Revised Standard Version, the New Revised Standard Version, the Jerusalem Bible, the New Century Version, the New Living Translation, the Good News Translation, the New International Version, Today's New International Version, the Contemporary English Version, The Message, the New American Bible, the Holman Christian Standard Bible, and the New International Reader's Version.

United Bible Societies' Greek New Testament

Like the Nestle-Aland Novum Testamentum Graece, the United Bible Societies' Greek New Testament is based on what biblical textual critics refer to as the "critical text," an eclectic text compiled by a committee that examined numerous Greek manuscripts and weighed them to determine which was thought to be closest to the lost original. Textual criticism enabled scholars to determine which of the variants contained in the manuscript copies was likely in the original autograph penned by the biblical author. The textual criticism they engaged in involved examining both the external evidence (date [earlier is better], source, geographical distribution, and its relationship to other manuscripts) and the internal evidence (the text itself, in which scholars watch for possible accidental or intentional corruptions). Like the Nestle-Aland Novum Testamentum Graece, the United Bible Societies' Greek New Testament includes some of the recently discovered manuscripts, such as the Chester Beatty Papyri and the Bodmer Papyri.

2. Primary Old Testament Textual Sources

Septuagint

The Septuagint is a translation of the Hebrew Old Testament Scriptures into Greek for the Jews living in Alexandria, a Greek-speaking city. The term *Septuagint* literally means "seventy," referring to the roughly 70 translators who produced the translation in the third century B.C. The translation was used for reading aloud in synagogues in Greek-speaking cities, including Corinth and many in Rome. The backdrop is that many of the Jews who grew up in these cities could no longer speak Hebrew, and hence a translation in their native language of Greek became necessary.

Targums

The Targums are Aramaic paraphrases of the Old Testament Scriptures. Some of these were discovered among the Dead Sea Scrolls. The need for an Aramaic translation of the Old Testament is rooted in the fact that the common language of the Jews in the postexilic period was Aramaic, not Hebrew. The Targums were designed for the common people, and hence interpretive elements, often involving paraphrases, were introduced so that people would understand the message of Scripture.

Syriac Peshitta

This translation became the version of choice in the Syriac (eastern Aramaic) church. It was designated "Peshitta," a word meaning "simple" or "plain." Scholars are unsure why the translation was designated this way. It could be that the translation was intended for popular use among the common people, and hence it was "simple" or "plain." Or perhaps it is called "simple" and "plain" because it omits explanatory glosses and annotations in the text. In other words, it is a *plain* rendering. The truth is that scholars know very little about the history of the Syriac Peshitta, but some speculate that it may have been intended as a reworking of the Aramaic Targums into Syriac.

Latin Vulgate

The Vulgate is a fourth century Latin translation done primarily by Jerome, a leading scholar of his day, as commissioned by Pope

Damasus I in A.D. 382. The term "Vulgate" literally means "common version" or "popular edition." It was intended to replace the Old Latin version (the "Itala").

Jerome first revised the Old Latin Gospels. His original work on translating some of the Old Testament books was done from the Septuagint, a Greek translation of the Old Testament Hebrew Scriptures (see above). Later, however, he decided the Septuagint was unsatisfactory and began translating the Old Testament from the original Hebrew manuscripts. Since Jerome's time, various editors and correctors have produced revised texts of the Vulgate over the years. In 1546 the Roman Catholic Council of Trent decreed that the Vulgate was the exclusive Latin authority for the Bible, though a scholarly revision was called for.

Dead Sea Scrolls

Khirbet Qumran, on the western shores of the Dead Sea, is the site of one of the most magnificent manuscript discoveries of all time. An Arab shepherd boy accidentally discovered the first of these long-hidden Essenic writings in the spring of 1947. Since then, thousands of fragments belonging to 800 manuscripts have been discovered in 11 different caves in Qumran. Generally speaking, these include Old Testament books, commentaries on Old Testament books, apocryphal and pseudepigraphal texts, thematic collections of Old Testament passages, hymns, and sectarian writings of the Qumran community.

Among the specific manuscripts discovered are: Isaiah, Exodus, Leviticus, Numbers, Deuteronomy, The Manual of Discipline, The Thanksgiving Psalms, The War Scroll, Pesher on Habakkuk, The Genesis Apocryphon, Tobit, Ecclesiasticus, the Book of Jubilees, the Book of Enoch, Testaments of the Twelve Patriarchs, the Sayings of Moses, the Vision of Amram, the Psalms of Joshua, the Prayer of Nabonidus, the Book of Mysteries, the Hymn of the Initiates, Poems from a Qumran Hymnal, Lament for Zion, and Hymns of Triumph.

The scrolls serve to verify the great accuracy in which biblical manuscripts were copied. In these scrolls discovered at Qumran in 1947, we have Old Testament manuscripts that date about a thousand years earlier (150 B.C.) than the other Old Testament manuscripts previously in our possession (which date to A.D. 980). When one compares the two sets of manuscripts, it is clear that they are essentially the same, with very few changes. The fact that manuscripts separated by a thousand years are essentially the same indicates the incredible accuracy of the Old Testament's manuscript transmission.

Masoretic Text

The Masoretic Text is the traditional Hebrew text of the Old Testament, meticulously assembled and codified. Work on the Masoretic Text took place from the sixth to the tenth centuries A.D. at Talmudic academies in Babylonia and Palestine. The goal of these Jewish scholars was, as far as humanly possible, to reproduce the original text of the Old Testament. They wanted to transmit to future generations the authentic Word of God. Toward this end, they utilized Hebrew manuscripts as well as any oral traditions that were available to them.

Those who participated took great care in their work, checking every word and every letter. The rigorous care given to the Masoretic Text in its preparation accounts for the remarkable consistency found in Old Testament Hebrew texts since that time.

Rudolf Kittel's Biblia Hebraica

Biblia Hebraica is a Latin phrase meaning "Hebrew Bible." It is a term traditionally used to refer to printed editions of the Old Testament. Often the phrase is used more specifically in reference to the three editions of the Hebrew Bible edited by Rudolf Kittel. The first two editions of Kittel's Biblia Hebraica appeared in 1906 and 1913. There is very little difference between the two, except for a correction of some errors. Included in these editions were footnotes that contained possible corrections to the Hebrew text that were based on the Samaritan Pentateuch, the Septuagint, the Latin Vulgate, and the Syriac Peshitta.

The third edition of Kittel's Biblia Hebraica (which appeared in installments from 1929 to 1937) reproduced the text of the Leningrad Codex, the oldest complete Hebrew Bible still preserved. The new edition also featured completely revised footnotes.

Biblia Hebraica Stuttgartensia

The Biblia Hebraica Stuttgartensia is considered a definitive edition of the Hebrew Bible, and is now claimed to be the most widely used original-language edition among scholars. It is a revision of the third edition of the Biblia Hebraica edited by Rudolf Kittel, the first Bible to be based on the Leningrad Codex. The Leningrad Codex is the oldest complete Hebrew Bible still preserved. The text is a nearly exact copy of the Masoretic Text as recorded in the Leningrad Codex. In the margin are Masoretic notes. These are based on the codex but have been edited to make them more consistent and easier to understand. Footnotes record possible corrections to the Hebrew text that are based on the Samaritan Pentateuch, the Dead Sea Scrolls, the Septuagint, the Latin Vulgate, and the Syriac Peshitta.

3. Translation Guide: Textual Sources

The King James Version

English Basis: Bishops Bible (1568), Tyndale's Bible (1535)
Old Testament: Masoretic Text
New Testament: Textus Receptus

The Revised Standard Version

English Basis: American Standard Version (1901)
Old Testament: Masoretic Text, Dead Sea Scrolls, Septuagint
New Testament: Nestle-Aland Novum Testamentum Graece (17th Edition)

The Amplified Bible

English Basis: American Standard Version (1901)

Old Testament: Rudolf Kittel's Biblia Hebraica, Dead Sea Scrolls, Septuagint

New Testament: Westcott-Hort Greek New Testament, Nestle-Aland Novum Testamentum Graece (26th Edition)

The New American Standard Bible

English Basis: American Standard Version

Old Testament: Rudolf Kittel's Biblia Hebraica (3rd Edition), Dead Sea Scrolls, Biblia Hebraica Stuttgartensia (consulted for the 1995 NASB update)

New Testament: Nestle-Aland Novum Testamentum Graece (26th Edition)

The Good News Translation

Old Testament: Rudolf Kittel's Biblia Hebraica (3rd Edition)

New Testament: United Societies' Greek New Testament (3rd Edition)

The New International Version

Old Testament: Biblia Hebraica, Dead Sea Scrolls, Septuagint, Latin Vulgate, Aramaic Targums, Syriac Peshitta, and other ancient manuscripts

New Testament: United Societies' Greek New Testament (1st and 2nd Editions)

The New King James Version

English Basis: King James Version

Old Testament: Stuttgart Biblia Hebraica (1977), Septuagint, Latin Vulgate, Dead Sea Scrolls

New Testament: Textus Receptus, though footnotes contain data from Nestle-Aland Novum Testamentum Graece

The New Revised Standard Version

English Basis: Revised Standard Version

Old Testament: Biblia Hebraica Stuttgartensia (1st Edition), Dead Sea Scrolls, Septuagint, Latin Vulgate, Syriac Peshitta, Aramaic Targums

New Testament: United Societies' Greek New Testament (3rd Edition), Nestle-Aland Novum Testamentum Graece (26th Edition)

The Revised English Bible

English Basis: New English Bible

Old Testament: Biblia Hebraica Stuttgartensia (1977), Dead Sea Scrolls, Septuagint

New Testament: Nestle-Aland Novum Testamentum Graece (26th Edition)

The New Century Version

Old Testament: Biblia Hebraica Stuttgartensia, Septuagint

New Testament: United Societies' Greek New Testament (3rd Edition)

GOD'S WORD

English Basis: The New Testament in the Language of Today

Old Testament: Biblia Hebraica Stuttgartensia

New Testament: Nestle-Aland Novum Testamentum Graece (26th Edition)

The New Living Translation

English Basis: Living Bible

Old Testament: Biblia Hebraica Stuttgartensia (1977 Edition),

Dead Sea Scrolls, Septuagint, Latin Vulgate, Syriac Peshitta, and other ancient manuscripts
New Testament: United Societies' Greek New Testament (4ᵗʰ Edition), Nestle-Aland Novum Testamentum Graece (27ᵗʰ Edition)

New International Reader's Version
English Basis: New International Version
Old Testament: Biblia Hebraica, Dead Sea Scrolls, Septuagint, Latin Vulgate, Aramaic Targums, Syriac Peshitta, and other ancient manuscripts
New Testament: United Societies' Greek New Testament (1ˢᵗ and 2ⁿᵈ Editions), Eclectic Text

The English Standard Version
English Basis: Revised Standard Version
Old Testament: Biblia Hebraica Stuttgartensia (2ⁿᵈ Edition), Dead Sea Scrolls, Septuagint, Syriac Peshitta, Latin Vulgate, and other ancient manuscripts
New Testament: United Societies' Greek New Testament (4ᵗʰ Edition), Nestle-Aland Novum Testamentum Graece (27ᵗʰ Edition)

The NET Bible
Old Testament: Biblia Hebraica Stuttgartensia
New Testament: Nestle-Aland Novum Testamentum Graece (27ᵗʰ Edition), with some alterations

The Message
Old Testament: Biblia Hebraica
New Testament: Greek New Testament

The Holman Christian Standard Bible
Old Testament: Biblia Hebraica Stuttgartensia (5th Edition)
New Testament: Nestle-Aland Novum Testamentum Graece (27th Edition), United Societies' Greek New Testament (4th Edition)

Today's New International Version
English Basis: New International Version
Old Testament: Biblia Hebraica, Dead Sea Scrolls, Septuagint, Latin Vulgate, and other ancient manuscripts
New Testament: Nestle-Aland Novum Testamentum Graece (27th Edition), United Societies' Greek New Testament (4th Edition)

The New Jerusalem Bible (Catholic)
French Basis: La Bible de Jerusalem
Old Testament: Masoretic Text, Septuagint
New Testament: Eclectic Greek texts

The New American Bible (Catholic)
Old Testament: Masoretic Text, Septuagint, Latin Vulgate, Dead Sea Scrolls, and other texts
New Testament: Nestle-Aland Novum Testamentum Graece (26th Edition), United Societies' Greek New Testament (3rd Edition)

The Rendering of Divine Names

ONE OF THE GREAT DIFFICULTIES for Bible translators pertains to how the Old Testament divine name should be rendered into English. God first revealed Himself to Moses at the burning bush in the form of four Hebrew consonants, YHWH (see Exodus 3). Though scholars are unsure of the exact pronunciation, most consider it to be "Yahweh." The term is found over 6,000 times in the Hebrew Old Testament.

The New Jerusalem Bible, which is a Roman Catholic Bible, renders the divine name as "Yahweh," as does its predecessor, the Jerusalem Bible. Most other translations today, however, do not follow this practice. Most translations follow the lead of the King James Version in rendering YHWH as "the LORD" (using small capitals). Others render it as "the LORD" (using capitals). This is distinguished from "Lord" (in title case), which refers to *Adonai*, another Old Testament Hebrew name of God. The Old Testament Hebrew term *Elohim* is rendered as "God" in most English translations.

Old Testament Name	Rendering in Most English Translations
YHWH	LORD (using small capitals), or LORD (using capitals)
Adonai	Lord (using title case)
Elohim	God

An exception occurs where we find reference to *Adonai* YHWH in the Old Testament (for example, Amos 3:11). According to the chart above, this would be rendered "Lord LORD." To avoid awkwardness, many translations render the phrase "the Lord GOD."

What About the Name *Jehovah?*

The American Standard Version of 1901 rendered YHWH as "Jehovah." It may surprise some to learn that the word *Jehovah* is a man-made term. The backdrop is that the ancient Jews had a superstitious dread of pronouncing the name YHWH. They felt that if they uttered this name, they might violate the third commandment, which deals with taking God's name in vain (Exodus 20:7). To avoid the possibility of breaking this commandment, the Jews for centuries substituted the name *Adonai* (Lord) or some other name in its place whenever they came across it in public readings of Scripture.

Eventually, the fearful Hebrew scribes decided to insert the vowels from *Adonai* (a-o-a) within these Hebrew consonants, YHWH. The result was *Yahowah,* or *Jehovah.* Hence, the word *Jehovah* is derived from a consonant-vowel combination from the words *YHWH* and *Adonai.*

Pronouns

While Bible translations are consistent in capitalizing the various names used of God, they are not consistent in capitalizing pronouns referring to deity. Among the translations that *do* capitalize pronouns used of God are the New King James Version, the New American

Standard Bible, and the Amplified Bible. Interestingly—and likely surprising to many—the King James Version is among those that do not capitalize pronouns used of deity. Both renderings, however, are perfectly acceptable. No slight is intended against God in those translations that do not capitalize such pronouns, for, indeed, there were no distinctions in the original Hebrew or Greek between pronouns used to address people and those used to address God.

APPENDIX C

Does the Apocrypha Belong in the Bible?

THE APOCRYPHA REFERS to 14 or 15 books of doubtful authenticity and authority that were written between the time of the Old and New Testaments. These include Tobit, Judith, the Additions to Esther, the Additions to Daniel (the Prayer of Azariah and the Three Young Men, Susanna, and Bel and the Dragon), the Wisdom of Solomon, Ecclesiasticus (also called Sirach), Baruch (also called 1 Baruch), the Letter of Jeremiah, 1 Maccabees, and 2 Maccabees.

Roman Catholics decided these books belonged in the Bible sometime following the Protestant Reformation (sixteenth-century). The Catholic Council of Trent (A.D.1545–1563) canonized these books. This canonization took place largely as a result of the Protestant Reformation. Martin Luther had criticized the Catholics for not having scriptural support for such doctrines as praying for the dead. By canonizing the Apocrypha, the Catholics obtained "scriptural" support for this and other distinctively Catholic doctrines (see 2 Maccabees 12:45).

Roman Catholics argue that the Septuagint (the Greek translation of the Hebrew Old Testament that predates the time of Christ) contained the Apocrypha. As well, church fathers such as Iraneaus, Tertullian, and Clement of Alexandria used the Apocryphal books in public worship and accepted them as Scripture. Further, it is argued, Augustine viewed these books as inspired.

Protestants have responded by pointing out that no New Testament writer ever quoted from any of these books as Holy Scripture or gave them the slightest authority as inspired books, even though they often quoted from the Old Testament as Scripture. Jesus and the disciples virtually ignored these books, something that would not have been the case if they had considered them to be God-inspired Scripture.

Moreover, even though certain church fathers spoke approvingly of the Apocrypha, there were other early church fathers—notably Origin and Jerome—who denied their inspiration. Further, even though the early Augustine acknowledged the Apocrypha, in his later years he rejected these books as being outside the canon and considered them inferior to the Hebrew Scriptures.

The Jewish Council of Jamnia, which met in A.D. 90, rejected the Apocrypha as Scripture. In addition, there are clear historical errors in the Apocrypha, such as the assumption that Sennacherib was the son of Shalmaneser instead of Sargon II (see Tobit 1:15). Further, unlike many of the biblical books, there is no claim in any Apocryphal book in regard to divine inspiration. Nor is there any predictive prophecy in the Apocryphal books, as there is in many Old and New Testament books.

Those who wish to see a full discussion of this issue may consult my book *Reasoning from the Scriptures with Catholics* (Harvest House Publishers, Eugene, OR: 2000).

Assessing the
"King James Only" Controversy

SOME PEOPLE BELIEVE the King James Version is the only legitimate Bible. With all due respect, however, this cannot possibly be the case.

We first observe that the King James Version we universally accept today is not an exact copy of the edition released in A.D.1611. The Bible that circulates today as the "Authorized" King James Version is actually the fourth revision of 1769. A simple way to verify this is by reading John 3:7 in today's King James Version. The spelling of the individual words in this sentence is entirely different from that of the original 1611 version. I must also point out that the punctuation, capitalization, and use of italics have been changed as each respective edition came out. It is therefore fair to ask, "Which King James Version is the 'only legitimate Bible'?"

Moreover, if the King James Version is the only legitimate Bible, then what was God's inspired Word prior to 1611? It is highly revealing that some of the translators of the King James Version continued to use earlier English versions long after the publication of the King James Version. They even approvingly quoted from one of these Bibles—the Geneva Bible—in the original preface to the King James Version.

Also relevant to this discussion is the question of whether English is the only language that has God's inspired Word. What about people living in France or Spain or Russia? Are they required to learn the English language so they can use the King James Version?

Finally, it is a historical fact that the 1611 King James Version included the Apocrypha. Yet few if any who claim exclusive inspiration for the King James Version's English text would accept the Apocrypha as God's Word.

Please do not misunderstand. I say all this not to malign the King James Version. I say this only to stress the point that it is not the only legitimate version.

For those interested in a more detailed treatment, there are good resources available.[1]

A Warning About Cultic Translations

A BOOK ON BIBLE TRANSLATIONS would be remiss not to address several prominent cultic translations that are in wide circulation. I have in mind the Mormon Inspired Version and the Jehovah's Witnesses' New World Translation. Let us take a brief look at these.

The Mormon Inspired Version

Mormon founder Joseph Smith is credited with the "translation" of the Inspired Version of the Bible. Actually, Smith did not come up with a new translation at all. Rather, he took the King James Version of the Bible and added to and subtracted from it—not by examining Hebrew, Aramaic, and Greek Bible manuscripts, but allegedly by "divine inspiration."

As Bruce McConkie, an apostle of the Mormon church, put it, "At the command of the Lord and while acting under the spirit of revelation, the Prophet [Joseph Smith] corrected, revised, altered, added to, and deleted from the King James Version of the Bible to form what is now commonly referred to as the Inspired Version of the Bible."[1] Virtually thousands of changes were introduced into the King James Version by Joseph Smith.[2]

Smith did not do any manuscript study whatsoever. Rather he simply rewrote certain Bible passages in the light of supposed new revelations from God.[3] This means that Smith's "translation" cannot be verified by any objective means. There is virtually no evidence to verify Smith's "translational" work at all.

It is also worth noting that while it took a large group of the world's greatest Bible scholars (who knew Hebrew, Aramaic, and Greek) several years to finish their work on the King James Version, it took Joseph Smith a mere three years to complete his work—despite the fact that he had virtually no knowledge of the biblical languages.

A significant passage that was added by Joseph Smith in Genesis 50 predicts Smith's own coming: "And that seer will I bless...and his name shall be called Joseph, and it shall be after the name of his father...for the thing which the Lord shall bring forth by his hand shall bring my people unto salvation."[4] This fact alone more than amply shows the true character of this alleged "translation."

It is interesting to observe that this "inspired version" has caused a dilemma for the Mormon Church. David A. Reed and John R. Farkas, authors of several Christian books on Mormonism, explain the problem this way:

> Some of Smith's revisions to the King James text fail to agree with the same passages as quoted [from the KJV] in the Book of Mormon. Other portions [of the Inspired Version] contradict current Mormon doctrine. Therefore, fully endorsing it could prove embarrassing, but flatly rejecting it as erroneous would discredit Smith as a prophet. Instead, LDS leaders have sidestepped the issue by alleging that the work Smith began in 1831 was left unfinished at his untimely death in 1844; numerous errors remain in the

uncorrected portions of the King James text, and therefore publication would be inappropriate. However, in a letter Smith wrote dated July 2, 1833 at Kirtland, Ohio, he states that he "this day finished the translating of the Scriptures" (*History of the Church,* vol. 1, p. 368).[5]

In assessing this "version" of the Bible, one cannot help but note that Smith claimed an authority that was not even claimed by Jesus Christ Himself—namely, the authority to *alter* the text of Scripture. In Matthew 5:18 we read the very words of Jesus: "Truly, I say to you, until heaven and earth pass away, not an iota, not a dot, will pass from the Law until all is accomplished." Jesus considered the Word of God as absolutely authoritative. How, then, could Joseph Smith claim to have an authority to change the Scriptures which Christ Himself considered absolutely authoritative?

Note, also, that when Jesus was being tempted by the devil for 40 days, the devil misquoted Scripture in an attempt to thwart Christ. Christ responded, however, by pointing to the absolute authority of Scripture by saying, "It is written..." (Matthew 4:4,7,10). Quite clearly, the honor and respect Jesus had for the Word of God is completely dissimilar to Smith's attitude toward Scripture.

It is significant that some of the changes Smith made to the Bible were found in the book of Revelation. Revelation 19:15 in the King James Version says, "And out of his mouth goeth a sharp sword, that with it he should smite the nations: and he shall rule them with a rod of iron." But Joseph Smith changed the verse to say, "And out of his mouth proceedeth the word of God, and with it he will smite the nations; and he will rule them with the word of his mouth."

Revelation 5:6 in the King James Version says, "And I beheld, and, lo, in the midst of the throne and of the four beasts, and in the midst of the elders, stood a Lamb as it had been slain, having seven horns and seven eyes, which are the seven Spirits of God sent forth into all the earth." But Joseph Smith changed this to read, "Having twelve horns and twelve eyes, which are the twelve servants of God, sent forth into all the earth." These are obviously substantive changes that significantly alter the meaning of the text.

I mention this, because making such changes in the Word of God is forbidden in the Book of Revelation itself. We read in Revelation 22:18-19: "I warn everyone who hears the words of the prophecy of this book: if anyone adds to them, God will add to him the plagues described in this book, and if anyone takes away from the words of the book of this prophecy, God will take away his share in the tree of life and in the holy city, which are described in this book."

The Jehovah's Witnesses' New World Translation

The New World Translation is an utterly unreliable translation produced by the Jehovah's Witnesses to support their heretical brand of theology. The translation strips Jesus of His full deity and inserts the term "Jehovah" throughout the Bible.

Dr. Robert Countess, who wrote a doctoral dissertation on the Greek of the New World Translation, concluded that the translation "must be viewed as a radically biased piece of work. At some points it is actually dishonest. At others it is neither modern nor scholarly."[6] No wonder British scholar H.H. Rowley asserted, "From beginning to end this volume is a shining example of how the Bible should not be translated."[7] Indeed, Rowley said, this translation is "an insult to the Word of God."[8]

Dr. Julius Mantey, author of *A Manual Grammar of the Greek New Testament,* called the New World Translation "a shocking mistranslation."[9] Dr. Bruce M. Metzger, professor of New Testament at Princeton University, called it "a frightful mistranslation," "erroneous," "pernicious," and "reprehensible."[10] Dr. William Barclay concluded that "the deliberate distortion of truth by this sect is seen in their New Testament translation…It is abundantly clear that a sect which can translate the New Testament like that is intellectually dishonest."[11]

In view of this universal "thumbs down" by legitimate biblical scholars, it is highly revealing that the Watchtower Society has always resisted efforts to identify members of the New World Translation committee. The claim was that they preferred to remain anonymous and humble, giving God the credit and glory for this translation. However, such anonymity also shielded the translators from scrutiny by legitimate biblical scholars.[12]

It must have been utterly embarrassing for the Watchtower Society when it became public who the translators of the New World Translation were. The reason for this is that the translation committee was completely unqualified for the task. Four of the five men in the committee had no Hebrew or Greek training whatsoever (they had only a high school education). The fifth—Fred W. Franz—claimed to know Hebrew and Greek, but upon examination under oath in a court of law in Edinburgh, Scotland, was found to fail a simple Hebrew test. Note the following cross-examination, which took place November 24, 1954 in this court:

"Have you also made yourself familiar with Hebrew?"

"Yes."

"So that you have a substantial linguistic apparatus at your command?"

"Yes, for use in my biblical work."

"I think you are able to read and follow the Bible in Hebrew, Greek, Latin, Spanish, Portuguese, German, and French?"

"Yes."[13]

The following day, Franz was put on the stand again, and the following interview took place:

"You, yourself, read and speak Hebrew, do you?"

"I do not speak Hebrew."

"You do not?"

"No."

"Can you translate that into Hebrew?"

"Which?"

"That fourth verse of the second chapter of Genesis?"

"You mean here?"

"Yes."

"No."[14]

The truth of the matter is that Franz—like the others who participated in the New World Translation committee—could not translate Hebrew or Greek. In fact, he dropped out of the University of Cincinnati after his sophomore year, and even while there, he had not been studying anything related to theological issues.

A good example of how the New World Translation is a biased translation is its rendering of Colossians 1:16-17. They mistranslate it in such a way as to make it appear that Christ was created *first* by the Father, and then Christ was used by the Father to create *all other* things in the universe. The New World Translation reads, "By means of him all *[other]* things were created in the heavens and upon the earth, the things visible and the things invisible, no matter whether they are thrones or lordships or governments or authorities. All *[other]* things have been created through him and for him. Also, he is before all *[other]* things and by means of him all *[other]* things were made to exist" (emphasis added). Thus, the Jehovah's Witnesses claim, "he is shown to be a created being, part of the creation produced by God."[15]

Biblical linguistic scholars say there is no justification from the Greek for inserting the word *other* into Colossians 1:16. This is a translation with a bias, the goal being to enforce the unorthodox doctrine that Jesus is a created being and is therefore not God Almighty. The fact is, Colossians 1:16 teaches that Christ created "all things"—and this being so, Christ Himself cannot be a created being. A good cross-reference is Isaiah 44:24, where God Himself asserts, "I am the LORD, who made *all things,* who alone stretched out the heavens, who spread out the earth *by myself* " (emphasis added). If Yahweh made all things by Himself, this obviously rules out the idea that Yahweh created Jesus first and then created everything else through Jesus. If Yahweh is called the Creator of the universe (Isaiah 44:24)—and if Jesus is called the Creator of the universe (Colossians 1:16; see also John 1:3)—then clearly this points to Jesus' identity as God. Hence, again, the New World Translation is shown to be utterly untrustworthy.

Reader Beware!

The above discussion of the Mormon Inspired Version and the Jehovah's Witnesses' New World Translation points us to the disconcerting reality that not all Bible translations are trustworthy or orthodox. Thankfully, most Bible translations in wide distribution today are much more reputable, as this book states.

Bibliography

Comfort, Philip. *Essential Guide to Bible Versions.* Wheaton, IL: Tyndale House, 2000.

Dewey, David. *A User's Guide to Bible Translations: Making the Most of Different Versions.* Downers Grove, IL: InterVarsity Press, 2004.

Duthie, Alan. *Bible Translations and How to Choose Between Them.* Greenwood, SC: Attic Press, 1985.

Fee, Gordon; and Strauss, Mark. *How to Choose a Translation for All Its Worth: A Guide to Understanding and Using Bible Versions.* Grand Rapids, MI: Zondervan, 2007.

Metzger, Bruce. *The Bible in Translation: Ancient and English Versions.* Grand Rapids, MI: Baker, 2001.

Ryken, Leland. *Choosing a Bible: Understanding Bible Translation Differences.* Wheaton, IL: Crossway, 2005.

Scorgie, Glen; Strauss, Mark; and Voth, Steven; eds. *The Challenge of Bible Translation: Communicating God's Word to the World.* Grand Rapids, MI: Zondervan, 2003.

Thomas, Robert. *How to Choose a Bible Version.* Ross-shire, Scotland: Mentor Books, 2000.

White, James. *The King James Only Controversy: Can You Trust the Modern Translations?* Minneapolis, MN: Bethany House, 1995.

Notes

Introduction

1. Alan Duthie, *Bible Translations and How to Choose Between Them* (Greenwood, SC: Attic Press, 1985), p. 10.
2. Bruce M. Metzger, *The Bible in Translation: Ancient and English Versions* (Grand Rapids, MI: Baker Books, 2001), p. 13.
3. Bruce Metzger, however, claimed, "It is doubtful whether Wycliffe himself took any direct part in the work of translating the Scriptures; he died at Lutterworth of a stroke on December 31, 1384. One need not, however, have any qualms about referring to the Wycliffe Bible, for it was under his inspiration that the work was done. In fact, two complete versions of the Scriptures were produced by his pupils and colleagues, John Purvey and Nicholas of Hereford." See Metzger, p. 57.
4. John Wycliffe, cited in Daniel B. Wallace, "The History of the English Bible: From Wycliffe to King James (The Period of Challenge)," downloaded from www.bible. org, insert added.
5. Wallace, "The History of the English Bible."
6. Metzger, p. 57.
7. David Dewey, *A User's Guide to Bible Translations* (Downers Grove, IL: InterVarsity Press, 2004), p. 118.
8. Martin Luther, cited in Gordon Fee and Mark Strauss, *How to Choose a Translation for All Its Worth* (Grand Rapids, MI: Zondervan, 2007), p. 30.
9. William Tyndale, cited in Dewey, p. 120.
10. Scott Jones, "William Tyndale—A Lasting Influence," downloaded from www .bible.org.
11. Fee and Strauss, p. 137.
12. Jones, "William Tyndale—A Lasting Influence."
13. Fee and Strauss, p. 137.

14. Wallace, "The History of the English Bible," insert added.
15. Daniel B. Wallace, "Why So Many Versions?" downloaded from www.bible.org.

Chapter 1

1. "Translation," Dictionary.com.
2. Sid Litke, "Translations," downloaded from www.bible.org.
3. Daniel B. Wallace, "Why So Many Versions?" downloaded from www.bible.org.
4. Denny Burk, "Why All the Translations?" North American Mission Board, www.namb.net.
5. David Dewey, *A User's Guide to Bible Translations* (Downers Grove, IL: InterVarsity Press, 2004), p. 102.
6. Alan Duthie, *Bible Translations and How to Choose Between Them* (Greenwood, SC: Attic Press, 1985), p. 21.
7. Dewey, p. 56.
8. Gordon Fee and Mark Strauss, *How to Choose a Translation for All Its Worth* (Grand Rapids, MI: Zondervan, 2007), p. 62.
9. See Fee and Strauss, p. 63.
10. Wallace, "Why So Many Versions?"
11. Fee and Strauss, p. 92.
12. Dewey, p. 61, insert added.
13. Fee and Strauss, pp. 30-31.
14. *The Challenge of Bible Translation*, eds. Glen Scorgie, Mark Strauss, and Steven Voth (Grand Rapids, MI: Zondervan, 2003), p. 52.
15. *The Challenge of Bible Translation*, p. 26.
16. Litke, "Translations."
17. Duthie, p. 44.
18. Dewey, p. 41.
19. F.F. Bruce, "New Bible Translations: A Short Survey," *Inter-Varsity* (Autumn 1953): 15-19.

Chapter 2

1. Daniel B. Wallace, "Why So Many Versions?" downloaded from www.bible.org.
2. Gordon Fee and Mark Strauss, *How to Choose a Translation for All Its Worth* (Grand Rapids, MI: Zondervan, 2007), p. 26.
3. Leland Ryken, *Choosing a Bible: Understanding Bible Translation Differences* (Wheaton, IL: Crossway, 2005), p. 27.
4. Ryken, pp. 8-9.
5. David Dewey, *A User's Guide to Bible Translations* (Downers Grove, IL: InterVarsity Press, 2004), pp. 39-40.
6. Alan Duthie, *Bible Translations and How to Choose Between Them* (Greenwood, SC: Attic Press, 1985), p. 35.

7. Robert Young, cited in Fee and Strauss, p. 35.
8. *The Challenge of Bible Translation,* eds. Glen Scorgie, Mark Strauss, and Steven Voth (Grand Rapids, MI: Zondervan, 2003), p. 93.
9. Duthie, p. 41.
10. Dewey, p. 51.
11. Wallace, "Why So Many Versions?"
12. Ryken, pp. 8-9.
13. Ryken, p. 11.
14. Ryken, pp. 15-16.
15. Fee and Strauss, p. 36.
16. Sid Litke, "Translations," downloaded from www.bible.org.
17. Fee and Strauss, p. 29.
18. Michael H. Burer, "Why So Many Translations? The Present State of English Bible Translation," downloaded from www.bible.org.

Chapter 3

1. Richard Ostling, "Evangelicals Are Battling Each Other Over the Use of Gender," AP Worldstream, February 13, 2002, HighBeam Research.
2. "100 Christian Leaders Cannot Endorse TNIV Bible Translation," *U.S. Newswire,* May 28, 2002, Highbeam Research.
3. Vern Poythress and Wayne Grudem, *The Gender-Neutral Bible Controversy: Muting the Masculinity of God's Words* (Nashville, TN: Broadman and Holman, 2000), online edition.
4. Darrell L. Bock, "Do Gender Sensitive Translations Distort Scripture? Not Necessarily," downloaded at www.bible.org.
5. Bock, "Do Gender Sensitive Translations Distort Scripture? Not Necessarily."
6. Robin Galiano Russell, "Bible Translation Stirs Gender Debate," *Dallas Morning News,* February 16, 2005, HighBeam Research.
7. Russell, "Bible Translation Stirs Gender Debate."
8. Ron Minton, "Gender-Inclusive Bible Translations," *Chafer Theological Journal* 9 (Spring 2003), electronic online version.
9. *The Challenge of Bible Translation: Communicating God's Word to the World,* eds. Glen Scorgie, Mark Strauss, and Steven Voth (Grand Rapids, MI: Zondervan, 2003), p. 195.
10. "Do Inclusive-Language Bibles Distort Scripture?" Wayne Grudem (Yes) and Grant Osborn (No), Part 1, *Christianity Today,* October 27, 1997, online edition.
11. "Do Inclusive-Language Bibles Distort Scripture?"
12. "Do Inclusive-Language Bibles Distort Scripture?"
13. As noted by E. Calvin Beisner, "The Bible and Gender-Inclusive Language," AR-Talk List.
14. Beisner, "The Bible and Gender-Inclusive Language."

15. Some of the examples in this section are derived from "Do Inclusive-Language Bibles Distort Scripture?"

16. Poythress and Grudem, *The Gender-Neutral Bible Controversy.*

17. "Do Inclusive-Language Bibles Distort Scripture?"

18. See "Do Inclusive-Language Bibles Distort Scripture?"

19. "Do Inclusive-Language Bibles Distort Scripture?"

20. This chart is based on David Dewey, *A User's Guide to Bible Translations* (Downers Grove, IL: InterVarsity Press, 2004), p. 92.

21. Bock, "Do Gender Sensitive Translations Distort Scripture? Not Necessarily."

22. Bock, "Do Gender Sensitive Translations Distort Scripture? Not Necessarily."

23. These agreements are discussed at length in Mark Strauss, "Current Issues in the Gender-Language Debate," in *The Challenge of Bible Translation.*

24. *The Challenge of Bible Translation,* p. 196. Dewey notes, however, that the liberal translation, *The New Testament and Psalms: An Inclusive Version* (1995, published in the USA by Oxford University Press), removes masculine pronouns and other language forms relating to God. He notes that "'Father' becomes 'Father-Mother' or 'Parent.' 'God' is no longer 'King' but 'Ruler' or 'Sovereign.' And Jesus becomes 'God's Child,' not 'God's Son.' The Holy Spirit is portrayed as female." (Dewey, pp. 97-98.)

25. Gordon Fee and Mark Strauss, *How to Choose a Translation for All Its Worth* (Grand Rapids, MI: Zondervan, 2007), p. 102.

26. Fee and Strauss, *How to Choose a Translation for All Its Worth,* p. 101.

27. "Do Inclusive-Language Bibles Distort Scripture?"

Chapter 4

1. However, as Robert Thomas notes, there is no official act of authorization recorded anywhere. See Robert Thomas, *How to Choose a Bible Version* (Great Britain: Christian Focus Publications, 2000), p. 24.

2. Gordon Fee and Mark Strauss, *How to Choose a Translation for All Its Worth* (Grand Rapids, MI: Zondervan, 2007), p. 138.

3. David Dewey notes: "This method of translation set an important precedent for subsequent Bible versions, many of which have followed a similar committee approach to crosschecking and final editing." See David Dewey, *A User's Guide to Bible Translations* (Downers Grove, IL: InterVarsity Press, 2004), p. 127.

4. *The Challenge of Bible Translation: Communicating God's Word to the World,* eds. Glen Scorgie, Mark Strauss, and Steven Voth (Grand Rapids, MI: Zondervan, 2003), p. 183.

5. Dewey, p. 128.

6. Dewey, p. 128.

7. Fee and Strauss, p. 138.

8. Daniel B. Wallace, "The Reign of the King James (The Era of Elegance)," downloaded from www.bible.org.

9. See Fee and Strauss, p. 51.

10. *The Challenge of Bible Translation*, p. 184.

11. Daniel B. Wallace, "Why I Do Not Think the King James Bible Is the Best Translation Available Today," downloaded from www.bible.org.

12. Wallace, "Why I Do Not Think the King James Bible Is the Best Translation Available Today."

13. See Wallace, "The Reign of the King James."

14. See Philip Comfort, *Essential Guide to Bible Versions* (Wheaton, IL: Tyndale House, 2000), p. 147.

15. See Adolf Deissmann, *New Light on the New Testament: From Records of the Graeco-Roman Period* (Edinburgh: T. & T. Clark, 1908).

Chapter 5

1. Bruce M. Metzger, *The Bible in Translation: Ancient and English Versions* (Grand Rapids, MI: Baker Books, 2001), p. 118.

2. Philip Comfort, *Essential Guide to Bible Versions* (Wheaton, IL: Tyndale House, 2000), p. 166.

3. Robert Thomas, *How to Choose a Bible Version* (Great Britain: Christian Focus Publications, 2000), p. 27.

4. David Dewey, *A User's Guide to Bible Translations* (Downers Grove, IL: InterVarsity Press, 2004), p. 144.

5. Dewey, p. 143; see also Metzger, p. 119.

6. The Apocrypha refers to 14 or 15 books of doubtful authenticity and authority that the Roman Catholics decided belonged in the Bible sometime following the Protestant Reformation. The Catholic Council of Trent (1545–1563) canonized these books. See Appendix C—"Does the Apocrypha Belong in the Bible?"

7. The Septuagint is the Greek translation of the Hebrew Old Testament that predates the time of Christ.

8. For more on Eastern Orthodoxy and Roman Catholicism, see my book *The Complete Guide to Christian Denominations* (Eugene, OR: Harvest House Publishers, 2005).

9. Note, however, that many scholars continue to justify the RSV rendering of Isaiah 7:14. They point out that the Hebrew word *almah* does indeed mean "young woman," according to our best Hebrew lexicons. The debate continues.

10. See also Bruce Metzger, "English Translations of the Bible, Today and Tomorrow," *Bibliotheca Sacra*, October-December 1993, p. 399.

11. See Daniel B. Wallace, "Why So Many Versions?" downloaded from www.bible.org.

12. See Cyrus Gordon, "Almah in Isaiah 7:14," *Journal of the American Academy of Religion*, 1953, Vol. 21, No. 2, p. 106.

13. Wallace, "Why So Many Versions?" downloaded from www.bible.org.

Chapter 6

1. Amplified Bible Web site.

2. Amplified Bible Web site.
3. Amplified Bible preface.
4. Amplified Bible Web site.
5. Amplified Bible Web site.
6. Gordon Fee and Mark Strauss, *How to Choose a Translation for All Its Worth* (Grand Rapids, MI: Zondervan, 2007), p. 149.
7. Alan Duthie, *Bible Translations and How to Choose Between Them* (Greenwood, SC: Attic Press, 1985), p. 60.
8. Amplified Bible Web site.
9. Duthie, p. 60.
10. Fee and Strauss, p. 149.
11. David Dewey, *A User's Guide to Bible Translations* (Downers Grove, IL: InterVarsity Press, 2004), p. 147.
12. See "George M. Lamsa: Christian Scholar or Cultic Torchbearer," *Christian Research Journal,* 1989, vol. 12, no. 2.

Chapter 7

1. Gordon Fee and Mark Strauss, *How to Choose a Translation for All Its Worth* (Grand Rapids, MI: Zondervan, 2007), p. 147.
2. "NASB preface," NASB Web site.
3. NASB Web site.
4. "NASB preface."
5. "NASB Translation Principles," NASB Web site.
6. NASB Web site.
7. David Dewey, *A User's Guide to Bible Translations* (Downers Grove, IL: InterVarsity Press, 2004), p. 173.
8. See Philip Comfort, *Essential Guide to Bible Versions* (Wheaton, IL: Tyndale House, 2000), pp. 171-72.
9. Daniel B. Wallace, "Why So Many Versions?" downloaded from www.bible.org.
10. Wallace, "Why So Many Versions?" insert added, emphasis added.

Chapter 8

1. David Dewey, *A User's Guide to Bible Translations* (Downers Grove, IL: InterVarsity Press, 2004), pp. 157-58. See also Gordon Fee and Mark Strauss, *How to Choose a Translation for All Its Worth* (Grand Rapids, MI: Zondervan, 2007), p. 154.
2. "Good News Translation preface," Good News Translation Web site.
3. Bruce M. Metzger, *The Bible in Translation: Ancient and English Versions* (Grand Rapids, MI: Baker Books, 2001), p. 168.
4. Robert Martin, *Accuracy of Translation* (Carlisle: Banner of Truth, 1989), p. 15.

Chapter 9

1. According to Gordon Fee and Mark Strauss, *How to Choose a Translation for All Its Worth* (Grand Rapids, MI: Zondervan, 2007), p. 149.
2. "NIV preface," NIV Web site.
3. Bruce M. Metzger, *The Bible in Translation: Ancient and English Versions* (Grand Rapids, MI: Baker Books, 2001), pp. 138-39.
4. David Dewey, *A User's Guide to Bible Translations* (Downers Grove, IL: InterVarsity Press, 2004), p. 161.
5. Daniel B. Wallace, "Why So Many Versions?" downloaded from www.bible.org.
6. See Robert Thomas, "Dynamic Equivalence: A Method of Translation or a System of Hermeneutics?" *The Master's Seminary Journal*, 1:2 (Fall 1990), p. 157.
7. Fee and Strauss, pp. 120-21.
8. Daniel B. Wallace, "Why So Many Versions?"
9. "NIV preface."
10. Some critics say the NIV is too interpretive on occasion. See Robert Thomas, *How to Choose a Bible Version* (Great Britain: Christian Focus Publications, 2000), p. 180.
11. Metzger, p. 140.
12. For example, Philip Comfort, *Essential Guide to Bible Versions* (Wheaton, IL: Tyndale House, 2000), p. 189.

Chapter 10

1. Gordon Fee and Mark Strauss, *How to Choose a Translation for All Its Worth* (Grand Rapids, MI: Zondervan, 2007), p. 148.
2. See Arthur L. Farstad, *The New King James Version: In the Great Tradition* (Nashville: Thomas Nelson, 2003).
3. "NKJV preface," NKJV Web site.
4. "NKJV preface."
5. "NKJV preface."
6. "NKJV preface."
7. "NKJV preface."
8. Daniel B. Wallace, "Why So Many Versions?" downloaded from www.bible.org. Elsewhere, however, Wallace concedes the NKJV is a good option for those who like the Elizabethan English of the KJV. See Daniel Wallace, "Inspiration, Preservation, and New Testament Textual Criticism," *Grace Theological Journal*, 12.1 (1992), p. 22.
9. Not all textual critics agree that the earliest manuscripts are the most accurate. The majority does, however.
10. Wallace, "Why So Many Versions?" For the Old Testament, the NKJV used the 1967/1977 Stuttgart edition of the *Biblia Hebraica for the Old Testament*. However, comparisons were also made to the Bomberg edition of 1524-25, which was used for the King James Version. The Septuagint (Greek) Version of the Old Testament

and the Latin Vulgate also were consulted, as well as relevant manuscripts from the Dead Sea caves.

11. Steven Sheeley and Robert Nash, *The Bible in English* (Nashville, TN: Abingdon, 1997), pp. 50-51.

12. See Philip Comfort, *Essential Guide to Bible Versions* (Wheaton, IL: Tyndale House, 2000), p. 173. The NKJV preface tells us that these footnotes "objectively present the facts without such tendentious remarks as 'the best manuscripts omit' or 'the most reliable manuscripts read.' Such notes are value judgments that differ according to varying viewpoints on the text."

Chapter 11

1. This material is adapted from Daniel Wallace, "Why So Many Versions?" downloaded from www.bible.org.

2. "NRSV preface," NRSV Web site.

3. David Dewey, *A User's Guide to Bible Translations* (Downers Grove, IL: InterVarsity Press, 2004), p. 170.

4. "NRSV preface."

5. Mark Strauss, *Distorting Scripture?* (Downers Grove, IL: InterVarsity Press, 1998), pp. 44-46.

6. Daniel B. Wallace, "Why So Many Versions?" downloaded from www.bible.org.

Chapter 12

1. David Dewey, *A User's Guide to Bible Translations* (Downers Grove, IL: InterVarsity Press, 2004), p. 168.

2. Bruce M. Metzger, *The Bible in Translation: Ancient and English Versions* (Grand Rapids, MI: Baker Books, 2001), p. 153.

3. "Revised English Bible preface."

4. Robert Thomas, *How to Choose a Bible Version* (Great Britain: Christian Focus Publications, 2000), p. 41.

5. "Revised English Bible preface," insert added.

6. See Gordon Fee and Mark Strauss, *How to Choose a Translation for All Its Worth* (Grand Rapids, MI: Zondervan, 2007), p. 152.

7. "Revised English Bible preface."

Chapter 13

1. See Robert Thomas, *How to Choose a Bible Version* (Great Britain: Christian Focus Publications, 2000), p. 46.

2. "NCV preface," NCV Web site.

3. "NCV preface."

4. See Philip Comfort, *Essential Guide to Bible Versions* (Wheaton, IL: Tyndale House, 2000), p. 196.

5. "NCV preface."

6. See Delphine Soulas, "Bible Gets Hip for Teenage Males," *The Washington Times,* March 13, 2004, p. C11; "New Generation Connects With the New Century; New Century Version Bible Sales Soaring Among Younger Demographics," *PR Newswire,* January 25, 2005; "NCV Jumps from #11 to #5 in Translation Standings," *Business Wire,* February 13, 2004, HighBeam Research.

Chapter 14

1. These facts are based on "The History of Our Translation," posted at the GOD'S WORD Web site.
2. GOD'S WORD Web site.
3. See Philip Comfort, *Essential Guide to Bible Versions* (Wheaton, IL: Tyndale House, 2000), p. 198.
4. Gordon Fee and Mark Strauss, *How to Choose a Translation for All Its Worth* (Grand Rapids, MI: Zondervan, 2007), p. 155.

Chapter 15

1. "NLT FAQ," NLT Web site.
2. "NLT preface," NLT Web site.
3. See Bruce M. Metzger, *The Bible in Translation: Ancient and English Versions* (Grand Rapids, MI: Baker Books, 2001), p. 182.
4. Alan Jacobs, "A Bible for Everyone," *First Things: A Monthly Journal of Religion and Public Life,* December 2003, Issue 138, p. 10.
5. See Philip Comfort, *Essential Guide to Bible Versions* (Wheaton, IL: Tyndale House, 2000), pp. 200-201.
6. "New Living Translation Outranks King James Version," *PR Newswire,* November 27,1996, HighBeam Research. See also Ernest Tucker, "Bible Sellers Nationwide Put Up Strong Numbers," *Chicago Sun-Times,* August 30, 1998, HighBeam Research.
7. This view is often referred to as "forensic justification." "Forensic" comes from a Latin word meaning "forum." This word has its roots in the fact that in the ancient Roman forum, a court could meet and make judicial or legal declarations. Forensic justification, then, involves God's judicial declaration of the believer's righteousness before Him. The believer is legally acquitted of all guilt and the very righteousness of Christ is imputed to his account. Henceforth, when God sees the believer He sees him in all the righteousness of Christ.
8. See Robin Galiano Russell, "Bible Translation Stirs Gender Debate," *Dallas Morning News,* February 16, 2005, HighBeam Research.

Chapter 16

1. John Sawyer, "Spirituality in the 21st Century," *USA Today,* July 1, 2002, HighBeam Research.
2. Robert Thomas, *How to Choose a Bible Version* (Great Britain: Christian Focus Publications, 2000), p. 46.

3. See Mark Strauss, "Linguistic and Hermeneutical Fallacies in the Guidelines Established at the 'Conference on Gender-Related Language in Scripture,'" *Journal of the Evangelical Theological Society,* June 1, 1998, HighBeam Research.

4. NIrV Web site.

5. NIrV Web site.

6. NIrV Web site.

7. NIrV Web site.

8. See Phil Anderson, "Graham's Daughter Looks to John's Gospel for Inspiration," *The Capital-Journal,* June 24, 2000, HighBeam Research.

Chapter 17

1. An edition of the ESV with the Apocrypha will be published in 2009 by Oxford University Press.

2. See Gordon Fee and Mark Strauss, *How to Choose a Translation for All Its Worth* (Grand Rapids, MI: Zondervan, 2007), p. 148.

3. ESV Bible Web site.

4. "ESV preface," ESV Bible Web site.

5. "ESV preface."

6. See Robert Thomas, *How to Choose a Bible Version* (Great Britain: Christian Focus Publications, 2000), p. 32.

7. "ESV preface."

8. "ESV preface."

9. "ESV preface."

10. "ESV preface."

11. See Richard Ostling, "New Gender-Neutral Bible Planned," Associated Press, January 28, 2002, HighBeam Research.

12. See Richard Ostling, "Why Can't We Have One Bible for All?" *The Cincinnati Post,* March 5, 2004, HighBeam Research.

13. David Dewey, *A User's Guide to Bible Translations* (Downers Grove, IL: InterVarsity Press, 2004), p. 190.

Chapter 18

1. Robert Thomas, *How to Choose a Bible Version* (Great Britain: Christian Focus Publications, 2000), p. 47.

2. "Preface," NET Bible.

3. W. Hall Harris, "The NET Bible," downloaded from www.bible.org.

4. "Preface."

5. "Preface."

6. "Preface."

7. "Preface."

8. See Peter Davids, "Three Recent Bible Translations: A New Testament Perspec-

tive," *Journal of the Evangelical Theological Society,* September 1, 2003. See also Michael Lyons and William Tooman, "Three Recent Bible Translations: An Old Testament Perspective," *Journal of the Evangelical Theological Society,* September 1, 2003, HighBeam Research.

9. Harris, "The NET Bible."
10. Harris, "The NET Bible."
11. Harris, "The NET Bible."

Chapter 19

1. See Daniel Ritchie, "Three Recent Bible Translations: A Literary and Stylistic Perspective," *Journal of the Evangelical Theological Society,* September 1, 2003. See also Matthew Brady, "Christians Turn to Other Books but Not the Bible," *The News and Record,* January 26, 1998, HighBeam Research.
2. Clint Kelly, "Getting the Message: Eugene Peterson's Contemporary Translation of the Bible has Enjoyed Immediate Acclaim," *Presbyterian Record,* December 1, 2001, HighBeam Research.
3. See, for example, David Dewey, *A User's Guide to Bible Translations* (Downers Grove, IL: InterVarsity Press, 2004), p. 77.
4. Eugene Peterson, "Version Information," The Message Web site.
5. Gordon Fee and Mark Strauss, *How to Choose a Translation for All Its Worth* (Grand Rapids, MI: Zondervan, 2007), p. 156.
6. Eugene Peterson, "Introduction," The Message New Testament.
7. Tom Laceky, "Folksy Bible," *The Milwaukee Journal Sentinel,* August 10, 2002, HighBeam Research.
8. See, for example, Dewey, p. 77. See also Robert Thomas, *How to Choose a Bible Version* (Great Britain: Christian Focus Publications, 2000), p. 47.
9. See Bruce M. Metzger, *The Bible in Translation: Ancient and English Versions* (Grand Rapids, MI: Baker Books, 2001), p. 183.
10. Philip Comfort, *Essential Guide to Bible Versions* (Wheaton, IL: Tyndale House, 2000), p. 198.
11. Metzger, p. 183.
12. Eugene Peterson, "Preface," *The Message: The Bible in Contemporary Language* (Colorado Springs, CO: NavPress, 2002), 8.

Chapter 20

1. Robert Thomas, *How to Choose a Bible Version* (Great Britain: Christian Focus Publications, 2000), p. 49.
2. John Dart, "Gender and the Bible," *The Christian Century,* July 3, 2002, vol. 119, issue 14, pp. 11-12.
3. David Dewey, *A User's Guide to Bible Translations* (Downers Grove, IL: InterVarsity Press, 2004), pp. 192-93.
4. Gordon Fee and Mark Strauss, *How to Choose a Translation for All Its Worth* (Grand Rapids, MI: Zondervan, 2007), p. 151.

5. "Translation Philosophy," Holman Christian Standard Bible Web site.

6. Press Release, "Broadman & Holman Publishers Announces New Bible Translation," posted at Broadman & Holman Publishers Web site, May 7, 1999.

7. The Holman Christian Standard Bible Web site tells us: "Yahweh is used more often in the Holman CSB than in most Bible translations because the word LORD in English is a title of God and does not accurately convey to modern readers the emphasis on God's name in the original Hebrew."

8. Holman Christian Standard Bible Web site.

Chapter 21

1. Promotional comments on the TNIV, Zondervan Web site.

2. "TNIV preface."

3. Gordon Fee and Mark Strauss, *How to Choose a Translation for All It's Worth* (Grand Rapids, MI: Zondervan, 2007), p. 150.

4. TNIV Debate Between Dr. Wayne Grudem and Dr. Mark Strauss, Concordia University, Irvine, California, May 21, 2002, transcribed by Wayne Leman, posted at: http://www.salemthesoldier.us/TNIV_concordia_debate.html.

5. Promotional comments on the TNIV, Zondervan Web site.

6. "TNIV preface."

7. John Kohlenberger, "What About the 'Gender Accurate' TNIV?" *Priscilla Papers,* Spring 2002, 16:2, p. 3.

8. "TNIV preface."

9. Kohlenberger, p. 2.

10. Promotional comments on the TNIV, Zondervan Web site.

11. See, for example, Fee and Strauss, p. 150.

12. Kohlenberger, p. 1.

13. John Dart, "Gender and the Bible," *The Christian Century,* July 3, 2002, vol. 119, issue 14, p. 11; Ellen Sorokin, "Groups Pan Gender-Neutral Bible," *The Washington Times,* January 29, 2002, p. 3; Victoria Pierce, "Religious Scholars Debate Changes in New Bible Translation," *Daily Herald,* February 23, 2002, Highbeam Research; Robin Galiano Russell, "Bible Translation Stirs Gender Debate," *The Dallas Morning News,* February 16, 2005, Highbeam Research; Mark I. Pinsky, "Evangelicals Battling Over New Bible Translation," *The Orlando Sentinel,* April 5, 2002, HighBeam Research.

14. Dan Allen, "New Bible Is Gender-Free, but Imprecise," *Lancaster New Era,* May 3, 2002, HighBeam Research.

15. Craig Blomberg, "Today's New International Version: The Untold Story of a Good Translation," downloaded from www.bible.org.

16. Blomberg, "Today's New International Version."

17. Blomberg, "Today's New International Version."

18. "TNIV preface."

Chapter 22

1. David Dewey, *A User's Guide to Bible Translations* (Downers Grove, IL: InterVarsity Press, 2004), p. 153.
2. Dom Henry Wansbrough, "General Editor's Foreword," New Jerusalem Bible (New York: Doubleday, 1989).
3. Bruce M. Metzger, *The Bible in Translation: Ancient and English Versions* (Grand Rapids, MI: Baker Books, 2001), p. 151.
4. Wansbrough, "General Editor's Foreword."
5. Gordon Fee and Mark Strauss, *How to Choose a Translation for All Its Worth* (Grand Rapids, MI: Zondervan, 2007), p. 152.
6. "NJB Foreword."
7. Metzger, p. 151.
8. Dewey, p. 165.

Chapter 23

1. "New American Bible preface."
2. "New American Bible preface."
3. Gordon Fee and Mark Strauss, *How to Choose a Translation for All Its Worth* (Grand Rapids, MI: Zondervan, 2007), p. 152; Robert Thomas, *How to Choose a Bible Version* (Great Britain: Christian Focus Publications, 2000), p. 35.
4. "New American Bible preface."
5. John Dart, "Gender and the Bible," *The Christian Century,* July 3, 2002, vol. 119, issue 14, pp. 11-12.
6. Bruce M. Metzger, *The Bible in Translation: Ancient and English Versions* (Grand Rapids, MI: Baker Books, 2001), p. 128.
7. "New American Bible preface."
8. See, for example, David Dewey, *A User's Guide to Bible Translations* (Downers Grove, IL: InterVarsity Press, 2004), p. 155.
9. Richard John Neuhaus, "The New American Bible," *First Things: A Monthly Journal of Religion and Public Life,* November 2007, issue 177, p. 72; Richard John Neuhaus, "More on Bible Babel," *First Things: A Monthly Journal of Religion and Public Life,* January 2006, issue 159, p. 61.
10. See Metzger, p. 129.
11. Metzger, p. 128.
12. "New American Bible preface."

Chapter 24

1. David Dewey, *A User's Guide to Bible Translations* (Downers Grove, IL: InterVarsity Press, 2004), p. 107.
2. Gordon Fee and Mark Strauss, *How to Choose a Translation for All Its Worth* (Grand Rapids, MI: Zondervan, 2007), p. 130.

3. Bruce Metzger, *The Making of the New Revised Standard Version of the Bible* (Grand Rapids, MI: Eerdmans, 1991), p. 62.

Appendix A

1. Daniel B. Wallace, "Why I Do Not Think the King James Bible Is the Best Translation Available Today," downloaded from www.bible.org.
2. Wallace, "Why I Do Not Think the King James Bible Is the Best Translation Available Today."

Appendix D

1. See, for example, James White, *The King James Only Controversy: Can You Trust the Modern Translations?* (Minneapolis, MN: Bethany House, 1995).

Appendix E

1. Bruce R. McConkie, *Mormon Doctrine*, 2d ed. (Salt Lake City, UT: Bookcraft, 1966), p. 383, insert added.
2. John A. Widtsoe, *Evidences and Reconciliations* (Salt Lake City, UT: Bookcraft, 1987), p. 97f.
3. See Anthony A. Hoekema, *The Four Major Cults* (Grand Rapids, MI: Eerdmans, 1978), p. 19.
4. Joseph Smith, Genesis 40:33, Inspired Version.
5. David A. Reed and John R. Farkas, *Mormons Answered Verse by Verse* (Grand Rapids, MI: Baker Books, 1992), p. 29, inserts added.
6. Robert H. Countess, *The Jehovah's Witnesses' New Testament* (Phillipsburg, NJ: Presbyterian and Reformed Publishing Co., 1982), p. 91.
7. H.H. Rowley, cited in Countess, p. 91.
8. Rowley, cited in Countess, p. 91.
9. Julius R. Mantey; cited in Erich and Jean Grieshaber, *Exposé of Jehovah's Witnesses* (Tyler, TX: Jean Books, 1982), p. 30.
10. Bruce Metzger, cited in Grieshaber, p. 30.
11. William Barclay, cited in Grieshaber, p. 31.
12. David Reed, *Jehovah's Witnesses Answered Verse by Verse* (Grand Rapids, MI: Baker Book House, 1992), p. 71.
13. Grieshaber, p. 100.
14. Grieshaber, p. 100.
15. *Reasoning from the Scriptures* (Brooklyn, NY: Watchtower Bible and Tract Society, 1989), p. 409.

Why Do Bad Things Happen If God Is Good?

Ron Rhodes

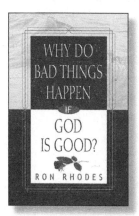

Have you ever wanted to reach out to someone who was hurting, but you didn't know what to say? Have you wondered if God really has everything under control? Have you ever asked, *Why did this happen to me?*

Bible teacher and speaker Ron Rhodes flags the religious and philosophical dead-ends that can make tough situations even worse. His thoughtful but easy-to-understand analysis of the existence of evil will help you find purpose and meaning in every experience...and help you affirm that even when bad things happen, God is good.